The People's Quiz Book

THE PEOPLE'S QUIZ BOOK

BANTAM PRESS

LONDON · TORONTO · SYDNEY · AUCKLAND · JOHANNESBURG

TRANSWORLD PUBLISHERS
61–63 Uxbridge Road, London W5 5SA
a division of The Random House Group Ltd
www.booksattransworld.co.uk

First published in Great Britain
in 2007 by Bantam Press
a division of Transworld Publishers

Published in association with
the Fever Media television series
for BBC1 *The People's Quiz**

Copyright © Fever Media 2007

Fever Media has asserted its right under the Copyright, Designs
and Patents Act 1988 to be identified as the author of this work.

A CIP catalogue record for this book
is available from the British Library.

ISBN 9780593059098

Addresses for Random House Group Ltd companies outside the UK
can be found at: www.randomhouse.co.uk
The Random House Group Ltd Reg. No. 954009

The Random House Group Ltd makes every effort to ensure that the papers
used in its books are made from trees that have been legally sourced from
well-managed and credibly certified forests. Our paper procurement
policy can be found at: www.randomhouse.co.uk/paper.htm

Typeset in Angie by Falcon Oast Graphic Art

Printed in the UK by
CPI Mackays, Chatham, ME5 8TD

2 4 6 8 10 9 7 5 3 1

*BBC and the BBC logo are trademarks of
the British Broadcasting Corporation and
are used under licence. Logo © BBC 1996

Contents

Acknowledgements

There are many people who have helped make both *The People's Quiz* television series and *The People's Quiz Book* happen and it's great to get the opportunity to say thank you.

Firstly, we'd like to thank the BBC for commissioning the series and giving us their support – Peter Fincham, Elaine Bedell, Jon Beazley, Sumi Connock, George Dixon, Jay Hunt, Jo Wallace.

A very big thanks to our presenter Jamie Theakston, and our fearsome quiz panel – Kate Garraway, Myleene Klass, William G. Stewart.

Martyn Fox and Rebecca Sanderson from Camelot have been very supportive.

Thanks to the Fever development team for developing the quiz and their constant work on the format – James Fox, Tim Harcourt, Tom Joseph, Michael Sutherland, Tali Walters.

The team who have been busy for months writing, verifying and compiling all the different question lists used in the national auditions, the BBC1 studio shows and the BBC2 *People's Quiz Wildcard* series deserve a special mention – Jimmy Baker, Alan Bone, Alison Code, Ian Cross, Morgan Davies, Brenda Haugh, Luke Kelly, Shannon Leary, Sarah Letheran and her team, Angharad Lloyd, Stephen Lovelock, Rob Maplethorpe, Terri Marzoli, Andy Mayer, Yasmine Richardson, Tom Sutton.

The lovely team at Jump Design for the beautiful graphics they have created – Richard Norley, Chris Skinner.

The team at Transworld Publishers – Emma Musgrave, Doug Young and Becky Jones.

All the production team and crew – of whom there are dozens – have worked long and hard. There is a lot of work that goes on behind the scenes to pull off a national event like this and every single member of the team has contributed.

Lastly, we want to thank everyone who loves quizzes, and particularly the thousands of contestants who have applied to and taken part in *The People's Quiz*.

Eileen Herlihy
Richard Hopkins
David Mortimer
Executive Producers

Introduction

Britain is certainly a nation of quiz lovers – we love the skill in answering the questions and the element of luck in getting the right questions at the right time. That's why we at Fever Media have teamed up with the BBC to bring you their biggest quiz show ever. There are more contestants, more questions and a bigger cash prize than ever before. But *The People's Quiz* isn't different just because it's bigger. To add extra elements of skill and chance we're publishing here almost all the questions we'll ask on the show (mixed with quite a few extras). Maybe the questions you've read will come up . . . and one of the questions in this book could be the £200, 700 question!

In *The People's Quiz Book* we have tried to replicate the TV series as faithfully as possible. You can decide whether you use the book to play along, or simply to test and build your general knowledge. Questions in Part 1 of the book, from our audition round, have tripped up many quiz masters – they may appear easy at first glance, but just one wrong answer will knock you out of the game.

The sign of a true quiz genius is the ability to answer questions correctly in a wide variety of subjects. Part 2 – General Knowledge – is designed to test just that.

In Part 3 – Specialist Subjects – we give you sets of questions from all forty categories used on the TV show. You can use these questions to identify your strengths and weaknesses.

If you need some light relief, in Part 4 we've included some of the silliest answers given by contestants in the national auditions. When you're faced with our panel firing questions at you, the strangest things can come out of your mouth . . .

INTRODUCTION

Whether you devour *The People's Quiz Book* from cover to cover, or simply enjoy a few rounds with friends, we hope you'll come away inspired by what you find in it! Maybe next year you could be a grand finalist . . .

The People's Quiz Book

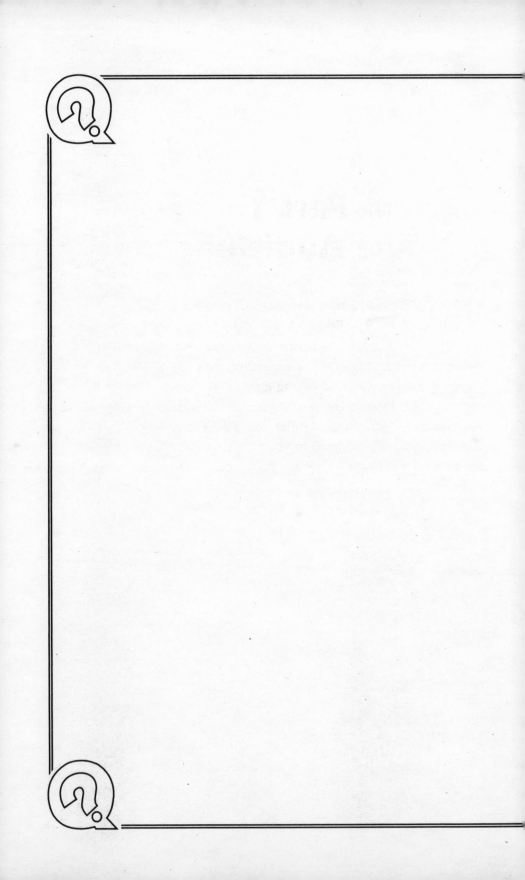

Part 1
The Auditions

THE QUESTIONS here are taken from the national auditions for *The People's Quiz 2007*. They are a random selection, each set containing a cross-section of subjects. Contestants must successfully complete a run of ten questions, with no wrong answers or passes, before proceeding to the next stage. The audition sets are divided by age group: Under 25s, 25–40 and 40+. But don't just test yourself in your own age group: see how you would do in other age categories.

──────────── *Under 25s* **SET 1** ────────────

1 Which is the largest of Spain's Balearic Islands?

2 Who wrote the hugely successful Harry Potter series of books?

3 In England and Wales, how many jury members are there in a Crown Court on a criminal case?

4 Which 1990s TV show, first shown on BBC2, featured gladiatorial contests between home-made robots?

5 The annual Scottish tradition of holding a 'Burns Supper' is in honour of which Scottish writer?

6 Which member of the bear family is white but has black eye patches, ears, legs, feet, chest and shoulders?

7 In 2001, which British boyband had a UK number one hit with the single 'If You Come Back'?

8 In rhyming slang, 'Rosie Lee' stands for which beverage?

9 Gemma Rose Owen is the daughter of which England footballer?

10 In which 1999 film does Julia Roberts play Anna, a Hollywood actress who falls in love with a London bookshop owner?

──────────── *Under 25s* **SET 2** ────────────

1 Which Hollywood actress starred in the hit film *Legally Blonde*?

2 In the original arcade game, what did Super Mario do for a living?

3 Which nineteenth-century Dutch artist cut off his left ear following a quarrel?

4 In 2006, which member of the Royal Family joined girlfriend Chelsy Davy in Cape Town to celebrate her twenty-first birthday?

5 In the 1990s, brothers Rory and Tony Underwood represented England at which sport?

6 What name is given to the series of interconnected underground tunnels in which wild rabbits live?

7 Which stripy animal has given its name to a type of pedestrian crossing?

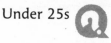

8 In 2002, which singer released the controversial single 'Shoot The Dog', which had a video that ridiculed Tony Blair?

9 Politician David Cameron has been credited with reviving the fortunes of which British political party?

10 In 2002, who was Patrick Kielty's co-host on the first series of the TV talent show *Fame Academy*?

────────────────── *Under 25s* **SET 3** ──────────────────

1 How many legs does a spider have?

2 Which actor played the title character in the 1994 comedy movie *Ace Ventura: Pet Detective*?

3 San Marino is a tiny republic completely landlocked by which European country?

4 In 1086, which king ordered the property survey known as the Domesday Book?

5 According to an Old Testament story, who was left in a basket of reeds at the edge of the river Nile?

6 From which country of the UK does tennis player Andy Murray come?

7 Which popular alcoholic spirit has a name which means 'little water' or 'dear water' in Russian?

8 'There's No Other Way', 'Parklife' and 'Girls And Boys' were UK Top 10 hits for which band in the 1990s?

9 Which word connects a dance-club style and a building where a car is kept?

10 How is Lawrence Tureaud, who played B. A. Baracus in *The A-Team*, better known?

────────────────── *Under 25s* **SET 4** ──────────────────

1 A solar eclipse occurs when the Sun cannot be seen from the Earth because of the position of which other heavenly body?

2 In the children's nursery rhyme, which small, carnivorous mammal is said to go 'Pop'?

3 The TV presenter Matt Baker fronted which popular long-running children's programme before leaving in 2006?

4 What is the official language of the island of Barbados?

5 'Old Glory' is the nickname for the flag of which nation?

6 Born in 1954, which actor and martial artist starred as Detective Inspector Lee in the *Rush Hour* films?

7 What name is given to an electrically operated machine used for washing and drying dishes and cutlery?

8 Which animated band had UK Top 10 hits in 2005 with 'Dare', 'Feel Good Inc' and 'Dirty Harry'?

9 At which battle did the American folk hero Davy Crockett die?

10 In which city in Northern Ireland was footballer George Best born?

—————————— *Under 25s* **SET 5** ——————————

1 Montego Bay is a popular tourist resort on which Caribbean island?

2 In 1996, Zoe Ball and Jamie Theakston presented which Saturday morning children's TV series?

3 Who wrote Handel's *Messiah*?

4 Who is the Greek equivalent of the Roman god Neptune?

5 In a standard game of pool, what colour is the cue ball?

6 Usually eaten cold with drinks, small pieces of crisply cooked pork crackling are generally known as pork . . . what?

7 Which US duo had UK Top 10 chart hits with 'Ms Jackson' and 'Hey Ya!'?

8 In mathematics, which Greek name is given to the number roughly equal to 3.14?

9 Complete the title of the William Golding novel: *Lord of the* . . . what?

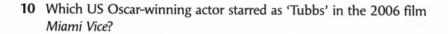

10 Which US Oscar-winning actor starred as 'Tubbs' in the 2006 film *Miami Vice*?

—————————— *Under 25s* **SET 6** ——————————

1 Which colourfully named pop singer has had hits with 'You Make Me Sick' and 'Just Like A Pill'?

2 The English civil wars between the Houses of Lancaster and York are referred to as the 'Wars of the ...' what?

3 147 is the maximum break attainable without penalty points in which indoor sport?

4 Which animated Disney film features the songs 'Under The Sea' and 'Kiss The Girl'?

5 Which musical instrument features on the euro coins of Ireland?

6 Which country in the UK holds an annual poetry and music competition in August known as the National Eisteddfod?

7 In 1863, which US president announced his Emancipation Proclamation, which led to the abolition of slavery there?

8 Actor Ralf Little starred as Caroline Aherne's screen brother in which hit British TV sitcom?

9 Which word describes a chemical with a pH value of more than seven?

10 According to the proverb, 'One man's meat is another man's ...' what?

—————————— *Under 25s* **SET 7** ——————————

1 'Exterminate, exterminate' is a common phrase said by which creatures in TV's *Doctor Who*?

2 The bestselling children's book *A Series of Unfortunate Events* was written by Lemony who?

3 Which type of triangle has three sides of equal length?

4 In the 2001 film *The Princess Diaries* who played Queen Clarisse Renaldi of Genovia?

5 What colour are the petals of the snowdrop?

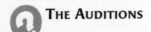
6 Along with eggs, salt, and milk or water, what is the main ingredient needed to make pancakes?

7 What nationality is the hip-hop musician Ms Dynamite?

8 Which term, meaning 'new art' in French, is given to a style of decorative art and design of the late nineteenth century?

9 The international organization the Arab League has its headquarters in which Egyptian city?

10 Named after the Welsh village where it was first bred, the Sealyham is a breed of which domestic animal?

——————————— *Under 25s* **SET 8** ———————————

1 Which continent has a name that means 'opposite the Arctic'?

2 What is the official currency of the Netherlands?

3 The Bernabeu Stadium is the home of which Spanish football team?

4 In which century did King Henry VIII die?

5 In the UK, which organization is known by the abbreviation YHA?

6 In 2001, which British boyband had a UK number one hit with the single 'Let's Dance'?

7 Supermodels Elle Macpherson, Claudia Schiffer and Naomi Campbell opened the 'Fashion Café' in which US city?

8 Famous for his spiky hair, which celebrity chef owns the restaurant Rhodes 24?

9 In which film did the Blue Fairy say, 'A lie keeps growing and growing until it's as clear as the nose on your face'?

10 Which Essex-born comedian is a permanent guest on the TV quiz *QI*?

——————————— *Under 25s* **SET 9** ———————————

1 Which iconic twentieth-century Spanish artist was born in 1881 on the Costa del Sol?

2 At which football ground does Liverpool Football Club play its home matches?

3 What name is given to a curved, flat piece of wood that can be thrown so as to return to the thrower?

4 Which Egyptian queen has given her name to two stone obelisks, or needles, one in London and the other in New York?

5 In 2000, which US illusionist spent 72 hours 'Frozen in Time'?

6 In the drink known as a G & T, for what does the 'G' stand?

7 George Canning, Stanley Baldwin and Clement Attlee have all held which political position?

8 In the TV series *Cracker*, which Scotsman plays Doctor Edward Fitzgerald?

9 In 2002, which Irish singer had a solo UK number one hit with the single 'Tomorrow Never Comes'?

10 Actors Corey Haim, Jason Patric and Kiefer Sutherland all starred in which hit 1987 vampire film?

───────────── *Under 25s* **SET 10** ─────────────

1 To which European country does the Caribbean island of Martinique belong?

2 According to tradition, how many leaves should a clover have to bring good luck?

3 In 2000, which European nation was added to the Five Nations Rugby Championship to make it a Six Nations Championship?

4 Actress Tamzin Outhwaite played the character of Melanie in which TV soap?

5 In 1998, which girl group had a UK number one hit with the single 'Bootie Call'?

6 Which poisonous, colourless gas is formed by fuels burning incompletely and can be found in car exhausts?

7 In 1988, prior to her marriage to Jude Law, Sadie Frost was married to which Spandau Ballet star?

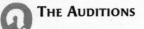

8 Which British actress starred as Evelyn in the 1999 film *The Mummy* opposite Brendan Fraser?

9 Which multi-millionaire businessman owns Stringfellows club in London?

10 Which comic-book hero is often referred to as 'the Man of Steel'?

──────────── *Under 25s* **SET 11** ────────────

1 Mark Owen is a member of which hugely successful boyband?

2 The Bullring shopping centre is situated in which West Midlands city?

3 The Japanese word 'bonsai', meaning 'tray planting', is usually used in connection with which plant?

4 Which Hollywood actress played the character Storm in the *X-Men* movies?

5 Which Spanish team won the 2006 UEFA Champions League final at the Stade de France?

6 Which popular TV gameshow featured the characters 'Wolf', 'Jet', 'Lightning' and 'Cobra'?

7 Which Native American princess is said to have saved English explorer John Smith from the Algonquian Indians?

8 A traditional game in which a blindfolded player tries to catch others is known as 'Blind Man's . . .' what?

9 Which religious leader is protected by a unit known as the Swiss Guard?

10 'The Red Lion' and 'The Rose and Crown' are traditional names in Britain for which type of establishment?

──────────── *Under 25s* **SET 12** ────────────

1 With which of his daughters did Ozzy Osbourne record the song 'Changes' in 2003?

2 *Gerrard: My Autobiography* was the 2006 bestseller of which Liverpool football player?

3 The lines on a globe that circle the Earth parallel to the equator are lines of what?

4 The ancient Roman building known in Italian as the *Colosseo* has which name in English?

5 How many wheels has the traditional Asian hand-drawn vehicle known as a rickshaw?

6 Which alcoholic spirit is traditionally added to pineapple and coconut to make a Piña Colada?

7 Which Spanish tennis player did Roger Federer defeat in the 2006 Wimbledon singles final?

8 The BBC science fiction series *Torchwood* is based in which British city?

9 In which hit 2003 film comedy did actress Martine McCutcheon star as Natalie?

10 If Christmas Day falls on a Monday, on which day of the week does New Year's Day fall?

———————————— *Under 25s* **SET 13** ————————————

1 Complete the 1992 song title by Whitney Houston: 'I Will Always . . .' what?

2 What is the only cultivated British fruit to have its seeds on the outside and not the inside?

3 According to legend, in which forest did Robin Hood and his Merry Men hide out?

4 In the UK, who was the first woman to become prime minister?

5 Which South American city has a name that means 'River of January' in Portuguese?

6 What colour is the 'tape' that refers to bureaucratic delay, with excessive attention to rules and regulations?

7 By which acronym is the Union of European Football Associations commonly known?

8 In the 2002 film *Harry Potter and the Chamber of Secrets*, which British comedy actor played Nearly Headless Nick?

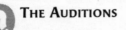
9   Which of Bob Geldof's daughters has written articles for *ELLE Girl* magazine and the *Daily Telegraph*?

10 In which TV drama series does actress Miranda Raison play MI5 spy Jo Portman?

——————————— *Under 25s* SET 14 ———————————

1   Singer Dannii Minogue is the sister of which Australian pop artist?

2   In which time-travelling film of 1985 did Michael J. Fox star as Marty McFly?

3   Which castle on the River Dee in Scotland is a private residence of the Queen?

4   In which motor sport is Italy's Valentino Rossi one of the world's leading competitors?

5   The traditional children's kissing game, in which a player pretends to be a postman, is known as 'Postman's . . .' what?

6   Which English playwright wrote *A Midsummer Night's Dream*?

7   Which medical name is given to the condition where body temperature falls to an abnormally low level?

8   What word, meaning 'pink' in French, is given to a type of wine coloured by only brief contact with red grape skins?

9   Which British Dame played Detective Superintendent Jane Tennison in TV's *Prime Suspect*?

10 Louisa Lytton was voted Sexiest Female at the 2006 Soap Awards for her performance as which character in *EastEnders*?

——————————— *Under 25s* SET 15 ———————————

1   Which girl group has had hits with 'Hole In The Head', 'Freak Like Me' and 'Push The Button'?

2   Found in the human body, what is the common name for the scapula?

3   What name is given to the seat on a bicycle?

4   Which children's TV cartoon features the toddling characters of Chuckie, Tommy and Angelica?

5 In 2006, with a net worth of 50 billion dollars, who was the richest person on the planet according to *Forbes* magazine?

6 What name is given to the tough fibrous tissue that binds bones and cartilage together at the joints?

7 François Mitterrand was president of which European country from 1981 to 1995?

8 Which US pop diva starred in the 2005 film comedy *Monster-in-Law*?

9 In UK greengrocers, the small basket in which fruit such as strawberries are sold is popularly known by what name?

10 In slang, which vegetable goes with the word 'couch' to describe someone who spends hours slumped in front of the TV?

––––––––––––––*Under 25s* SET 16––––––––––––––

1 What name is given to the system of printing with raised dots that enables blind people to read?

2 In 2000, who was elected President of the US?

3 Liz McClarnon, Natasha Hamilton and Jenny Frost were members of which English girl group?

4 The alternative medical practice of reflexology applies pressure points to the hands and where else in the human body?

5 In economics, a general rise in prices and fall in the purchasing power of money is known by what technical term?

6 What name is given to a tapering structure hanging from a cave roof, formed from the dripping of mineral-rich water?

7 The meat of which bird is the main ingredient in the casserole often known by the French name of 'coq au vin'?

8 The hit 1994 stage show *Riverdance* showcases the traditional dancing of which country?

9 Which Hollywood actress starred with Jack Black in the movie *Shallow Hal*?

10 The character Joe Mangel is most closely associated with which Australian TV soap?

―――――――――――――*Under 25s* **SET 17** ―――――――――

1 What is the name of Tony Blair's youngest child?

2 In 1998, which pop group covered the Bee Gees' hit single 'Tragedy'?

3 In which 1998 Oscar-nominated film did actor Jim Carrey discover his entire life to be a TV show?

4 In Hans Christian Andersen's tale 'The Princess and the Pea', what did the queen put under the mattress?

5 Thomas Crapper is widely credited with inventing the flushing mechanism for which bathroom appliance?

6 Which British military decoration was originally made from the metal of Russian cannons captured in the Crimean War?

7 In November 2006 against Holland, which footballer scored his first goal for England in over a year?

8 The Looney Tunes character Wile E. Coyote spends most of his time devising increasingly elaborate schemes to catch whom?

9 Which boy's name completes the slang phrase for a fair division or distribution, 'even . . .' what?

10 Which citrus fruit gets its name from Tangiers, the port in Morocco from where it was originally exported?

―――――――――――――*Under 25s* **SET 18** ―――――――――

1 Which popular children's character had a UK number one hit in 2000 with the song 'Can We Fix It'?

2 What colour is the dragon that features on the flag of Wales?

3 Boston is the capital of which US state?

4 The summer Olympic Games are held every how many years?

5 Which nineteenth-century scientist famously sailed to South America and the Galapagos Islands on board HMS *Beagle*?

6 By what name is a German Shepherd dog also known?

7 Which disease, common in tropical areas, derives its name from the Italian for 'bad air'?

8 In 2006, which British supermodel made a cameo appearance for Comic Relief in a *Little Britain* live show?

9 Joaquin Phoenix received an Oscar nomination for his role as Johnny Cash in which hit 2005 film?

10 In 2003, which US celebrity became the first black woman to appear in *Forbes* magazine's list of billionaires?

Under 25s SET 19

1 The Charles Bridge is a major tourist attraction in which central European capital city?

2 In the title of Eric Carle's children's story what type of creepy-crawly is 'Very Hungry'?

3 Which Disney film features the song 'Everybody Wants To Be A Cat'?

4 Which popular presenting duo had a hit single with 'Let's Get Ready To Rhumble'?

5 Which *Friends* character, played by Matt LeBlanc, was given a spin-off TV series of his own?

6 What is the first name of the German philosopher to whom the political philosophy Marxism is attributed?

7 International Nurses Day is held on 12 May, the anniversary of which famous nurse's birth?

8 Often used in medical emergencies, a defibrillator is designed to treat which organ of the body?

9 Which Winter Olympic freestyle skiing event takes place on a course studded with numerous bumps and two large jumps?

10 In November 2006, which Australian actress did the UK press report had become Hollywood's highest-paid film actress?

——————————*Under 25s* **SET 20**——————————

1 Of which American boyband was Justin Timberlake a member?

2 In the 2004 Olympic Games, which British rower won his fourth consecutive Olympic gold in the men's coxless four?

3 What is the full name of the UK's national museum of decorative art, often abbreviated as the V&A?

4 Which narrow Scottish loch became internationally famous for the monster that is supposed to live within it?

5 The 2004 film *The Motorcycle Diaries* is based on a road trip taken by which famous Cuban revolutionary?

6 What is the official language of Mexico?

7 Hydroelectric power is generated by the flow of what?

8 Adapted from the words 'charity' and 'mugger', what term is used for someone who asks for donations in the street?

9 Which Australian supermodel was originally named Eleanor Nancy Gow?

10 'Garlic bread, it's the future, I've tasted it', is said by which comedian, playing Brian Potter, in *Phoenix Nights*?

——————————*Under 25s* **SET 21**——————————

1 On which river is Stoke-on-Trent situated?

2 Moussaka and Souvlaki are dishes from which country of mainland Europe?

3 How many days are there in the month of May?

4 The Basenji breed of dog is famous for not doing what?

5 Whose book known as *The Origin of Species* caused controversy when it was published in 1859?

6 In which Scottish city is the Hearts versus Hibernian football match a local derby?

7 Which US pop diva starred as Terri in the 1997 film *Anaconda*?

8 Which English singer rose to fame when rapper Eminem sampled her song 'Thank You' into his song 'Stan'?

9 Which British actress and *Carry On* star is known affectionately as Babs?

10 When *Doctor Who* returned to the screen in 2005, which actor played the Doctor?

---------------------------*Under 25s* **SET 22** ---------------------------

1 The single entitled 'Bootylicious' was sung by which chart-topping American girl group?

2 Sometimes used to make furniture, which plant provides the panda with its diet?

3 Which city on the east coast of Scotland lies in the bay between the rivers Dee and Don?

4 In Olympic artistic gymnastics, the vault and which other event are performed by both men and women?

5 In which US TV series did Mikhail Baryshnikov appear as a love interest for Carrie, played by Sarah Jessica Parker?

6 The 2006 film *The Devil Wears Prada* was set in which US city?

7 In an orchestra, which instrument does a flautist play?

8 On 11 February 1990, which leading anti-apartheid campaigner was released from Victor-Verster prison?

9 A dish traditionally made of cooked cabbage, fried with cooked potatoes, is known as 'Bubble and . . .' what?

10 In 2004, which Australian actress was honoured as a 'Citizen of the World' by the United Nations?

---------------------------*Under 25s* **SET 23** ---------------------------

1 Found in the leg, the tendon that joins the heel and calf is named after which Greek hero?

2 In which sport do international teams compete for the Davis Cup?

3 With whom did Andrew Ridgeley form the 1980s pop group Wham!?

4 In the 1990 film *Edward Scissorhands*, which US actor played the title role?

5 The Tasman Sea is a large body of water separating Australia and which other country?

6 Weighing up to 120 tonnes, what is the heaviest living animal?

7 How many of his six wives did Henry VIII have executed?

8 Until New York's Chrysler Building was completed in 1930, which French landmark was the world's tallest structure?

9 Craig Phillips, Brian Dowling and Kate Lawler were the first three winners of which UK TV reality gameshow?

10 What is the first name of Queen Elizabeth II's husband?

―――――――――――― *Under 25s* **SET 24** ――――――――――――

1 *Raiders of the Lost Ark* was the first in a series of films about which archaeologist hero?

2 In painting, which colour is formed when blue and yellow are mixed together?

3 The John F. Kennedy Airport uses which three-letter code?

4 Lisa, Claire, Faye, Lee and 'H' were collectively known as which 1990s British pop group?

5 Which Victorian engineer designed ships called the *Great Western*, *Great Eastern* and *Great Britain*?

6 Zermatt and Davos are popular ski resorts in which European country?

7 Dan Castellaneta, Nancy Cartwright and Hank Azaria provide voices on which long-running TV cartoon series?

8 In which popular song do participants put their 'left leg in' and their 'left leg out'?

9 In 1999, which basketball player did the US sports network ESPN vote as the greatest athlete of the twentieth century?

10 In the 2001 film *Captain Corelli's Mandolin,* which Spanish actress plays the doctor's daughter?

————————————— *Under 25s* **SET 25** —————————————

1 Which biblical hero foolishly revealed to Delilah that the secret of his strength was his uncut hair?

2 Which country of the UK had a population of roughly 2.9 million at the 2001 census?

3 What was the name of the red-nosed reindeer in the Christmas song recorded by the 'singing cowboy' Gene Autry?

4 In mathematics, what is the name given to an angle of less than 90°?

5 Which girl group had their first UK number one hit in 1998 with the single 'Never Ever'?

6 What name is given to a person who doesn't eat dairy products, eggs or any other animal products?

7 In football, a goal inadvertently scored by a player against his own team is known as what?

8 Which heiress said, 'I think every decade has an iconic blonde – like Marilyn Monroe – and right now, I'm that icon'?

9 In the mid-1800s, the blight of which crop caused a famine in Ireland?

10 Which 1990 film featured a large deadly spider from the jungles of South America accidentally transported to the US?

————————————— *Under 25s* **SET 26** —————————————

1 Which actress recorded the song 'Somethin' Stupid' with Robbie Williams?

2 Which fourteenth-century Scottish king defeated the English army at the Battle of Bannockburn?

3 Which traditional children's singing game ends with the words 'A-tishoo! A-tishoo! We all fall down'?

4 Which part of the body is most usually affected by the condition known as 'corns'?

5 In European geography, for which country does the abbreviation ROI stand?

6 The name of which county can precede the word 'pudding' to describe an item traditionally served with roast beef?

7 In the TV series *Lois & Clark: The New Adventures of Superman*, which US actress played Lois Lane?

8 What nationality is the fashion designer Tommy Hilfiger?

9 Which *Friends* actor starred with Bruce Willis in the 2004 movie *The Whole Ten Yards*?

10 In 2006, Melanie Slade shot to fame as the girlfriend of which teenage England footballer?

————————— *Under 25s* **SET 27** —————————

1 Which Hollywood actress starred alongside Richard Gere in the 1990 film *Pretty Woman*?

2 Which former US president also had a career as an actor in Hollywood?

3 In the children's story, which little girl narrowly escapes from three bears after eating their porridge?

4 Which government body, based in Llantrisant in Wales, is primarily responsible for providing UK coinage?

5 Dr John Carter, Dr Doug Ross and Dr Mark Greene are characters in which long-running US TV medical drama?

6 In 1995, singer Robbie Williams left which boyband?

7 With which sport is the name Thierry Henry most associated?

8 In which US state is Anaheim, where Walt Disney opened his first theme park in 1955?

9 In 2006, which *Desperate Housewives* actress published an autobiographical book entitled *Burnt Toast*?

10 The dish traditionally consisting of bread coated in egg and milk and fried is known as 'French . . .' what?

———————————— *Under 25s* SET 28 ————————————

1 The Campaign for Nuclear Disarmament is a pressure group more commonly known by which three initials?

2 Glamis Castle in Scotland was the childhood home of which late member of the British Royal Family?

3 *Titus Andronicus* and *Troilus and Cressida* are both plays by which world-famous English playwright?

4 The Year of the Dragon is a feature of which country's calendar?

5 In the traditional children's song, what colour are the ten bottles standing on the wall?

6 In the US, which type of meat is especially associated with the term 'southern-fried'?

7 Which animated TV comedy features the characters of Bender, Fry and Dr Zoidberg?

8 In UK law, what four-letter word is the temporary release of a person awaiting trial on payment of a sum as surety?

9 In 2003, the Kumars teamed up with which TV talent show singer on the UK number one hit 'Spirit In The Sky'?

10 Which former wrestling star played the title role in the 2002 film *The Scorpion King*?

———————————— *Under 25s* SET 29 ————————————

1 In 1996, which girl group shot to fame with the single 'Wannabe'?

2 Mary Queen of Scots was imprisoned for nineteen years during the reign of which English queen?

3 Which British mammal with distinctive black and white markings is traditionally referred to as 'Brock'?

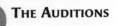
4 Which tennis player won the women's singles at Wimbledon a record nine times?

5 Which pack of seventy-eight playing cards is often used for fortune-telling and includes the suits of cups and wands?

6 Founded in 1945, the name of which international organization is abbreviated to UN?

7 In the TV show *Doctor Who*, by what acronym is 'Time and Relative Dimension in Space' better known?

8 Ra or Re is the name of the sun god in the ancient mythology of which country?

9 Which blonde former *Baywatch* star posed naked in Stella McCartney's shop window to protest against the use of fur?

10 In the 1987 film *Dirty Dancing*, what was the first name of the character played by Patrick Swayze?

—————————— Under 25s SET 30 ——————————

1 How many strings does a standard guitar usually have?

2 Which legendary area of the Atlantic is thought to be responsible for mysterious disappearances of ships and planes?

3 In mathematics, what name is given to a number that can only be divided by itself and 1?

4 The famous line 'All animals are equal but some animals are more equal than others' is from which George Orwell novel?

5 Which pop star was the author of the 2003 children's book *The English Roses*?

6 The term 'insomniac' describes a person who is unable to do what?

7 In sport, a team that wins a quarter-final progresses to which round?

8 *The Wrath of Khan*, *The Voyage Home* and *The Search for Spock* are films in which sci-fi series?

9 What name is given to the method of cooking an egg by cracking the contents into a pan of boiling water?

10 In which TV sitcom did Hugo Horton, played by actor James Fleet, marry Alice Tinker?

────────────── *Under 25s* **SET 31** ──────────────

1 How many players are required in a game of noughts and crosses?

2 *The Bends* and *OK Computer* were hit 1990s albums for which British pop group?

3 In the children's classic *Through the Looking Glass*, the fat, quarrelsome twins are called Tweedledum and . . . what?

4 The Ming Tombs and the Temple of Heaven are located in which Chinese city?

5 In 2006, which ex-*EastEnders* actress appeared on *The Catherine Tate Show* as a 'Gingers for Justice' protester?

6 The Ryder Cup is a golf event played by a combined team from Europe against golfers from which country?

7 Which film was the 2004 sequel to 2001's *Ocean's Eleven*?

8 In the French language, the word *pois* refers to which small green vegetable?

9 Born in 2006, Moses Bruce Anthony Martin is the son of which Coldplay singer?

10 If Boxing Day falls on a Saturday, on which day of the week did Christmas Eve fall?

────────────── *Under 25s* **SET 32** ──────────────

1 What was the name of the world's first postage stamp?

2 The character of Wilbur the Pig appears in which classic children's story by E. B. White?

3 Which gas, with the chemical symbol Ne, is used in fluorescent lamps?

4 Which pop group had their first UK number one hit in 1999 with the single 'Bring It All Back'?

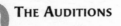

5 Between AD 54 and 68, Nero was emperor of which ancient civilization?

6 A friend of the TV puppet Sooty, what type of animal is Sweep?

7 In horse racing, in which month of the year does the Grand National traditionally take place?

8 In human anatomy, what is the name given to the fleshy lower part of the external ear?

9 Which male first name is shared by the Hollywood actors Modine, Broderick and McConaughey?

10 Which Bank of England banknote is the lowest value denomination?

─────────────── *Under 25s* **SET 33** ───────────────

1 In which country of the United Kingdom was politician Gordon Brown born?

2 According to the famous story, which Anglo-Saxon king is said to have allowed a housewife's cakes to burn?

3 In which country is the city of Mecca located?

4 What mode of transport was a penny farthing?

5 How many members were there in the original line-up of the boyband Blue?

6 Which actress played the role of Ling Woo in the US TV series *Ally McBeal*?

7 With which profession in the fashion industry is Nicky Clarke most closely associated?

8 Under the 2006 Formula 1 points system, how many points are awarded to the constructors winning a Grand Prix race?

9 In the Burgundy region of France, the grape variety called pinot noir is principally used to make wine of which colour?

10 In which 1989 Oscar-winning film is Robin Williams a teacher at Welton Academy?

───────────── 25–40 **SET 1** ─────────────

1 Which country is known as 'Cymru' in its native language?

2 Central America is an isthmus that connects North America with which continent?

3 Which hit by Abba begins with the line, 'You can dance, you can jive, having the time of your life'?

4 Which French city in east central France has given its name to a type of mustard?

5 Which Scottish snooker player holds the record for winning the World Snooker Championship seven times?

6 Which word is used to describe animals that have a backbone or spinal column?

7 Meaning 'rebirth' in French, what name is given to the period of European history that followed the Middle Ages?

8 According to the Highway Code, the traffic sign for 'no overtaking' depicts how many cars?

9 In 2006, which female TV presenter hosted the daily BBC2 show *Strictly Come Dancing: It Takes Two*?

10 Which 1998 British gangster film featured the characters Nick the Greek and 'Hatchet' Harry Lonsdale?

───────────── 25–40 **SET 2** ─────────────

1 Who is Hollywood star Kirk Douglas's famous actor son?

2 How many players are needed for the card game Patience?

3 In which 1995 Disney animated film did a Native American girl and a soldier share a romance?

4 Lazio and Juventus are professional football clubs in which country?

5 Which comedian had a 2005 number one single with the Tony Christie song 'Is This The Way To Amarillo'?

6 Which nineteenth-century British prime minister asked British tea merchants to produce a tea blended with bergamot oil?

7 In which European capital city is the Van Gogh Museum located?

8 In the animal world, the withers are the highest part of which animal's back?

9 In 1889, which Austrian psychiatrist published a book entitled *The Interpretation of Dreams*?

10 In which TV gameshow were contestants able to win a 'Bendy Bully' and a tankard?

—————————— *25–40* **SET 3** ——————————

1 Created by Agatha Christie, which elderly spinster detective lived in St Mary Mead?

2 In Greek mythology, the gorgon Medusa's hair was made of which creatures?

3 In the TV series, which letter does Superman wear on his chest?

4 Which sport is affectionately referred to as the 'Beautiful Game'?

5 Of what is Earl Grey a variety?

6 Which city in Scotland is nicknamed 'the Granite City' for the stone used in its buildings?

7 In 1923, which French fashion designer began the trend for tanning when she was accidentally sunburned on a cruise?

8 Which word, Chinese for 'great wind', is given to a tropical cyclone in the central and southern region of China?

9 In 2002, which TV talent show winner had a UK number one hit with the single 'Light My Fire'?

10 Which Asian country provides the setting for the 2003 movie *The Last Samurai*?

—————————— *25–40* **SET 4** ——————————

1 Complete the title of a novel by C. S. Lewis, *The Lion, the Witch and the* . . . what?

2 Which long hairstyle for men shares its name with a type of fish?

3 Which US actor played the part of Captain Jack Sparrow in the 2003 film *Pirates of the Caribbean*?

4 Which university is the oldest institution of higher learning in the United States?

5 In which city is the Sherlock Holmes Museum found?

6 Which fatty acid that is said to benefit the heart's health is found in oily fish?

7 In international Rugby Union, how many players are there in each team when a game is in play?

8 After ten years apart, which boyband re-formed in 2006 and released the album *Beautiful World*?

9 In which country of the UK was comedian Dawn French born?

10 Which actress played Ricky Tomlinson's on-screen wife in both *Brookside* and *The Royle Family*?

—————————— *25–40* **SET 5** ——————————

1 In 1988, which politician resigned after wrongly claiming that most of Britain's eggs were infected with salmonella?

2 Galia and Piel de Sapo are both varieties of which fruit?

3 Lanzarote is part of which island group?

4 For which Premiership football club did Ryan Giggs make his début in March 1991?

5 How many teams compete in the semi-finals of a sporting competition?

6 Which 1980s and 90s US TV sitcom featured the characters Darlene, DJ and Dan Conner?

7 In 2003, which US pop singer had a UK number one hit with the single 'Beautiful'?

8 In which 1960 film Western did Charles Bronson, Steve McQueen and Yul Brynner star as 'magnificent' gun-slingers?

9 What nationality is the supermodel Christy Turlington?

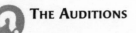
10 In the Harry Potter books, Crabbe and Goyle are the sidekicks of which unpleasant character?

25–40 SET 6

1 In the old nursery rhyme, which bridge '. . . is falling down'?

2 Which seventeenth-century English orange-seller turned actress became the lover of King Charles II?

3 Who is heir to the British throne?

4 With which English football club did David Beckham win the European Champions League in 1999?

5 Which Hollywood actress played Janet Weiss in the 1975 film *The Rocky Horror Picture Show*?

6 On which day of the week does Easter Day always fall?

7 In English, the name of which German city is given to a type of mild perfume?

8 Which city, located in South Australia, does the river Torrens flow through?

9 Long kept a secret, what was the first name of the TV detective Inspector Morse?

10 At the 2004 Superbowl, which singer performed with Janet Jackson and caused her infamous 'wardrobe malfunction'?

25–40 SET 7

1 A fictitious Slough paper merchants' premises provided the setting for which hit TV sitcom?

2 Which two-word Italian phrase is often used to describe eating in the open air?

3 'They think it's all over. It is now,' was said by Kenneth Wolstenholme during the 1966 final of which sporting event?

4 In which athletics field event was Ukrainian Sergey Bubka an outstanding competitor?

5 Between 1962 and 1979, which Bond film character was played by British actor Bernard Lee?

6 A Loiner is a native of which city in West Yorkshire?

7 With reference to motoring, what do the initials AA stand for?

8 In 1986, which British pop group had a UK hit when they covered the Frantic Elevators' song 'Holding Back The Years'?

9 According to the phrase, if you refuse to speak to someone, you are said to send them to which English city?

10 What is the official language of Liechtenstein?

––––––––––––––––––– *25–40* **SET 8** –––––––––––––––––––

1 Which US female singer-songwriter released the album *Songs in A Minor* in 2001?

2 The long-running TV series *Casualty* is set in which fictional hospital?

3 Which plant is the national emblem of Scotland?

4 In which year will the next leap year fall?

5 In the nursery rhyme, to which city did Doctor Foster go '. . . in a shower of rain'?

6 Writer Arthur C. Clarke is best known for which genre of novel?

7 The famous opera house known as La Scala is in which Italian city?

8 Russian Vaslav Nijinsky was most closely associated with which style of dance?

9 Which type of acid is extracted from the juice of lemons, oranges, limes and grapefruit?

10 Which Australian actor voiced the character of Roddy in the 2006 animated film *Flushed Away*?

––––––––––––––––––– *25–40* **SET 9** –––––––––––––––––––

1 In the TV series *Only Fools and Horses* which character does Trigger repeatedly and mistakenly call Dave?

2 In which TV soap is Ian Beale a longstanding character?

3 Which BBC radio station, that mostly plays classical music, broadcasts on 90 to 93FM?

4 Which football league team on the south coast has the nickname 'The Seagulls'?

5 'Heigh ho, heigh ho, it's off to work we go,' is a phrase from which 1937 Disney film musical?

6 From the Latin, how is the constellation Ursa Major more commonly known?

7 Who was the last British monarch before Oliver Cromwell became Lord Protector?

8 Who was lead singer of the British band Blur?

9 'White', 'Pink' and 'Ruby' are varieties of which citrus fruit?

10 The word 'dachshund' comes from which language?

─────────── 25–40 SET 10 ───────────

1 Which popular singer starred as Don in the 1963 film *Summer Holiday*?

2 The river Liffey flows through which Irish city?

3 Diana Prince is the alter-ego of which TV super-heroine?

4 Which country competes annually with England for Rugby Union's Calcutta Cup?

5 During the Second World War, which English singer was known as 'the Forces' Sweetheart'?

6 What is the popular name of the official report of everything that is said during debates in the British Parliament?

7 The songs 'One Day I'll Fly Away' and 'Almaz' were UK hits for which American female vocalist?

8 Which character from literary fiction has a companion called Sancho Panza?

9   Manzanilla is a sherry most closely associated with which country?

10   In which 1967 film does Warren Beatty's character say: 'We rob banks'?

─────────────── *25–40* **SET 11** ───────────────

1   The author and journalist Jane Goldman is married to which TV presenter?

2   Which British comic actor starred as Inspector Clouseau in five of the Pink Panther films?

3   In 2000, Kylie Minogue performed at the closing ceremony of which major sporting event in Sydney, Australia?

4   Which Derbyshire town has given its name to a tart of jam and almond-flavoured sponge?

5   Which US pop star had a UK number one hit in 1983 with the single 'Billie Jean'?

6   On which part of the body would a beret normally be worn?

7   The wizard, Merlin, is an important character in the tales of which legendary English king?

8   Who was British prime minister at the end of the First World War?

9   In the children's TV show *Teletubbies* what colour is the Teletubby, Po?

10   Which German word is used to wish good health to someone who has sneezed?

─────────────── *25–40* **SET 12** ───────────────

1   The singles 'Oye Mi Canto' and 'Anything For You' were hits for which Cuban-born pop star?

2   What is the name of Disney's flying elephant?

3   Mombasa is a port in which East African country?

4   In 2005, which Hollywood superstar married fellow actor Ashton Kutcher?

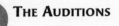

5 According to legend, which medieval king of England unsuccessfully commanded the sea to stop rising?

6 Which winter sport uses a vulcanized rubber disc called a puck?

7 With which field of the arts is the American Frank Lloyd Wright most associated?

8 Which invaders of Britain built the roads that are now called Ermine Street, Fosse Way and Watling Street?

9 In the 1990s, which character did actor Steve McFadden first play in TV's *EastEnders*?

10 In human anatomy, is the cornea located on the front or the back of the eye?

───────────── *25–40* **SET 13** ─────────────

1 Which comic character, played by Barry Humphries, was presented with the keys to Melbourne in 2006?

2 'Who Do You Think You Are Kidding, Mr Hitler?' was the theme song of which classic TV sitcom?

3 Which of Henry VIII's children reigned in England for forty-four years?

4 Which American cyclist won the Tour de France a record seven times between 1999 and 2005?

5 The commonly used name of which medical condition has the abbreviation RSI?

6 In which capital city is Westminster Abbey located?

7 What is the capital city of Switzerland?

8 In 2001, which British singer-songwriter had his first UK number one hit with the single 'Gotta Get Thru This'?

9 'Billy the Fish' and 'Biffa Bacon' can be found in which British comic?

10 Which 1985 film, starring Emilio Estevez and Rob Lowe, centred on a group of friends stuggling with adulthood?

─────────────────── *25–40* **SET 14** ───────────────────

1   In literature, which doctor is the friend and confidant of Sherlock Holmes?

2   Which supermodel created and presents the TV show *America's Next Top Model*?

3   What is the name given by Argentinians to the islands known in the UK as the Falklands?

4   Which Danish Euro-pop group had their first UK number one hit in 1997 with 'Barbie Girl'?

5   Which son of the late Formula 1 World Champion Graham Hill also won the world title?

6   Which fictional Londoner was portrayed by actor Warren Mitchell in the TV sitcom, *Till Death Us Do Part*?

7   Which astronaut said the famous line, 'One small step for man, one giant leap for mankind'?

8   Complete the title of the traditional singalong song, 'Show Me The Way To Go . . .' where?

9   Which member of Destiny's Child starred as Foxxy Cleopatra in the 2002 film *Austin Powers in Goldmember*?

10 In 1995, which low-cost airline was founded by Stelios Haji-Ioannou?

─────────────────── *25–40* **SET 15** ───────────────────

1   Which Hollywood star played a mountain rescue climber in the 1993 film *Cliffhanger*?

2   Born in 1756, which prolific Austrian composer's first name was Wolfgang?

3   In which seaside resort town in Devon was the TV sitcom *Fawlty Towers* set?

4   In 1977, the legendary disco, Studio 54, opened its doors in which US city?

5   In the nursery rhyme, who is described as '. . . quite contrary'?

6   Which English monarch did Anne of Cleves marry in 1540?

7 The Royal Northern College of Music and the Royal Exchange Theatre are based in which English city?

8 Which is the largest coral reef in the world?

9 Which British actress was born Amelia Driver?

10 In 2004, who became the UK's longest serving Chancellor of the Exchequer since the 1820s?

─────────── *25–40* **SET 16** ───────────

1 Which singer and actress played Daisy Duke in the 2005 film *The Dukes of Hazzard*?

2 At which northern English racecourse is the classic horse race, the St Leger, run?

3 In theatre, which musical features the love song 'Memory'?

4 In the nursery rhyme, which day's child is 'fair of face'?

5 Which composer changed the name of his Third Symphony from 'Bonaparte' to 'Eroica'?

6 'The Star-Spangled Banner' is the national anthem of which country?

7 At the court of Henry VIII, who was Lord Chancellor of England between 1529 and 1532?

8 Which carbohydrate food is the principal ingredient in the dish paella?

9 The Nikkei Index measures movements in share prices on the stock exchange of which city?

10 In 1981, which Swedish pop group had UK hits with the songs 'Lay All Your Love On Me' and 'One Of Us'?

─────────── *25–40* **SET 17** ───────────

1 *Broadway Danny Rose* and *Manhattan* are films from which New York director?

2 Which Shakespeare play features the Montague and the Capulet families?

3 Dim sum is a type of food associated with the cuisine of which Asian country?

4 Eindhoven and Utrecht are cities in which European country?

5 Which three-word Latin phrase is used to indicate an unacceptable or unwelcome person?

6 What colour are the cartoon characters The Smurfs?

7 Which chemical element with the symbol Na is a soft silver-white metal?

8 Which British singer duetted with Peter Gabriel on the 1980s Top 10 hit 'Don't Give Up'?

9 Which male first name is shared by the movie stars Redford, Carlyle and De Niro?

10 Which winter sport has traditionally been known as 'the roaring game' in Scotland?

—————————————— 25–40 SET 18 ——————————————

1 Who released the greatest hits album The Immaculate Collection in 1990?

2 Which US TV sitcom featured the nose-twitching witch Samantha Stephens, and her mortal husband Darrin?

3 Which spirit is made from the fermented juice of the Mexican agave plant?

4 Hokkaido, Kyushu and Shikoku islands are part of which Asian country?

5 Which railway tunnel is often referred to in the press as the 'Chunnel'?

6 In astrology, which star sign is represented by a scorpion?

7 In which ocean are the French Polynesian islands found?

8 In the Harry Potter films, which Scottish actor played the character of the half-giant, Rubeus Hagrid?

9 In terms of area, which is the second-largest state in the USA?

10 Which author created spymaster George Smiley?

———————————— *25–40* **SET 19** ————————————

1 Which style of shoe heel takes its name from the Italian word for dagger?

2 Which British pop star was born Georgios Panayiotou?

3 In the cult US TV cartoon series, who is the sidekick of Butt-Head?

4 Which US singer played Aunty Eternity in the 1985 film *Mad Max Beyond Thunderdome*?

5 Fencing, swimming, shooting, running and which other sport make up a modern pentathlon?

6 Which British pop group had a UK number one hit in 1967 with the single 'All You Need Is Love'?

7 Zürich is a city in which European country?

8 In 1620, in which present-day US state did the Pilgrim Fathers land?

9 Which North American natural tourist attraction can be viewed from the *Maid of the Mist*?

10 In the 1990s, which British prime minister launched a 'Back to Basics' campaign that soon backfired?

———————————— *25–40* **SET 20** ————————————

1 Which female vocalist sang the 2001 hit 'I'm Like A Bird'?

2 Which comedian, known for his deadpan style, succeeded Terry Wogan as presenter of *Blankety Blank*?

3 What was the name of the 1985 hit film set in Kenya that starred Meryl Streep as Danish writer Karen Blixen?

4 The most famous work of the late Douglas Adams is *The Hitchhiker's Guide to the . . .* what?

5 Which colour of flag is the universal symbol for surrender or truce?

6 What type of dial, usually situated in gardens, is a traditional device used for measuring time?

7 Of which fruit is the Blenheim Orange a variety?

8 Which sea lies directly north of Turkey?

9 What acronym is commonly used to refer to an official order restricting a person's anti-social behaviour?

10 With which sport is the name Andrew Murray most associated?

25–40 SET 21

1 The retina is part of which organ of the body?

2 Which word, meaning 'crib' in French, is used in English for a day nursery for young children?

3 Who was the first foreigner to coach the England football team?

4 Who stars as Marie Antoinette in the 2006 film of the same name?

5 The cobbled Royal Mile is a feature of which Scottish city?

6 Which US pop star had UK number one hits in 1986 with the songs 'Papa Don't Preach' and 'True Blue'?

7 Which author wrote the novel *1984*?

8 In which Australian city is Darling Harbour located?

9 In the British school curriculum, what do the initials PE stand for?

10 Which TV presenter and entertainer hosted the 1990s TV quiz *Didn't They Do Well!?*

25–40 SET 22

1 Which Edwardian poet and novelist wrote the much-quoted poem 'If'?

2 The TV drama series *Spooks* features which branch of the British security service?

3 On which river does Glasgow lie?

4 In 1995, which US actress starred in the romantic comedy *While You Were Sleeping*?

5 In which house does the British Cabinet traditionally meet every Thursday morning?

6 Which country and western singer wrote the hit song, 'I Will Always Love You'?

7 In Italian cuisine, what type of foodstuff is 'fettucine'?

8 Royal Birkdale and Royal Lytham & St Annes are venues for the Open Championship in which sport?

9 Which word comes from the Italian for 'forty days', and is used for the isolation of an animal that may spread disease?

10 In fashion, an elevated narrow platform on which models walk is known by what name?

——————————— 25–40 **SET 23** ———————————

1 Which fruit is the main ingredient of the dish guacamole?

2 Which British singer had his first UK number one hit in 1959 with 'Living Doll'?

3 American actor Dick Van Dyke plays the inventor of a flying car in which 1968 film musical?

4 Which TV comedy was set in the fictional village of Dibley?

5 Which US golfer won the Open Championship at Hoylake in 2006?

6 Who is third in the line of succession to the British throne?

7 In which Italian city is the Bridge of Sighs, which once connected the Doge's palace to the prison?

8 What is the name of Sylvester Stallone's flamboyant mother?

9 Which word can follow 'jelly', 'star' and 'gold' to form the names of three aquatic creatures?

10 The title of 'Mikado' was historically given to the emperors of which country?

——————————— 25–40 **SET 24** ———————————

1 In which country were the 2006 Oscars hosted?

2 The show *West Side Story* is a musical adaptation of which Shakespeare play?

3 Paella is perhaps the best-known dish of which European country?

4 The 1970s TV sitcom *The Liver Birds* was set in which English city?

5 Which English monarch began the construction of the Tower of London?

6 Kabbala is a form of mysticism that started in which major religion?

7 What nationality is the former Formula 1 driver Michael Schumacher?

8 In which castle are the Scottish Crown jewels held?

9 Which word is used for an animal that eats both plant and animal matter?

10 In 1969, which British pop group had its final UK number one hit with the single 'The Ballad Of John And Yoko'?

—————————— 25–40 SET 25 ——————————

1 In Daniel Defoe's novel, on which day of the week did Robinson Crusoe find his faithful servant and companion?

2 In the US, what is meant by 'sidewalk'?

3 Fran Healy is the lead singer of which Scottish rock band?

4 Muirfield is a famous venue in which sport?

5 In the human body, which is the only organ that is mainly composed of cardiac muscle?

6 In which country of the UK did Ayrshire cattle originate?

7 In which month is the Queen's official birthday?

8 In the UK honours system, which title for women is the equivalent to the title of 'Sir' for men?

9 The hit British TV quiz show *Blockbusters* was originally hosted by which presenter?

10 Which actor starred in both of the films *Seven Years in Tibet* and *Se7en*?

———————— *25–40* **SET 26** ————————

1 What is the name of the lead singer in the band Blondie?

2 What is the first name of Ozzy Osbourne's wife?

3 In the musical *Annie Get Your Gun*, what is Annie's surname?

4 'Call me Ishmael,' is a famous quote from which Herman Melville novel?

5 In 1605 which buildings did Guy Fawkes and his co-conspirators intend to blow up?

6 Which legendary gameshow host was the 'Bob' in *Bob's Your Uncle*?

7 Which actress famously shaved her head as part of her role in the film *GI Jane*?

8 What is a boater hat traditionally made of?

9 Excluding injury time or penalties, how long is a standard football match?

10 The Côte d'Azur is a holiday destination on the coastline of which sea?

———————— *25–40* **SET 27** ————————

1 Which breed of dog is most closely associated with the Queen?

2 In 1982, which son of a British prime minister went missing during a motor race in the Sahara desert?

3 Which type of insect would you find in a hive?

4 On which TV makeover show did designer Laurence Llewelyn-Bowen first come to national fame?

5 Which Russian novelist wrote *War and Peace*?

6 What nationality is the former England football manager Sven-Göran Eriksson?

7 Which comedy actor is the voice of Shrek in the 2001 hit film animation?

8 Which South American country uses the internet country code '.ar'?

9 'Money For Nothing' and 'Romeo And Juliet' were UK chart hits for which British band?

10 The omelettes known as 'tortillas' originated in which European country?

25–40 SET 28
---

1 In the Alexandre Dumas 1844 swashbuckling novel, how were Athos, Porthos and Aramis collectively known?

2 Which English pop duo had a number one hit with the 1987 single 'Always On My Mind'?

3 In UK weights and measures, how many pounds are there in one stone?

4 What is the predominant colour of the shirt, shorts and socks of the Liverpool FC home kit?

5 Which US actor played the grown-up Peter Pan in the 1991 Steven Spielberg film *Hook*?

6 Which English monarch said, 'I have the heart and stomach of a king, and of a king of England too'?

7 In the UK, in which decade did the one-pound coin become legal tender?

8 Whom did Jacques Chirac succeed as President of France in 1995?

9 'Dubya' is a nickname for which US politician?

10 A Jack O'Lantern is traditionally associated with which celebration?

25–40 SET 29
---

1 Which monarch did Prince Albert of Saxe-Coburg-Gotha marry in 1840?

2 Casablanca is a city in which North African country?

3 In metric measurement, how many millimetres are there in one metre?

4 Pink Lady is a variety of which fruit?

5 In the comic strip *Asterix*, what type of animal is Dogmatix?

6 Which living species of bird lays the largest egg?

7 According to the proverb, what type of waters 'run deep'?

8 Complete this line from the nursery rhyme, 'Remember, remember the fifth of November, gunpowder, treason and . . .' what?

9 Which 1964 musical film is based on the George Bernard Shaw play *Pygmalion*?

10 In 1984, which British rock band had a major UK hit with the single 'Radio Ga Ga'?

—————————— *25–40* **SET 30** ——————————

1 In Herman Melville's novel *Moby Dick*, what is Moby Dick?

2 How many players are in a standard cricket team?

3 What was the national currency of France prior to the euro?

4 The dish risotto is originally from which country?

5 In the 1994 blockbuster movie *The Shawshank Redemption*, which actor played Ellis Boyd Redding?

6 The Battle of the Somme took place during which war?

7 A final appearance or action is often called a 'swan . . .' what?

8 Originally from southern Africa, the Rhodesian ridgeback is a breed of which animal?

9 The name of which common plant comes from the French for 'teeth of the lion', due to the shape of its leaves?

10 In 1997, actress Nadia Sawalha appeared in which TV soap?

—————————— *25–40* **SET 31** ——————————

1 Which R&B vocalist had a UK number one hit in 1997 with 'I Believe I Can Fly'?

2 On which continent is the South Pole?

3 The Tony Awards are given for outstanding achievement in which field of the arts?

4 What colour is the cross on the flag of England?

5   In which epic 1962 film did Peter O'Toole star as the lead character T. E. Lawrence?

6   In UK weights and measures, how many ounces are there in one pound?

7   American author Samuel L. Clemens published several classic novels under which pen name?

8   The Andalusian and the Camargue are two breeds of which animal?

9   Which US soul singer was cautioned by police in 1999 over an alleged assault on a security officer at Heathrow Airport?

10 On TV, which furry creatures picked up litter on Wimbledon Common?

25–40 SET 32

1   By what name is the official aeroplane of the President of the United States commonly known?

2   The fruit known as a satsuma originated in which Asian country?

3   At which UK racecourse is the Grand National run?

4   Which actor has played the cult characters Michael Knight and Mitch Buchannon on TV?

5   In the world of international time-keeping, what do the initials GMT stand for?

6   In a play by Shakespeare, which king is the father of Cordelia, Goneril, and Regan?

7   In 1994, which US pop diva had a UK number one hit with a cover of the song 'Without You'?

8   In relation to music formats, what does the abbreviation CD stand for?

9   What time of day is applied to the shadowy beard appearing on a man's face usually towards the evening?

10 Which British-born actress was nominated for an Oscar for her role in the 1997 film *Good Will Hunting*?

────────── *25–40* SET 33 ──────────

1 What name is given to the pastry used to make profiteroles and eclairs?

2 Which US president came into office in 1961?

3 Actress Naomi Watts played the character Ann Darrow in a 2005 re-make of which classic film?

4 Which month is named after Augustus Caesar?

5 In which US state is the city of New Orleans found?

6 Which county shares its name with the cat featured in *Alice in Wonderland*, that disappears leaving only its smile?

7 Which traditional Maori dance do the All Black rugby team perform before each match?

8 Which name beginning with 'A' is given to the bony outgrowths on the heads of male deer?

9 Arthur Daley was a lovable rogue in which TV comedy series that ran from 1979 to 1994?

10 James Galway is a virtuoso on which instrument?

────────── *25–40* SET 34 ──────────

1 Which 1980 horror film starred Jack Nicholson as the rampaging killer Jack Torrance?

2 Which pulse is the main ingredient of the dish houmous?

3 Headingley Cricket Ground can be found in which Yorkshire city?

4 The term 'Matador' is most closely associated with which sport?

5 In 1975, which British singer became the lead singer of the rock group Genesis?

6 Julian, Dick, Anne, George and Timmy made up which gang in the series of books by Enid Blyton?

7 Mohamed Al-Fayed has been the owner of which department store in Knightsbridge, London since 1985?

8 With reference to tests of ability, for what do the letters IQ stand?

9 Which two-word French phrase is used as an expression of good wishes to someone beginning a journey?

10 Which celebrated Renaissance figure became court painter as well as a military engineer to the Duke of Milan in 1482?

────────────── *40+* **SET 1** ──────────────

1 How many members were there originally in the pop group S Club 7?

2 Which US president was known by the initials FDR?

3 Inzamam-ul-Haq has captained which country in Test match cricket?

4 The world's first railway, carrying passengers on steam trains, ran between Stockton and which other north-east town?

5 Which piece of embroidery, over seventy metres long, celebrates William the Conqueror's invasion of England?

6 In 1937, which award-winning author wrote the fantasy novel *The Hobbit*?

7 Which composer wrote the American folk opera *Porgy and Bess*?

8 The group of islands known as the Hebrides lie off the west coast of which country of the UK?

9 Ziggy Stardust is the alter ego of which British singer-songwriter?

10 For which 1956 film were James Dean and Rock Hudson both nominated for the Best Actor Oscar?

────────────── *40+* **SET 2** ──────────────

1 Which Derby-winning racehorse was kidnapped in 1983?

2 In chess, which piece can only move diagonally?

3 In which Turkish city is the Blue Mosque found?

4 The children's novel *Goodnight Mister Tom* is set in Britain during which war?

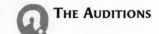

5 Which country and western singer played Truvy Jones in the 1989 tearjerker, *Steel Magnolias*?

6 The Coral Sea is part of which ocean?

7 Complete the title of the famous hymn, 'Onward, Christian . . .' what?

8 Which male first name is shared by the actors Swayze, Stewart and McGoohan?

9 In human anatomy, above which organ is the adrenal gland located?

10 Which pop artist designed the famous 'banana' cover for the 1967 album *The Velvet Underground & Nico*?

40+ SET 3

1 Which planet did William Herschel discover in 1781?

2 In the TV comedy series *Are You Being Served?*, what was the name of the character played by Mollie Sugden?

3 Complete the proverb: 'Charity begins at . . .'?

4 In the 2002 Bond film *Die Another Day*, which British actor played the role of gadget master 'Q' for the first time?

5 The South Pacific Cook Islands are a territory of which Commonwealth country?

6 In which country was astronomer Galileo Galilei born?

7 Which Russian ballerina gave her name to a dish made of meringue, cream and fruit?

8 The 1993 film blockbuster *Jurassic Park* was based on a book by which bestselling author?

9 By which title is the wife of a duke known?

10 In 1997, which Elton John song, rewritten in memory of Diana, Princess of Wales, was a UK number one hit?

40+ SET 4

1 Which famous female TV newsreader retired in 2006 after a career which included *Tomorrow's World* and *TV-AM*?

2 Eating which vegetable is commonly believed to help a person see in the dark?

3 Which mythological creature, resembling a horse, has a single horn on its forehead?

4 With which sport is the name Will Carling most closely associated?

5 Which Italian composer wrote the opera *Otello*, based on the Shakespeare play *Othello*?

6 Jung Chang's 1991 autobiography, entitled *Wild Swans*, was about growing up in which country?

7 Formed in 1949, which international organization is known by the acronym NATO?

8 A Galwegian is a native of which city on the west coast of Ireland?

9 Which legal term describes the person chosen by the writer of a will to carry out the requests expressed in it?

10 Which king summoned the parliament known as the Long Parliament in November 1640?

40+ SET 5

1 What nationality was Elvis Presley?

2 Mr T played Sergeant Bosco 'B. A.' Baracus in which TV series of the 1980s?

3 The Great Sphinx is a monument found in which country?

4 In the nursery rhyme tongue twister, who 'picked a peck of pickled peppers'?

5 In 1967, which Briton became the first person to sail round the world single-handed, stopping only once?

6 By what name is the writer and military tactician T. E. Lawrence better known?

7 Which spirit is the main alcoholic ingredient of the cocktail known as Planter's Punch?

8 In Greek mythology, who unwittingly killed his father and married his mother?

9 In the 1995 biopic *Nixon*, which Welsh-born actor played Richard Nixon?

10 Which stage musical features the 'Cotton Blossom', a floating theatre on the Mississippi river?

───────────────────── 40+ SET 6 ─────────────────────

1 Which US city is home to the famous Red Sox baseball team?

2 Which prime minister said: 'In politics if you want something said, ask a man. If you want anything done, ask a woman'?

3 Which fictional detective, created by Sir Arthur Conan Doyle, lived at 221B Baker Street, London?

4 In the Dennis Potter TV series first shown in 1986, Michael Gambon played Philip E. Marlow in *The Singing . . .* what?

5 Raised in 1982 from the bottom of the Solent, what was the name of King Henry VIII's flagship?

6 Who had a UK number one hit single in 1993 with 'I'd Do Anything For Love (But I Won't Do That)'?

7 The 2004 documentary film *Fahrenheit 9/11* was made by which American film-maker and anti-war activist?

8 First seen in the 1928 cartoon, *Steamboat Willie*, what is the name of Walt Disney's famous cartoon mouse?

9 What nationality was the Renaissance painter Sandro Botticelli?

10 In which Arthur Miller play does the travelling salesman Willie Loman appear?

——————————— **40+ SET 7** ———————————

1　*Humble Pie* is the name of the autobiography of which volatile TV chef?

2　Which Labour prime minister coined the phrase 'A week is a long time in politics'?

3　In the Marx Brothers films, which brother never spoke?

4　In 1936, in which Lincolnshire seaside town did Billy Butlin open his first holiday camp?

5　Which metal is the main component of steel?

6　In which national museum are the Rosetta Stone and the Elgin Marbles found?

7　According to the proverb, what have to be broken in order to make an omelette?

8　By which abbreviation is closed-circuit TV better known?

9　The singer-songwriter Errol Brown was the lead singer of which 1970s British pop band?

10　The character Cliff Barnes is most closely associated with which 1980s US TV soap?

——————————— **40+ SET 8** ———————————

1　Which debonair British actor wrote two autobiographies entitled *The Moon's a Balloon* and *Bring on the Empty Horses*?

2　Nicolae Ceauşescu was President of which eastern European country from 1974 until 1989?

3　In a 1950s children's TV sitcom, which overweight schoolboy was known as the 'Fat Owl of the Remove'?

4　Loch Ness is a large freshwater loch in which country?

5　In 1985, which tennis player won the Wimbledon men's singles title at the age of seventeen?

6　Jersey Royals are an early variety of which vegetable?

7 According to the saying, how many winks is a person said to have during a short nap?

8 Marti Pellow was the lead singer with which chart-topping pop group?

9 Which prolific US inventor was called 'the Wizard of Menlo Park'?

10 Which 1984 film comedy spoof features the rock star characters David St Hubbins, Nigel Tufnel and Derek Smalls?

———————— 40+ SET 9 ————————

1 Which band had UK 1980s hits with 'True' and 'Gold'?

2 Which heroic nurse was known as 'The Lady with the Lamp'?

3 In 1872, which American ship was famously found in perfect condition but abandoned in the North Atlantic?

4 Of which fruit is Cox's Orange Pippin a variety?

5 The fictional detective Sherlock Holmes famously wore which style of hat?

6 The thirteenth-century Rheims Cathedral was traditionally used to crown the kings of which European country?

7 In which animated TV series do the characters of Cartman, Kenny, Stan and Kyle regularly appear?

8 Bridgetown is the capital of which Caribbean island?

9 Which 1978 classic horror movie had the working title *The Babysitter Murders*?

10 The false bravado gained from drinking alcohol is popularly known as 'Dutch . . .' what?

———————— 40+ SET 10 ————————

1 Who sang the theme tune for the 1981 Bond film *For Your Eyes Only*?

2 Of which amphibian is the 'natterjack' a variety?

3 Which Olympic winter sport is often described as being similar to 'Chess on ice'?

4   Ross and Demelza were the lead characters in which 1970s TV drama series?

5   'Scrumpy' is a rough, unsweetened variety of which alcoholic drink?

6   The sports car company Lamborghini was founded in which European country?

7   From which Mediterranean island off the west coast of Italy did Napoleon Bonaparte escape in 1815?

8   In a restaurant, the name of which precious metal comes before the word 'service' to give a table waiting style?

9   In the human body, what is the common name for the thorax?

10 What is the French word for the colour red?

40+ SET 11

1   Which Russian monk was the subject of a 1978 disco hit by the group Boney M?

2   Which president of France died at the age of seventy-nine, in November 1970?

3   What is the name of the fictional 'King of the Jungle' in the novels by Edgar Rice Burroughs?

4   A popular feature of children's sports days is a race run with an egg balanced on what?

5   In the TV sitcoms *Only Fools and Horses* and *The Green Green Grass*, what is the name of Boycie's wife?

6   All Souls, Balliol and Merton colleges are part of which university?

7   The pawpaw fruit is more commonly known by which name?

8   Which Californian city is known as the 'City of Angels'?

9   Which ocean lies to the west of Australia?

10 Which comic actor played the title role in the 1998 film comedy *Patch Adams*?

—————— 40+ SET 12 ——————

1 Sunnydale, California was the setting for which 1997 cult teen horror series?

2 Made famous by a Beatles album cover, Abbey Road is located in which city?

3 In which sport was the Soviet Union's Nellie Kim an Olympic gold medallist?

4 'History is bunk,' is a saying generally attributed to which American motor manufacturer?

5 Which bestselling US novelist wrote *The Pelican Brief*?

6 What name was given to 1950s UK youths who wore Edwardian-style jackets, drainpipe trousers and crepe-soled shoes?

7 Which three-letter abbreviation is used for a sandwich that contains bacon, lettuce and tomato?

8 The Sahara desert is located on which continent?

9 The flag of which Scandinavian country is a golden yellow cross on a blue background?

10 Which female TV personality and wine expert co-authored *Entertaining With Food & Drink* in 1995?

—————— 40+ SET 13 ——————

1 Which nineteenth-century prime minister was known by the nickname Dizzy?

2 Which North American aviation company created the 747 jumbo jet?

3 Which US singer and actress had a UK number one hit in 1980 with 'Woman In Love'?

4 The Forbidden City and the Summer Palace are located in which Chinese city?

5 In the 1966 film *Born Free*, which animal was raised by Joy and George Adamson?

6 Which term, meaning 'foot to earth' in French, is used for a small flat, house, or room kept for occasional use?

7 'Checkmate' is a term used in which board game?

8 How many inches high is the net in table tennis?

9 In the 1960s and 70s TV series *Ironside*, which actor played the wheelchair-bound detective?

10 VE Day marks the end of the Second World War in Europe; in which month is it celebrated?

—————————— 40+ SET 14 ——————————

1 In 1971, which member of the Royal Family was chosen as the BBC Sports Personality of the Year for her horsemanship?

2 Temple Meads railway station is in which English city?

3 In which 1991 movie did Brad Pitt become famous for his role as Geena Davis's love interest, J. D.?

4 The Matterhorn, in the Alps, is situated on the border between Switzerland and which other country?

5 Complete the title of a comedy by Shakespeare, *The Comedy of . . .* what?

6 Which actor played café owner René Artois in the TV sitcom *'Allo 'Allo!*?

7 Which raw food is traditionally the main ingredient in the hangover cure known as a Prairie Oyster?

8 Which hairy green fruit lends its name to a person who tags along unwanted on a couple's date?

9 What nationality was the nineteenth-century composer Johann Strauss?

10 What is the star sign of someone born on 30 October?

—————————— 40+ SET 15 ——————————

1 In the children's TV series, who are Tinky Winky, Dipsy, Laa Laa and Po?

2 A 'gaggle' is a group of which farmyard fowl?

3 From 1990 to 1995, former electrician Lech Walesa was President of which East European country?

4 What is the first name of football legend George Best's son?

5 Which South American country has the largest population?

6 The texting and online abbreviation 'BTW' stands for which three words?

7 In 1983, which British rock singer had a UK number one hit with the single 'Baby Jane'?

8 Which sea is bordered by countries including Sweden, Germany, Finland and Russia?

9 The autobiography *The Life and Times of the Thunderbolt Kid* is about the early life of which US travel writer?

10 In which 1960 epic film did Laurence Olivier play Marcus Licinius Crassus?

―――――――――― *40+* **SET 16** ――――――――――

1 The singer-songwriter Damon Gough performs under the name of 'Badly Drawn . . .' what?

2 In 2006, who succeeded Sven-Göran Eriksson as the England football manager?

3 Who directed the 1993 film blockbuster *Jurassic Park*?

4 In the *Arabian Nights* story, what was inside Aladdin's lamp?

5 Arundel Castle, in West Sussex, is the seat of which dukes?

6 How is the West Highland White Terrier dog more popularly known?

7 Fitzgerald's Bar was a popular haunt in which TV drama series set in a small Irish village?

8 Spectacles are used to aid which of the five senses?

9 Which US president said 'Ich bin ein Berliner' during a 1963 visit to Berlin?

10 The French word *pantalon* refers to which item of clothing?

40+ SET 17

1 Who played the title role in the 1969 film *The Prime of Miss Jean Brodie*?

2 In which US city does the car race known popularly as the Indy 500 take place?

3 As used in lonely hearts columns, what does the abbreviation GSOH stand for?

4 What name is given to the classified telephone directory, often printed on yellow paper, listing services provided?

5 Which singer had UK number one hits in the 1980s with 'This Ole House' and 'Oh Julie'?

6 A sweet consisting of flavoured gelatin coated in icing sugar is known as 'Turkish . . .' what?

7 Which famous English forest lies between the rivers Severn and Wye in Gloucestershire?

8 In which decade was the Mir space station launched?

9 The Greater Horseshoe and Serotine are varieties of which flying mammal?

10 Which Welsh former choirboy presents TV's *Songs of Praise*?

40+ SET 18

1 Which 1960s female vocal group had hits with 'Baby Love' and 'You Keep Me Hanging On'?

2 Which city in Zimbabwe was once known as Salisbury?

3 'You were only supposed to blow the bloody doors off,' is a line from which 1969 comedy crime movie?

4 Which jeweller made famous gold and jewel-encrusted Easter eggs for the Russian royal family?

5 The Riesling grape is used to make which colour of wine?

6 Idaho is a state in which country?

7 The Hindu god of prophecy, Ganesh, has the head of which animal?

8 Which first name is shared by UK politicians Cameron, Miliband and Davis?

9 In the French language, the word *neige* refers to which type of weather precipitation?

10 Who wrote the children's book *The Wind in the Willows*?

——————————— 40+ SET 19 ———————————

1 Which Swedish actress played Anastasia in the 1956 film?

2 What is the length, in metres, of an Olympic swimming pool?

3 In Carlo Collodi's children's story, what type of toy was Pinocchio?

4 What nationality was the pop artist Andy Warhol?

5 At which Scottish university did Prince William and Kate Middleton first meet?

6 Which word follows 'blow', 'angel' and 'cat' to form the names of three aquatic creatures?

7 James Callaghan, British prime minister from 1976 to 1979, represented which UK party?

8 Which comedy actress played a different starring role in every episode of the TV series *Murder Most Horrid*?

9 Who recorded the hit album *Soprano in Red*?

10 The island of Gomera is in which group of islands?

——————————— 40+ SET 20 ———————————

1 The classic novel *Black Beauty* centres on the adventures of what type of animal?

2 Danny Zuko, Kenickie and Sandy are all characters from which film musical?

3 With which sport is the expression to 'tee off' most commonly associated?

4 In the 1981 war film *Gallipoli*, which Australian-raised actor played the role of Frank Dunne?

5 How many points does a star of David have?

6 In which 1990s TV comedy series did actress Caroline Quentin play the character Dorothy?

7 In 1851, which American author wrote the classic *Moby Dick*?

8 Which Elizabethan playwright's mother was born Mary Arden?

9 The word 'bomber' can be put before which item of clothing?

10 Which dark brown, syrupy vinegar is most closely associated with Modena in Italy?

—————————— 40+ SET 21 ——————————

1 In the children's nursery rhyme, Mary 'had a little . . .' what?

2 The Arsenal goalkeeper Jens Lehmann represented which country in the 2006 FIFA World Cup?

3 In August 2005, what name was given to the hurricane that swept through the southern states of America?

4 The phrase 'vis-à-vis' comes from which language?

5 Complete the title of a Gilbert and Sullivan comic opera: *The Pirates of* . . . what?

6 The 1980s TV series *The Jewel in the Crown* was set in which Asian country?

7 In 1930, which British aeronautical engineer patented the first jet engine?

8 Gianni, Donatella and Santo belong to which Italian fashion-designing dynasty?

9 Which Chinese-American detective, who works for the Honolulu Police, was created by author Earl Derr Biggers?

10 Which rating is used to measure the warmth of a duvet?

─────────── *40+* **SET 22** ───────────

1 The Yuan is the national currency of which Asian country?

2 What was the nickname of the English Crusader King, Richard I?

3 In which city in the UK is Queen's University found?

4 Peter Jackson's *Lord of the Rings* trilogy was famously filmed on location in which country?

5 Which actress played Patsy in the TV show *Absolutely Fabulous*?

6 Gunga Din is the name of a heroic Hindu water-carrier in a poem of army life by which English writer?

7 Which traditional form of entertainment is compèred by a ringmaster?

8 Which Wigan-born entertainer was famous for the songs 'Leaning On A Lamppost' and 'When I'm Cleaning Windows'?

9 Lady Grey is a variety of which beverage?

10 Which jockey opened a chain of restaurants called 'Frankie's' with celebrity chef Marco Pierre White?

─────────── *40+* **SET 23** ───────────

1 In 1996, which country won the Eurovision Song Contest for a record seventh time?

2 The Gladstone, the Royal Seaforth, and the Albert are docks in which English city?

3 Which stage musical features the songs 'One Night In Bangkok' and 'I Know Him So Well'?

4 Which actress played the Bond girl called 'Jinx' in the 2002 film *Die Another Day*?

5 Paul Merton and Ian Hislop are team captains on which long-running TV series?

6 In 1916, the Royal Navy fought which country's fleet at the Battle of Jutland?

7 What is the birth name of former boxer Muhammad Ali?

8 Which religious order did St Francis of Assisi found?

9 In the nursery rhyme 'Incey Wincey Spider', what did the spider climb?

10 How many days are there in the month of April?

─────────────── 40+ **SET 24** ───────────────

1 Golden Delicious is a variety of which fruit?

2 For which film did Bruce Springsteen record his Oscar-winning song 'Streets Of Philadelphia'?

3 The town of Timbuktu is located on the edge of which desert?

4 In human anatomy, the phalanges are located in the toes and which other part of the body?

5 To which animal does the word 'equestrianism' relate?

6 The Solomon Islands are situated in which ocean?

7 *The Order of the Phoenix* is part of which series of children's bestselling books?

8 Which French word, used in English to bid farewell, literally means 'to God'?

9 What is the only sign of the zodiac not represented by a human or creature?

10 Which British TV series about an antiques dealer featured the characters Tinker Dill and Eric Catchpole?

─────────────── 40+ **SET 25** ───────────────

1 According to the old proverb, 'A watched kettle never . . .' what?

2 Koalas are native to which country?

3 Who is Hollywood legend Henry Fonda's actress daughter?

4 In the 2002 film *Catch Me If You Can*, which US actor played professional con artist Frank Abagnale Junior?

5 In geometry, how many sides does a decahedron have?

6 On 6 June 1944, also known as D-Day, which country did the Allied Forces invade?

7 What is the national mapping agency of Britain called?

8 First published in 1897, who wrote the horror novel *Dracula*?

9 In 1980, which British band had a UK number one hit with 'Going Underground'?

10 Frangipane is a confection that takes its flavour from which nut?

—————————————— 40+ **SET 26** ——————————————

1 Apart from gravy, which sauce is traditionally served with roast beef?

2 Complete the title of a 1986 Woody Allen film, *Hannah and Her . . .* what?

3 At the 1992 Barcelona Olympic Games in which race did Linford Christie take gold?

4 Which bird is the wisest of Winnie the Pooh's friends?

5 In the natural world, what type of reptile is a Gila Monster?

6 Tommy Boyd, Mick Robertson and Susan Stranks all presented which 1970s children's TV series?

7 During his lifetime, Albert Einstein had Swiss citizenship, US citizenship and citizenship of which other country?

8 Spain's Costa Blanca lies on which body of water?

9 In English, which five letters are counted as vowels?

10 *Saint Joan* and *Mrs Warren's Profession* are plays by which Irish-born writer?

—————————————— 40+ **SET 27** ——————————————

1 Who wrote the opera *The Mastersingers of Nuremberg*?

2 Ferrari is a name most closely associated with what means of transport?

3 In the 1951 film *A Streetcar Named Desire*, which legendary US actor played the character Stanley Kowalski?

4 Which British athlete won the Olympic gold medal for the 1500 metres in both 1980 and 1984?

5 In 1844, which saint was born in the French town of Lourdes?

6 'Vienna' and 'Dancing With Tears In My Eyes' were Top 10 hits for which British band of the 1980s?

7 In the 1960s TV sitcom *The Munsters*, what is the name of Herman's son?

8 In which country are *Die Welt* and *Die Zeit* national newspapers?

9 Based at Thames House in London, what is the common name of the counter-espionage branch of the security services?

10 Ostia is the ancient port of which city?

───────────── 40+ SET 28 ─────────────

1 In his classic poem about daffodils, William Wordsworth wrote that he 'wandered lonely as a . . .' what?

2 The 1973 Elton John hit 'Candle In The Wind' was released as a tribute to which American screen legend?

3 In the nursery rhyme 'Ride a Cock Horse', where is the 'cock-horse' ridden to?

4 Prior to becoming US president, Bill Clinton was governor of which US State?

5 Which heroic character did Colin Farrell play in the title role of a 2004 film?

6 Which actress played the title role in the US TV series *Ally McBeal*?

7 In which decade did Sir Clive Sinclair launch the 'Sinclair C5'?

8 Which golfer is known as the 'Great White Shark'?

9 The 1840 Treaty of Waitangi established British colonial rule over which country?

10 In the world of beauty treatments, a manicure deals with which part of the body?

---------------------------------- 40+ **SET 29** ----------------------------------

1 Which US director's films include the comedies *Blazing Saddles* and *Young Frankenstein*?

2 Which fictional, nineteenth-century British naval officer was created by novelist C. S. Forester?

3 Grasmere and Derwentwater are in which English National Park?

4 In 1997, a branch of the Guggenheim Museum opened in which Spanish city?

5 Which US record producer of the 1960s is best known for his 'Wall of Sound'?

6 Hake, plaice and Dover sole are types of which species?

7 A phrase used to describe a state of total confusion and disorder is 'at sixes and . . .' what?

8 Scottish outlaw Robert MacGregor was better known by which nickname?

9 The word 'strudel' originated in which European language?

10 'Evening, all', were the opening words spoken by Jack Warner playing the role of a sergeant in which classic TV series?

---------------------------------- 40+ **SET 30** ----------------------------------

1 Mary Quant is most closely associated with popularizing which style of skirt in the 1960s?

2 Which Bond actor was born in Edinburgh, Scotland?

3 Composed by Igor Stravinsky, what is *The Rite of Spring*, a ballet or an opera?

4 Which Irish playwright declared that: 'Work is the curse of the drinking classes'?

5 Of which Middle Eastern country was King Hussein I monarch until his death in 1999?

6 In the TV cartoon, in which fictional park do Yogi Bear and Boo-Boo live?

7 The informal term 'hackette' is sometimes used to describe a female working in which field?

8 In 1958, which US rock 'n' roll legend had a UK number one hit with the single 'Jailhouse Rock'?

9 What, in the insect world, is a purple emperor?

10 In the 2002 film *Chicago*, which Hollywood actor played Billy Flynn?

────────────────── 40+ **SET 31** ──────────────────

1 What nationality was the nineteenth-century painter J. M. W. Turner?

2 The martial art t'ai chi comes from which Asian country?

3 Which two-word Latin phrase literally means 'without limit' or 'for ever'?

4 According to the proverb, 'Beggars can't be . . .' what?

5 Which 'p' is a five-letter slang word for cheap wine?

6 Jake Shears, Paddy Boom, Babydaddy, Del Marquis and Ana Matronic make up which US band?

7 On the Mohs scale of the hardness of minerals, which gemstone has the highest value of ten?

8 The 2006 film entitled *The Last King of Scotland* is based on the regime of which African dictator?

9 Cinnamon is a warm, sweet spice that comes from the bark of a tree native to which of the world's continents?

10 Which actress in the TV drama *Silent Witness* is the daughter of Edward Fox and Joanna David?

────────────────── 40+ **SET 32** ──────────────────

1 Which Premiership football team is known as 'The Magpies'?

2 The Clyde is the principal river of which UK country?

3 Which Andrew Lloyd Webber musical with a religious theme was made into a successful film in 1973?

4 'Hooray Hooray, It's A Holi-Holiday' was a big hit in 1979 for which pop group?

5 Which country has the national motto, 'In God We Trust'?

6 Which small landlocked country in southern Africa is situated in the highest part of the Drakensberg mountains?

7 Of which food product is Danish Blue a variety?

8 What is the English equivalent of the Spanish boy's name Eduardo?

9 Stephen Merchant and which comedian are the creators of the hit TV comedy *Extras*?

10 The sinister Mr Tod, who appears in several of Beatrix Potter's children's tales, is what type of animal?

––––––––––––––– 40+ **SET 33** –––––––––––––––

1 Which South American nation won the 2002 FIFA Football World Cup?

2 In London, the four training institutions for barristers and law students are known as the 'Inns of . . .' what?

3 Minnie Mouse, Pluto and Goofy were all invented by which US animator?

4 The Java Trench, also called the Sunda Trench, is situated in which ocean?

5 The last chapter of which Charlotte Brontë novel begins with the line, 'Reader, I married him'?

6 When referring to controlling the temperature in a building or car, what does the abbreviation AC stand for?

7 In the 1930s, which US actress received Oscars for her roles in the films *Jezebel* and *Dangerous*?

8 In post-Second World War Britain, in which decade did sweet rationing permanently end?

9 What was the name of the long-running BBC TV show that centred around sheepdog trials?

10 *The Unforgettable Fire* and *Achtung Baby* were bestselling albums for which Irish band?

Part 2
General Knowledge

THE GENERAL knowledge questions here are used for three rounds for mixed age groups. You can simply see how many questions you can answer or you can play the rounds from the show.

Two Minute Marathon

In this, the final audition weekend round, contestants must answer as many questions correctly as they can in two minutes. If you are playing in a group, the top scorer wins the round and the others can play again.

Only the Strong Survive

Only the Strong Survive is the first round of the studio show. A circle of contestants answer questions in turn against the clock. If you get one wrong, you are in the Red Zone and out of that game. When the time is up, those left standing face one more question on the buzzer to find out who goes through to the next round. The remaining players must try again in another game of Only the Strong Survive.

Brain Chain

In the second round of the studio show, players try again to build a run of correct answers, only this time there is a twist. Playing against the clock, each contestant has ninety seconds to build a chain by giving as many correct answers in a row as possible. However, the chain of questions only counts if you **save** it before you get a question wrong or the time is up.

―――――――――――― SET 1 ――――――――――――

1 In UK sporting circles, which form of racing is informally referred to as 'the dogs'?

2 Which Oscar-winning British actor and writer played Kilwillie in the TV series *Monarch of the Glen*?

3 Edele and Keavy Lynch were members of which 1990s Irish girl group?

4 The overthrow in 1989 of the communist regime in Czechoslovakia is known as what revolution?

5 Which bird, a member of the family Columbidae, is used as a symbol of peace?

6 In which BBC TV spy drama is Adam Carter played by Rupert Penry-Jones?

7 Which British rock star duetted with Tina Turner on the 1990 UK chart hit 'It Takes Two'?

8 Which 1974 Charlton Heston film saw an earthquake of unimaginable magnitude hit Los Angeles?

9 Who was vice-president of the US from 1989 to 1993?

10 In radio terminology, what do the initials 'DAB' stand for?

11 Which instrument is traditionally played by the leader of an orchestra?

12 On 14 November 1973, which member of the Royal Family was married at Westminster Abbey?

13 Tipperary, Meath and Kilkenny are counties in which European country?

14 Which playwright was killed in a fight in a tavern in Deptford in 1593?

15 Which shellfish are used in the French dish *moules marinières*?

16 What is the common name for the large bird that is sometimes called the South American Ostrich?

17 By which name is a five-sided polygon more commonly known?

18 In October 2006, the historic cricketing trophy known as 'The Ashes' left for a three-month tour of which country?

19 Which German composer's work includes nine symphonies, thirty-two piano sonatas and one opera?

20 Jerome K. Jerome's book *Three Men in a Boat* is an account of a boating holiday on which English river?

21 Of what is a panatella a type?

22 By what name was the French singer born Edith Giovanna Gassion better known?

23 Which leader of the Liberal Party resigned in 1976?

24 In tenpin bowling, a 'turkey' is the name commonly given to how many consecutive strikes?

25 In 1975, which leading Scottish actor married French-Moroccan painter Micheline Roquebrune?

26 A 'pride' is the collective noun used to describe a group of which carnivorous animals?

27 In 2004, who took over from Clive Woodward as head coach of the England Rugby Union team?

28 The First World War ended in which year?

29 Saint Andrew, the patron saint of Scotland, was the brother of which other saint?

30 What name is given to the batter 'pudding' that is traditionally served with a roast beef dinner?

31 Sometimes called *Glis glis*, the small mammal reared and fattened by ancient Romans is the Edible . . . what?

32 What is the correct technical term for the art of making and displaying fireworks?

33 In 1980, the question 'Who shot JR?' was asked in relation to which TV series?

34 In the anatomy of hearing, what is the non-technical name for the tympanic membrane?

35 Which London borough shares its name with a coach or carriage that is for hire?

36 The international airline QANTAS is based in which country?

37 In which country did the theatrical performance group 'The Blue Man Group' originate?

38 The Aberdeen Angus is a breed of which farm animal?

39 Of which hot drink is 'robusta' a variety?

40 From which country of the UK does snooker player Stephen Hendry come?

41 Which twentieth-century British prime minister was nicknamed 'Supermac'?

42 The moa, now extinct, was a large emu-like flightless bird native to which country?

43 What is the astronomers' name for the North Star or Pole Star?

44 In 1852, what was the English scholar Peter Mark Roget the first to publish?

45 Which international airport is located in the English county of Essex?

46 In which TV game show were the contestants invited to go 'wild in the aisles'?

47 Goth rock front man Brian Warner is better known by which name?

48 With which country's cuisine is a korma most closely associated?

49 In the TV series *The Good Life*, what was the name of Penelope Keith's character?

50 In the children's cartoon *The Rugrats*, what relation are the characters Phil and Lil to one another?

--------------------------------- SET 2 ---------------------------------

1 By what name are the larvae of moths and butterflies known?

2 What nationality was the 1962 Formula 1 champion Graham Hill?

3 Port Louis is the capital of which island country in the Indian Ocean?

4 Who was the lead singer of the band The Pretenders?

5 In which country is Mount Fuji found?

6 Which British supermodel released the single 'Love And Tears' in 1994?

7 Which type of golf club is designed to roll the ball along the surface of the green into the hole?

8 What was the name of the famous bomber aircraft used by the RAF in the audacious 'Dambusters' raid?

9 Which US blues legend famously has a guitar called 'Lucille'?

10 In which Scottish county is the royal residence of Balmoral?

11 Which Disney film musical features the songs 'The Bare Necessities' and 'I Wanna Be Like You'?

12 *Secrets and Lies* and *Vera Drake* are both films by which English director?

13 Between 1675 and 1948, which part of London was the home of the Royal Observatory?

14 Which film actor, famous for his roles in horror movies, was originally called William Henry Pratt?

15 In 1945, which US president famously met with Churchill and Stalin at the Yalta Conference?

16 The adjective 'equine' describes which type of animal?

17 Rock vocalist David Bowie made a guest appearance in the 2006 series of which BBC sitcom?

18 Which blonde former *Baywatch* star married Kid Rock in 2006?

19 In which European country did puy lentils originate?

20 The name of which traditional board game means 'I play' in Latin?

21 In the Second World War, the RAF named their inflatable life jackets after which actress?

22 Holden Caulfield is the teenage hero of which classic American novel?

23 With which type of food is celebrity TV chef Rick Stein most closely associated?

24 Which US singer-songwriter was born Steveland Judkins in 1950?

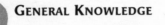

25 Born in 1935, in which sport has Gary Player won nine major championships?

26 What is the capital of Poland?

27 In 1997, Kofi Annan became the Secretary-General of which organization?

28 *The Mikado* is an operetta by W. S. Gilbert and which other composer?

29 Founded in 1853 by mill owner Titus Salt, which Yorkshire model town became a World Heritage Site in 2001?

30 In 1916, which British field marshal died on board HMS *Hampshire* when it struck a mine?

31 Which fantasy author wrote *The Two Towers*, the second part of a trilogy?

32 Holly Johnson was the lead singer of which 1980s UK band?

33 In 2003, who succeeded Keith Wood as captain of the Irish Rugby Union team?

34 Which Brazilian footballer won FIFA's Golden Shoe award for the top scorer at the 2002 World Cup?

35 With which sport is Lennox Lewis most closely associated?

36 What name is given to the Swiss dish of melted cheese served at the table in a large pot over a lighted burner?

37 What was the title of a 1968 book by US air force surgeon Kenneth Cooper that pioneered a new form of exercise?

38 Founded in the 1600s, which university city has the oldest botanic garden in Britain?

39 The Duke of Monmouth, executed in 1685 for leading a rebellion, was the son of which British monarch?

40 According to the song, what did Molly Malone sell on the streets of Dublin?

41 'Pen' is the female term for which aquatic bird?

42 Which sixth-century Greek writer is especially famous for his fables?

43 In which century was the Russian composer Sergei Prokofiev born?

44 Which female TV presenter first became famous as presenter of the people show *That's Life!*?

45 Ibiza belongs to which Spanish island group?

46 According to the Robert Browning poem, which rodents were enticed out of the German town of Hamelin by the Pied Piper?

47 Which TV cartoon series featured the characters of Spotty, Texas Pete and Bulk?

48 Which song title has been a hit for Huey Lewis and the News, Frankie Goes To Hollywood and Celine Dion?

49 From which animal does bacon come?

50 During the twentieth century, how many monarchs ruled Britain?

--- **SET 3** ---

1 In 1904, Sir Herbert Beerbohm Tree played a major role in founding which London drama school?

2 In cockney rhyming slang, which item of footwear is meant by the word 'canoes'?

3 In which arcade game would you find ghosts called Inky, Pinky, Blinky and Clyde?

4 Which item of make-up shares its name with the French word for red?

5 Which children's TV cartoon featured the characters Colonel K and Penfold?

6 According to the proverb, 'The hand that rocks the cradle, rules the . . .' what?

7 In 1531, Francisco Pizarro and his forces invaded which ancient South American civilization?

8 Used as a flavour enhancer in the food industry, what do the initials MSG stand for?

9 In 1962, the great American novelist John Steinbeck won which prestigious Prize for Literature?

10 Which nonflammable gas has the chemical symbol He?

11 Which 2001 song by the group Gorillaz takes its title from the name of an Oscar-winning actor and director?

12 In which European country is the Dáil the lower house of parliament?

13 What French word describes what the English traditionally call a 'French stick'?

14 Which teen star had a number one hit with 'The One And Only' in 1991?

15 Which international human rights organization won the Nobel Peace Prize in 1977?

16 What was the original name of Adrian IV, the only Englishman to become Pope?

17 The hard cheese known as Cantal originated in which European country?

18 Which German castle became a notorious Second World War prisoner of war camp and inspired a TV series bearing its name?

19 In the TV sitcom *The Fall and Rise of Reginald Perrin* which actor played the title role?

20 What is specifically studied by or collected by an oologist?

21 In the Looney Tunes cartoons, what is the name of the hunter who is always chasing Bugs Bunny?

22 Actress Nicole Kidman holds dual citizenship for Australia and which other country?

23 What was the name of the dog who featured in the *Famous Five* novels by Enid Blyton?

24 Because of the large holes in its leaves, the houseplant *Monstera Deliciosa* is popularly known as 'The Swiss . . .' what?

25 Which TV comedian's alter egos include Paul Calf and Alan Partridge?

26 In which US city is the world-famous Juilliard performing arts school?

27 What does a philatelist collect?

28 Published in 1897, which H. G. Wells novel is about a man who cannot be seen?

29 Which nation won the Rugby World Cup in 1999?

30 In 1945, who was US president at the end of the Second World War?

31 Which former editor of the *Sunday Times* presents TV's *This Week*?

32 What is the name of the popular brand of soft sweets, of various shapes and colours, all containing liquorice?

33 Singer KT Tunstall grew up in which country of the UK?

34 The musical *The Sound of Music* is set in which European country?

35 The cathedral city of Canterbury is located in which UK county?

36 In which decade of the twentieth century was the UK voting age lowered from twenty-one to eighteen?

37 Originating in the Low Countries, what type of food is Limburger?

38 The dance called the Lambada originated in which South American country?

39 Which British artist had songs in the 1980s with 'I Guess That's Why They Call It The Blues' and 'Little Jeannie'?

40 Before she married, what was singer and actress Madonna's maiden name?

41 By what stage name is the Irish singer-songwriter George Ivan Morrison better known?

42 Which colour was the body dye, known as woad, used by the ancient Britons?

43 From the French for 'red stick', what is the name of the Louisiana state capital?

44 Which group had hits in the 1960s with 'Ferry 'Cross The Mersey' and 'I Like It'?

45 In 1901, who became twenty-sixth president of the USA, following the assassination of President McKinley?

46 In mathematics, what is the opposite of multiplication?

47 In 2000, which popular author also starred in the West End production of his own play *The Accused*?

48 In 1998, which female gardening expert joined the TV series *Ground Force?*

49 Which world-famous ballet company is based in Moscow, Russia?

50 In which US state was President John F. Kennedy born?

———————————————— SET 4 ————————————————

1 'Vera Lynn' is cockney rhyming slang for which alcoholic drink?

2 Which leading singer of the twentieth century was nicknamed 'the Chairman of the Board'?

3 What type of animal is a bittern?

4 Which British city has an underground railway system nicknamed 'The Clockwork Orange'?

5 Which green-fingered Radio 4 programme, presented by Eric Robson, is sometimes known by the initials GQT?

6 Which two colours traditionally decorate a barber's pole?

7 Which Australian cricketer, who retired in 1948, holds the record for the highest career Test batting average?

8 A year in which there are twenty-nine days in February is known as a what?

9 In 335 BC, which Greek philosopher and student of Plato founded the school and library known as the Lyceum?

10 Which famous American highway connects Chicago to Los Angeles?

11 Which famous US motor racing circuit is nicknamed the 'Brickyard'?

12 In cricket, which team won the 2006 County Championship title?

13 In 2005, which BBC News reporter was made Chancellor of Roehampton University?

14 In ancient Rome, which emperor murdered his wife Octavia in order to marry Poppaea?

15 The ancient town of Delphi is in which European country?

16 Which Latin phrase, meaning 'in the glass', is used for biological techniques taking place outside a living organism?

17 In which country is the Neander Valley, where the remains of Neanderthal man were found in 1856?

18 NAFTA, or the North American Free Trade Agreement, was signed in the 1990s by the US, Canada and which other country?

19 Which Texan model appeared on the cover of Roxy Music's 1975 album *Siren*?

20 Which type of cabbage, grown for its edible buds, shares part of its name with the capital of Belgium?

21 What name is given to the 'stone', used as a skin abrasive, which is a light and porous form of solidified lava?

22 Which drink is sometimes referred to as Adam's ale?

23 The dessert known as chantilly cream originated in which European country?

24 Which game is the only card game that can legally be played for money in English pubs?

25 Which Italian composer wrote the opera *La Bohème*?

26 The Appaloosa is a breed of which animal?

27 Which former child star played Michael Alig in the 2003 film *Party Monster*?

28 The countries of Lithuania, Latvia and Estonia are known collectively by what name?

29 In the Communist era, the letters 'DDR' referred to the eastern part of which present country?

30 Which Dickens novel did Lionel Bart turn into a hit stage musical?

31 Which sharp-toothed, South American freshwater fish made an appearance in the 1967 Bond film *You Only Live Twice*?

32 The red wine Valpolicella is made in which European country?

33 In September 2005, Frank Hadden was named as the Rugby Union coach for which UK country?

34 Which American novelist, who lived from 1843 to 1916, wrote *Washington Square?*

35 In which country did the campaign known as the Great Leap Forward take place in the late 1950s and early 1960s?

36 In 1991, which Irish rock band had a UK number one hit with the single 'The Fly'?

37 With which London landmark are 'Beefeaters' most commonly associated?

38 Gado gado is a dish of mixed cooked vegetables with a peanut sauce from which Asian country?

39 Sir Joshua Reynolds was a famous name in which of the arts?

40 In which 1957 classic film does Audrey Hepburn play a model opposite Fred Astaire?

41 What was the name of the Roman goddess of the hearth, whose temple in Rome was tended by virgins?

42 Which US motor company founder is famous for saying, 'You can have any colour you like, so long as it's black'?

43 In which language was Samuel Beckett's play *Waiting for Godot* first published?

44 What are the offspring of a duck called?

45 Which cricket county plays its home matches at Lord's Cricket Ground?

46 In 2006, which US pop singer was rumoured to have dumped her husband by text message?

47 In 1721, who became Britain's first prime minister?

48 On which continent was singer Cliff Richard born?

49 Which Scotsman was the 2006 Snooker World Champion?

50 In imperial measurements, how many pints are there in a gallon?

———————————————— **SET 5** ————————————————

1 From 1836 to 1961, the UK publication known as 'Bradshaw' gave timetables for which form of transport?

2 Hooded and Carrion are two types of which dark-coloured British bird?

3 In 1940, who succeeded Neville Chamberlain as British prime minister?

4 What is the name of Charlie Brown's cartoon dog?

5 Historically, a vizier was a high-ranking official of which empire?

6 Médoc and Saint Émilion are districts within which major French wine-growing region?

7 Which romantic novel by Emily Brontë features the heroine Catherine Earnshaw?

8 In which language is the word *gracias* used to mean 'thanks'?

9 In which Asian country did the form of theatre known as 'Noh' originate?

10 Which British prime minister described Russia as 'a riddle wrapped in a mystery inside an enigma'?

11 Which is the first book of the New Testament?

12 An otologist is a specialist in the anatomy and structure of which part of the human body?

13 The Cannes film festival takes place in which country?

14 What is the name of the ancient temple in Rome that was built by Hadrian and dedicated to all the gods?

15 In the UK, in which decade did it become compulsory for car drivers to wear seatbelts?

16 Which European country has cities called Ghent, Namur and Liège?

17 In Greek mythology, whose unrequited love for Narcissus caused her to waste away until only her voice was left?

18 What name was given to the highest court of justice and the supreme council in ancient Jerusalem?

19 The word 'charade' originated in which European language?

20 Which TV comedy was set in the fictional town of Royston Vasey?

21 Which British businessman appeared in the 2006 film *Superman Returns*?

22 What is a Penny Black?

23 In 1979, the Puerto Rican winner of 'Miss World', Wilnelia Merced, married which British TV personality?

24 In pop music, what is the shared surname of siblings La Toya, Marlon, Randy and Michael?

25 Who took over from Christopher Eccleston as TV's Dr Who?

26 Teen movie *10 Things I Hate About You* is loosely based on which Shakespeare play?

27 In the 1960s, who had UK chart hits with 'I Second That Emotion' and 'Tracks Of My Tears'?

28 In the TV series *Thunderbirds*, what is the name of the evil protagonist?

29 A vixen is the female of which animal?

30 Of which US city was Rudy Giuliani mayor from 1993 to 2001?

31 In the Tomb Raider games, what is the profession of Lara Croft?

32 In which US state was President George W. Bush born?

33 By what name was the Italian painter Giovanni Antonio Canale better known?

34 What was the name of the character played by Rik Mayall in the TV comedy *The Young Ones*?

35 Which instrument in the percussion family has wooden bars which are struck with mallets?

36 Which trio had UK number one hits in the 1960s with 'Make It Easy On Yourself' and 'The Sun Ain't Gonna Shine Anymore'?

37 Which Formula 1 Grand Prix is staged at Monza?

38 In 1911, which actress founded a theatre school in London named after her?

39 The name of which martial art means 'Way of the Sword' in Japanese?

40 What is the collective noun for a group of rhinos?

41 Vert is the heraldic term for which colour?

42 In which decade was Margaret Thatcher first elected as British prime minister?

43 In a tennis match, what name is given to the official who sits in a high chair at one end of the net?

44 Football legend George Best played for which English club between 1963 and 1974?

45 Which silver-white metallic element has the chemical symbol Mg?

46 In 1990, which Soviet leader received the Nobel Peace Prize?

47 Which celebrity chef, a regular guest on TV's *Ready Steady Cook*, won *The Weakest Link Chef Special* in 2002?

48 Which Taiwanese director made the 2005 Oscar-winning film *Brokeback Mountain*?

49 The 'Undertaker', 'Ultimate Warrior' and Bret 'The Hitman' Hart are legends in which TV sport?

50 Which 2001 Kylie Minogue hit begins with the line 'La la la, la la la la la'?

SET 6
---

1 In which month does the UK move from British Summer Time to GMT?

2 Which famous British heavy metal band is named after a medieval torture device?

3 In skin products, what does the abbreviation SPF stand for?

4 What was the surname of the 1980s pop duo Mel and Kim?

5 Which sport is most closely associated with The Queen's Club in London?

6 Which Elizabethan playwright is credited with inventing such common words as 'bump', 'eventful' and 'lonely'?

7 In 1997, which UK-born entertainer was made an honorary US veteran for his decades of entertaining troops in war zones?

8 First run in 1779, which Classic horserace for three-year-old fillies is run at Epsom every year?

9 What type of shop was traditionally marked in the street by three golden balls?

10 Which theatre company is often known as the RSC?

11 In 1985, which British prime minister was refused an honorary degree by Oxford University?

12 Which US investigative organization has the motto 'Fidelity, Bravery and Integrity'?

13 In world geography, is Madagascar an island or a peninsula?

14 In the 2006 New Year Honours, John Whiteley was awarded an MBE for services to which sport?

15 In 1969, which British rock band had a UK number one hit with the single 'Honky Tonk Women'?

16 Of which small principality in the Alps did Prince Hans Adam II become the head of state in 1989?

17 Which German song, about a soldier's girlfriend, became popular with Allied troops during the Second World War?

18 In the 1980 film comedy *Gregory's Girl*, which Scottish actor played the gawky schoolboy, Gregory?

19 Which actress played the character Cathy Gale in the 1960s TV series, *The Avengers*?

20 In 2004, which former Bond star was the voice of Santa in the UNICEF cartoon *The Fly Who Loved Me*?

21 Born in 1718, the Yorkshire cabinet-maker who gave his name to an eighteenth-century style of furniture was Thomas . . . who?

22 What is the motto of the Boy Scout organization?

23 Which City of London arts centre, opened in 1982, did the Queen call 'one of the wonders of the modern world'?

24 Marking the end of the First World War, in which month of the year is Armistice Day?

25 What nationality was the seventeenth-century philosopher Spinoza?

26 Which Australian actress was born Catherine Elise Blanchett?

27 What was the name of the 'cross-eyed lion' in the classic 1960s TV series *Daktari*?

28 By which two-word name are burning meteoroids falling into the Earth's atmosphere more commonly known?

29 Which county plays its home cricket matches at Old Trafford?

30 Who was the second wife of Henry VIII?

31 Which UK military force, made up of part-time volunteer soldiers, is known by the initials TA?

32 Michelle Williams has a daughter, Matilda, with which Australian actor?

33 With which sport is Ireland's Ruby Walsh most closely associated?

34 Traditionally, the meat of which animal goes into a Shepherd's Pie?

35 Which Oscar-winning actor starred in the films *Guess Who's Coming to Dinner* and *In the Heat of the Night*?

36 What nationality is the feminist writer and broadcaster Germaine Greer?

37 In March 1982, at the outset of the Falklands War, what was the first island occupied by Argentinian forces?

38 Which English seafarer, who was a castaway on an island for twenty-eight years, was created by Daniel Defoe?

39 In the game of dominoes, how many pieces are there in a standard set?

40 Which singer came to prominence in the 1970s as lead vocalist of punk band Generation X?

41 In *Minder*, how did Arthur Daley refer to his wife?

42 Born in New York, who was the first wife of former Beatle Paul McCartney?

43 On a UK motorway, what is the maximum legal speed limit in mph for buses and coaches less than twelve metres long?

44 In 1987, which member of the Royal Family was a special guest on the 200th edition of *A Question of Sport*?

45 What nationality was the philosopher Martin Heidegger?

46 What is the name of the Roman road that ran from Lincoln to Exeter?

47 Which popular US TV sitcom of the 1980s and 90s was set in a Boston bar?

48 By what name was the painter Domenikos Theotokopoulos better known?

49 In 1988, which band was formed by ex-Bananarama singer Siobhan Fahey and US musician Marcella Detroit?

50 Released in 2005, *X & Y* was the title of the third album by which hugely successful British band?

_____ SET 7 _____

1 By which name is the toy doll Barbara Millicent Roberts better known?

2 From which type of flower are vanilla pods obtained?

3 The term 'ovine' refers to which type of animal?

4 The US vocalist Susannah Hoffs was the lead singer in which 1980s girl band?

5 What was the name of the house where the O'Hara family lived in *Gone With the Wind*?

6 The comedy screenwriter Richard Curtis is the co-founder of which UK charity?

7 Which cult sci-fi TV comedy has fans that are known as 'Dwarfers'?

8 In 1995, the heiress Jemima Goldsmith married which Pakistan cricket captain?

9 From 1910 Transvaal was a province in which African country?

10 In which 1971 gangster film did Michael Caine play the character Jack Carter?

11 Judo is derived from which other Japanese form of unarmed combat?

12 Which hit Bryan Adams song begins with the lines 'I got my first real six string, bought it at the five-and-dime'?

13　Which opera by Verdi features the lovers Violetta and Alfredo?

14　In the UK in 2006 at what age does a woman become eligible to receive the basic state pension?

15　The American Mustang is a breed of which animal?

16　Ikebana is the Japanese art of arranging what?

17　Of which US actress's performance did Dorothy Parker say: 'She ran the whole gamut of the emotions from A to B'?

18　Karaoke was invented during the late twentieth century in which country?

19　The dish moussaka is most closely associated with which Mediterranean country?

20　Which street in Lambeth, central London, gave its name to a popular dance and song of the 1940s?

21　Flowing from the Great Slave Lake to the Beaufort Sea, the Mackenzie River is the longest river in which country?

22　The 1966 film *Born Free* is set in which African country?

23　The science of herpetology is the study of amphibians and which other group of animals?

24　In Canada, on the 1st of which month does Canada Day fall?

25　Which former England cricketer took part in the 2006 series of TV's *Strictly Come Dancing*?

26　What does a thermometer measure?

27　The Chrysanthemum Throne is the common name given to the throne of which Asian country?

28　Which island in New York harbour was the historical gateway to the US for thousands of immigrants?

29　In which country is 'taoiseach' the name given to the head of government?

30　Who traditionally records a Christmas message to the Commonwealth?

31　Which author wrote the 2005 bestselling book *Yes Man*?

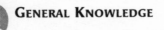

32 In Formula 1, Damon Hill succeeded Nigel Mansell in which team?

33 Munich and Stuttgart are cities in which European country?

34 In the NATO phonetic alphabet, the name of which drink is used to represent the letter 'W'?

35 Which female Olympic athlete won the 2004 BBC Sports Personality of the Year award?

36 In tennis, the US Open, French Open, Australian Open and which other event make up the 'Grand Slam'?

37 On which side of the road do cars drive in India?

38 Which prominent name on the US Declaration of Independence is often used to mean a signature?

39 In the EU, what type of 'policy' do the initials CAP stand for?

40 *Ficus elastica* is the botanical name of which houseplant?

41 With which international cuisine is the dish of gefilte fish associated?

42 In which country was the guerrilla leader Che Guevara killed in 1967?

43 In which game are there tiles named Bamboos, Circles, Characters, Dragons and Winds?

44 The musical *Fame* is set in which US city?

45 Which country's Rugby Union team is known as the Springboks?

46 Which kidney-shaped nut is edible when roasted and is often eaten salted?

47 Re-recorded in 2006 by Katie Price and Peter Andre, the Oscar-winning song 'Whole New World' was from which film?

48 Which indoor ball game is also known as ping-pong?

49 The decommissioned Royal Yacht *Britannia* is now permanently moored in which Scottish city?

50 Which Hollywood film star married fellow actor Geena Davis in 1987?

─────────────────── **SET 8** ───────────────────

1 Which US singer was born Michael Bolotin?

2 In 1400, Owen Glendower proclaimed himself Prince of which part of Britain?

3 What is the name of the ancient art form which fastens pieces of tiles or glass to create a picture or design?

4 The Galician Blond is a breed of cattle originally from which European country?

5 Which King of Denmark was also crowned King of England in 1016?

6 Which site in Cornwall is the westernmost point in England?

7 In 1982, which Yorkshire presenter hosted the very first edition of the gameshow *Countdown*?

8 Set in the courtroom, which TV series starring Leo McKern ran from 1978 to 1992?

9 Which successful BBC TV drama starring Robert Vaughn features a group of élite London con artists?

10 In 1980, which Hollywood star married a dental nurse named Robyn Moore?

11 Kevin Pietersen first played which sport for England in 2004?

12 Which hit TV series was set in the fictitious town of Crinkley Bottom?

13 In 2002, which *Pop Idol* singer became famous for his stammer?

14 Which US poet wrote the acclaimed poem *The Waste Land*?

15 A person born on 30 June would belong to which sign of the zodiac?

16 The 'Glorious Twelfth' of August is the first day of the season in Scotland for shooting which birds?

17 By what name is the sport of 'tauromachy' better known?

18 With which pastime is Mrs Beeton most closely associated?

19 What was the surname of the post-war Tory cabinet minister whose nickname, based on his intials, was 'Rab'?

20 In 1990, which *Star Wars* actress wrote a novel, detailing her marriage to Paul Simon, called *Surrender the Pink*?

21 *Helianthus* is the Latin name of which tall flower?

22 The 1957 film *The Seventh Seal* was the work of which Swedish director?

23 The fashion designer Ralph Lauren was born in which country?

24 The French word *papillon* denotes which winged insect?

25 In July 2002, Steve Fossett became the first person to fly solo around the world in which mode of transport?

26 In 1988, which British reggae band had their only UK number one hit with the single 'Don't Turn Around'?

27 Which country manufactured the Stuka divebomber in the Second World War?

28 Kaiser Wilhelm II was the last emperor of which European country?

29 In pop music, what is the shared surname of siblings Rebbie, Jackie, Tito, Janet and Jermaine?

30 With which Asian country is the dish tempura most closely associated?

31 Bedford Falls was the setting for which 1946 film classic?

32 What does the word *secco* on a bottle of Italian wine mean?

33 Which Shakespearean character was the Prince of Denmark?

34 In which country are the ruins of the ancient city of Troy?

35 During the First World War, 'Chloride of Lime' was used to purify what?

36 In music notation, how many quavers are there in a crotchet?

37 Which 1957 Oscar-nominated film starring Henry Fonda focused on a jury's deliberations in a capital murder case?

38 Which actress played Denise Royle in the hit TV sitcom *The Royle Family*?

39 Which King led the Royalist army at the Battle of Edgehill in 1642?

40 Which ventriloquist had a dummy called Lord Charles?

41 Kamakura is a coastal town in which Asian country?

42 Which Danish pop group had UK number one hits in 1998 with the singles 'Doctor Jones' and 'Turn Back Time'?

43 Which TV personality published an autobiography entitled *Memoirs of an Unfit Mother*?

44 An attractive book, designed to be looked at rather than read, is often given the name of which piece of furniture?

45 Wasps and Saracens are leading English clubs in which sport?

46 Who began presenting *Radio 1's Chart Show* in March 2005?

47 Huey, Dewey and Louie are nephews of which Disney cartoon character who first appeared in 1934?

48 According to legend, which English king held his court at Camelot?

49 To which country does the Caribbean island of Anguilla belong?

50 Which bright star, also known as the Dog star, is found by following the line of Orion's belt downwards?

──────────────── SET 9 ────────────────

1 Cape Horn is the southernmost point of which continent?

2 TV comedian Rowan Atkinson was born and bred in which city?

3 In 1834, which Dorset village became known for six 'Martyrs' who were transported to Australia after joining a union?

4 In 2006, Patrick Swayze made his West End début in which stage musical?

5 Cable stitch is a term used in which leisure activity?

6 Centurion, Tiger and Sherman are all types of which military vehicle?

7 TV personality Priscilla White is better known by which name?

8 Who was the British prime minister at the time of the Suez Crisis in 1956?

9 Who was chancellor of West Germany from 1969 to 1974?

10 Which band had its only UK number one hit in 1968 with the single 'Albatross'?

11 In 1984, which British ice-dance duo won an Olympic gold in Sarajevo?

12 In 1964, which US singer-songwriter had a UK number one hit with the single 'It's Over'?

13 What is the name of the house situated at No. 3764 Elvis Presley Boulevard in Memphis, Tennessee?

14 Of which African country was Jan Smuts prime minister from 1919 to 1924, and again from 1939 to 1948?

15 Who became the first chancellor of the German Empire in 1871?

16 Catcher, Short Stop and Third Baseman are fielding positions in which US sport?

17 What colour are the petals of the forget-me-not flower?

18 In 1907, which English author and poet won the Nobel Prize for Literature?

19 Born in Venice, which famous eighteenth-century author and libertine was at one time director of the Lottery in Paris?

20 Who won Best Actress Oscars for roles in 1979's *Norma Rae* and 1984's *Places in the Heart*?

21 In the 2006 remake of *The Pink Panther* which actor played Inspector Clouseau?

22 When looking forward, port is on which side of a ship?

23 Which long-running Radio 4 programme features the Grundy and Aldridge families?

24 Which British commander in the Napoleonic Wars was known to his troops as 'Old Nosey'?

25 What was Olympic champion Jonathan Edwards's sporting event?

26 Who was the first person pictured on a British postage stamp?

27 How were Frank Sinatra, Dean Martin and Sammy Davis Junior collectively known in 1950s Hollywood?

28 In 2000, which British pop group had a UK number one hit with the single 'Stomp'?

29 'Banana Rock' and 'Minuetto Allegretto' were 1970s hits for which furry pop group?

30 Who received the title Princess Royal from the Queen in 1987?

31 Which England football captain of the 1950s was married to one of the Beverley Sisters?

32 Often used to indicate an alternative name for something, what does the abbreviation AKA stand for?

33 Which animated children's TV series has characters called Dizzy, Scoop and Muck?

34 Which town in Essex was called Camulodunum by the Romans?

35 Complete the title of a 1978 novel by John Irving, *The World According to . . .* what?

36 From 1994 to 2003, actor Jon Tenney was married to which *Desperate Housewives* actress?

37 Supermodel Heidi Klum married which British soul artist in 2005?

38 How many days does the first month of the year have?

39 Which hip-hop singer did Whitney Houston marry in 1992?

40 Which Shakespeare play was made into a film directed by Baz Luhrmann in 1996?

41 In the nursery rhyme, what did Humpty Dumpty fall off?

42 Which British pop artist had his only UK number one hit in 1983 with the Marvin Gaye song 'Wherever I Lay My Hat'?

43 'Dirty old river, must you keep rolling, flowing into the night', are the opening lines from which 1967 Kinks hit?

44 Champagne is named after a wine-making region of which country?

45 The US actor Jon Voight is the father of which present-day Hollywood actress?

46 Professor Moriarty is the clever, evil enemy of which famous fictional detective?

47 In 1624, which cardinal did King Louis XIII of France appoint as his chief minister?

48 The Oscar-winning 2004 film *Ray* is a biopic of which American music star's life?

49 The kakapo is a large flightless parrot native to which country?

50 In which decade was legendary film star James Dean killed in a car crash?

SET 10
---

1 The dessert Tiramisu is traditionally made using which Italian cheese?

2 Who was president of Yugoslavia from 1953 to 1980?

3 What name is given to the flat biscuit with currants in the middle, popularly known as 'squashed fly biscuit'?

4 On a right-angle triangle, by what name is the side opposite the right angle better known?

5 In music, what name is given to the highest female singing voice?

6 Which children's TV puppet had the catchphrase 'Izzy whizzy let's get busy!'?

7 Which society for the brainy, founded in Oxford in 1946, uses intelligence tests as the qualification for membership?

8 How many balls in total are there on a snooker table when a player breaks at the start of a new frame?

9 Actor Kevin Costner played Lieutenant John Dunbar in which 1990 Oscar-winning film?

10 Which Scottish city has a fruit cake named after it?

11 With which sport is the name Aaron Lennon most associated?

12 Born in 1770, which German composer continued to write music even after he had lost his hearing?

13 Which religious movement was started in the nineteenth century by Joseph Smith and Brigham Young?

14 Eggplant is another name for which vegetable?

15 By which informal name is the famous London teaching hospital, St Bartholomew's, better known?

16 In 2006, which female TV presenter took over from Kelly Brook as the co-presenter of TV's *Love Island*?

17 In which country was the reggae singer-songwriter Bob Marley born?

18 With which animal is the job of a farrier most closely associated?

19 In 1906, which US president, nicknamed 'Teddy', won the Nobel Peace Prize?

20 What name is given to a column rising from the floor of a cave, formed of calcium salts deposited by dripping water?

21 Who was the eldest son of Indira Gandhi and her successor as Indian prime minister in 1984?

22 In 1960, which dance-craze was kicked off by a Chubby Checker hit record of the same name?

23 In the title of a 1915 novel by John Buchan, how many steps are there?

24 Eric Arthur Blair is the real name of which twentieth-century English author?

25 Who is the youngest daughter of the Duke of York?

26 Peachick is the name given to the young of which bird?

27 In 1958, which Welsh singer had her first UK number one hit with the single 'As I Love You'?

28 In the 1940s, Aneurin Bevan presided over the creation of which national institution?

29 In Italian cuisine, what type of foodstuff is 'tagliatelle'?

30 Which Japanese word is used for a high sea wave capable of inflicting great damage?

31 Which place near Marble Arch in London was the site of public hangings until the eighteenth century?

32 In British place names, to what does the Latin word 'regis' refer?

33 What colour is the centre scoring zone of an archery target?

34 Which sauce is traditionally served in England with roast lamb?

35 What does the 'L' stand for in the abbreviation RNLI?

36 Of which country was Jean Chrétien prime minister from 1993 to 2003?

37 Buck is the adult male of which animal that is more often known as a 'billy'?

38 What was the name of the black cartoon cat created and animated by Otto Messmer in 1919?

39 Which famously witty playwright and poet once said, 'Life imitates art far more than art imitates life'?

40 In 2006, Lisa Butcher and Mica Paris became the new presenters of which BBC TV makeover show?

41 What is the capital city of Brazil?

42 Which former First Lady in the Philippines is famed for her extensive shoe collection?

43 In Greek mythology, which hero had to perform twelve 'labours'?

44 In 2004, which country imposed Europe's first nationwide smoking ban?

45 On which date in July does the USA celebrate its independence?

46 Of which US psychedelic rock band was the late Jerry Garcia both the lead singer and guitarist?

47 In which Norfolk residence does the Royal Family traditionally spend Christmas?

48 Which English designer and authoress is famously quoted as saying that 'Life is too short to stuff a mushroom'?

49 Which nineteenth-century British prime minister wrote novels entitled *Coningsby* and *Sybil*?

50 Who was Prime Minister of Australia when the Queen made a state visit in 1992?

———————————— SET 11 ————————————

1 Which American pioneer of modern dance died in 1927 when her long scarf became entangled in the wheels of a car?

2 Which TV journalist took over from Andrew Marr as BBC political editor in 2005?

3 In which 1994 Disney film did Whoopi Goldberg provide the voice of a hyena called Shenzi?

4 In 2006, which Danish pop group had hits with the singles 'From Paris To Berlin' and 'Self Control'?

5 *The Evacuees* and *Bar Mitzvah Boy* were both TV dramas by which award-winning TV writer?

6 Which small low-powered binoculars are used by audiences in theatres and opera houses?

7 Which fictional, sword-wielding, masked crime-fighter takes his name from the Spanish word for fox?

8 Which British singer had 1980s hits with the songs 'Another Day In Paradise' and 'One More Night'?

9 In chemistry, what is the name of the chart that contains all of the known chemical elements?

10 Which is the ninth month of the year?

11 Which British monarch was publicly executed in London in 1649?

12 Who was prime minister when the United Kingdom entered the EEC in 1973?

13 The 2005 film *The New World* is loosely based on the life of which Native American princess?

14 Who became Queen of Scotland in December 1542 when she was only six days old?

15 Which 1971 film musical features the song 'If I Were A Rich Man'?

16 Which Italian term is used in music notation for 'gradually getting louder'?

17 Which tennis player's autobiography is called *You Cannot Be Serious*?

18 Which Lancashire city's football team is called 'North End'?

19 Smoked bacon and egg ice cream and sardine on toast sorbet are amongst the creations of which award-winning UK chef?

20 Which presenter of *Newsnight* also wrote the bestselling book *The English*?

21 Which British rock band had their first UK number one hit in 1995 with the single 'Some Might Say'?

22 Which former leader of the Tory Party has claimed that as a young man he often drank fourteen pints of beer in a day?

23 The greengage is a variety of which small edible fruit?

24 To which group of animals does the 'dab' belong?

25 The Palace of Holyroodhouse is in which Scottish city?

26 In which US state is the Churchill Downs racecourse?

27 Which London-born singer of the 1960s was originally called Mary O'Brien?

28 In 1994, which Oxford college became the last all-women college at the university?

29 Which US singer and musician is backed by 'The Heartbreakers'?

30 In the nursery rhyme, which creature frightened 'Little Miss Muffit'?

31 First published in 2001, which US author wrote the bestselling novel *Deception Point*?

32 Principally noted for his spy novels, what is the pen-name of British novelist David John Moore Cornwell?

33 Who released the single 'Kiss From A Rose' in 1994?

34 Which Italian city has the local name Napoli?

35 In which century was the League of Nations formed?

36 In 1983, which *Star Wars* actor married US screenwriter Melissa Mathison?

37 Which city, famous for its swords, was the capital of Spain until 1560?

38 Who was president of the United States from 1981 to 1989?

39 Of which North African country was Gamal Abdel Nasser president from 1956 to 1970?

40 Pecorino Romano is a hard sheep's milk cheese from which European country?

41 A popular houseplant with hinged leaves designed to trap and digest small insects is known as the 'Venus . . .' what?

42 What was the first name of naval commander Admiral Nelson?

43 The Krakow Film Festival takes place in which country?

44 Jenny Shipley served as the first female prime minister of which country from 1997 to 1999?

45 Which singer played the Acid Queen in the 1975 film, *Tommy*?

46 Which name is shared by a Second World War fighter-bomber and the Eurofighter now in service with the RAF?

47 Which 1940 Disney film features the character Jiminy Cricket?

48 Gordon, English and Irish are all varieties of which breed of dog?

49 Which 1974 film is the only sequel to have won a Best Picture Oscar?

50 Which member of the Beatles was known as 'The Quiet One'?

—— SET 12 ——

1 In which European country were Prince and Princess Michael of Kent married?

2 In a hospital, what do the letters ICU stand for?

3 What was the first name of Queen Elizabeth II's father?

4 The Dandie Dinmont terrier is named after a character in a novel by which Scottish author?

5 The vegetable bok choy originated in which Asian country?

6 Which fictitious, secret diarist features in the series of books by English writer, Sue Townsend?

7 The playwright Sir Alan Ayckbourn has run a theatre in which Yorkshire seaside resort since 1972?

8 In 1996, Benjamin Netanyahu became prime minister of which Middle Eastern country?

9 In 2003, Danny Wallace started a 'Karma Army' where members carried out 'Random acts of . . .' what?

10 Macadamia nuts are native to which country?

11 In the southern hemisphere, the longest day falls in which month?

12 The 1981 film _The Final Conflict_ was the second sequel to which 1976 horror film starring Gregory Peck?

13 Of which country was Pierre Trudeau prime minister from 1968 to 1979, and from 1980 to 1984?

14 In which 2001 hit comedy film did Ben Stiller play a clueless male model?

15 In the traditional British dish of 'bangers and mash', what are the 'bangers'?

16 In which 2002 film did Steve Coogan play the role of the record producer Tony Wilson?

17 The pipistrelle is the smallest and most common type of which British mammal?

18 Whom did Charles Darwin's portrait replace on the back of a ten-pound note?

19 In which type of motorsport is Sebastian Loeb a multiple world champion?

20 The clock of which children's TV town told the time 'steadily, sensibly, never too quickly, never too slowly'?

21 What type of reptile is a skink?

22 In 1854, Britain allied with France to fight Russia in which war?

23 In which children's TV series could the Soup Dragon, the Froglets and the Glow Buzzers be found?

24 The 'Anschluss', in 1938, was the annexation by Germany of which country?

25 Which nineteenth-century French painter died on a South Pacific island in 1903?

26 According to the zodiac, Sagittarians are born in November and which other month?

27 What is the name given to the tough, outer sheath that protects the trunk and branches of a tree?

28 'Burlington Bertie' is rhyming slang in horseracing for which betting price?

29 In personal advertisements, what do the letters SWF stand for?

30 The lotus is the national flower of which Asian country?

31 Which Bond actor appeared in the 2002 film *Road to Perdition*?

32 In English history, which powerful, fifteenth-century northern earl was called 'the Kingmaker'?

33 In the nineteenth century, Kid McCoy and Gentleman Jim Corbett were world champions in which sport?

34 What name is given to the ballet shoes which enable a dancer to stand on the tips of the toes?

35 Brothers Martin Kemp and Gary Kemp were members of which 1980s band?

36 Which former *TV-AM* newsreader once famously threw a glass of wine over Jonathan Aitken at a party?

37 Which former presenter of *Changing Rooms* also took part in the 2006 series of *Strictly Come Dancing*?

38 In which country was the composer Frédéric Chopin born?

39 In which North African country are the ruins of the ancient city of Memphis?

40 In 1980, which British rock trio had a UK number one hit single with 'Don't Stand So Close To Me'?

41 In 1963, which British band had a UK number one hit with the single 'Sweets For My Sweet'?

42 Which band had UK chart hits in the1980s with 'Road To Nowhere' and 'Once In A Lifetime'?

43 Established in 1804, with which pastime is the RHS most closely associated?

44 The White Stripes' single 'I Just Don't Know What To Do With Myself' featured which supermodel poledancing in the video?

45 Which word is a blend of the words 'motor' and 'calvacade'?

46 In 1964, who was the first female British athlete to win an Olympic gold and set a world record in the long jump?

47 What is the breed name of the small dog that is affectionately known as a 'Staffy'?

48 In 2004, which former England cricketer received a BBC Lifetime Achievement Award?

49 Which former Hollywood wild child's band is called Juliette and the Licks?

50 In 2002, which presenter of the BBC programme *The Clothes Show* wrote a book entitled *Fashion UK*?

SET 13

1 In which limb of the body are the triceps muscles found?

2 What is the young of a kangaroo called?

3 From June 1948 to May 1949, which blockaded European city was supplied with necessities by an airlift?

4 In which equestrian sport did Nick Skelton and Robert Smith compete for Great Britain at the 2004 Olympics?

5 Who is the female presenter of TV's *Springwatch*?

6 Brothers Gary and Phil Neville have both represented England in which sport?

7 A cardiologist is a doctor specializing in the treatment of which part of the body?

8 In 1948, which famous British composer established an annual music festival in the small Suffolk resort of Aldeburgh?

9 Earl Grey tea is flavoured with the essence of what?

10 The Broadway musical *South Pacific* is set during which twentieth-century historical event?

11 Who was lead singer with the 1970s rock band Sweet?

12 Ventriloquist Nina Conti is the daughter of which British actor?

13 Which Tudor mansion in Buckinghamshire serves as the country residence of the British prime minister?

14 Between 1675 and 1710, which English architect re-built St Paul's Cathedral?

15 Which US actress played the title role in the 1996 film *Emma*?

16 Which green-leafed herb, sometimes called cilantro, is often used to flavour curries?

17 Lincoln, Leicester and Romney are breeds of which animal?

18 For which country does the cricketer Sachin Tendulkar play?

19 The theme park 'Lotte World' is located in which South Korean city?

20 Which pop duo had UK chart hits in the 1980s with 'Agadoo' and 'Do The Conga'?

21 Which leading Rugby League team in Lancashire is called the Warriors?

22 The warthog is a wild pig indigenous to which continent?

23 The bilby, also known as the rabbit-eared bandicoot, is native to which country?

24 Who was the lead singer with the 1960s pop group The Troggs?

25 In November 2006, which British celebrity chef opened his first New York restaurant in the London NYC Hotel?

26 On the flag of Vietnam, how many gold stars are there?

27 The Royal Shakespeare Company is based in which Warwickshire town?

28 The 1960s TV quiz show *Criss Cross Quiz* was based on which traditional game?

29 In 2006, which supermodel appeared as Katie Pollard in a stage version of the TV comedy *Little Britain*?

30 In the area of trade, what do the initials EFTA stand for?

31 At the 1996 Olympic Games, which US athlete won both the 200m and 400m events?

32 Globe and Jerusalem are both types of which edible thistle?

33 In relation to time, 'Julian' and 'Gregorian' are both types of what?

34 Often used as a ski lodge, by what name is a traditional Swiss wooden mountain hut better known?

35 In Ireland, what word is used for alcohol made illicitly, typically from potatoes?

36 Which German chemist designed a type of adjustable gas burner in 1855, which is used in scientific work?

37 By which name is the sea parrot more commonly known?

38 What nationality was the sixteenth-century prophet Nostradamus?

39 In the US what is celebrated on 2 February and is also a film starring Bill Murray?

40 Founded in the UK in the 1850s, what do the initials YWCA stand for?

41 David Miller, Sebastien Izambard, Urs Bühler and Carlos Marin make up which international 'poperatic' group?

42 David Byrne was the lead singer of which US pop group of the 1970s and 80s?

43 What does the 'W' stand for in the name of US President George W. Bush?

44 Which King of England took part in the Third Crusade to the Holy Land?

45 What are the offspring of a deer called?

46 In a 1934 novel by James Hilton, what is the nickname of Mr Chipping, the schoolmaster hero?

47 In which Shakespeare tragedy does he refer to jealousy as a 'green-eyed monster which doth mock'?

48 Brandon Flowers is the frontman of which US rock band?

49 In Roman mythology, who was the twin brother of Romulus?

50 Dasher, Dancer, Prancer and Vixen are traditionally four of whose reindeer?

———————————— **SET 14** ————————————

1 The Stadium of Light is the home ground of which English football team?

2 What is the common name, meaning 'earth pig' in Afrikaans, given to the mammal sometimes called an 'African Ant Bear'?

3 Which TV chatshow host was born in the Yorkshire town of Barnsley?

4 The adjective lupine describes which type of animal?

5 The meat stew 'goulash' is originally from which European country?

6 For which Spanish club did footballing superstar Ronaldinho sign in July 2003?

7 In which decade of the twentieth century did Sir Edmund Hillary and Tenzing Norgay reach the summit of Mount Everest?

8 The phrase 'spag bol' is an informal abbreviation for which Italian dish?

9 Peking Duck is a dish from which Asian country?

10 Which ancient Greek king of Lydia was renowned for his wealth?

11 In 1297, which patriot led a Scottish army to victory over the English at the Battle of Stirling Bridge?

12 The fictional detective Hercule Poirot appeared in novels written by which British crime writer?

13 What is the civilian profession of Lance Corporal Jones in the TV sitcom *Dad's Army*?

14 Which former British prime minister was known as the 'grey man' of politics?

15 On which Caribbean island did calypso music originate?

16 Which US actor partnered Walter Matthau in the films *The Odd Couple* and *Grumpy Old Men*?

17 According to a myth, which creature's repeated efforts encouraged Scotsman Robert the Bruce to fight the English again?

18 What does an ammeter measure?

19 The 1960s slow dance music known as 'rock steady' originated on which Caribbean island?

20 In the natural world, what colour are the spots on a common, seven-spot ladybird?

21 Which Brazilian author wrote *The Alchemist*?

22 Darjeeling is a type of tea that comes from which country?

23 Ichthyology is the study of which type of animal?

24 Which word is both a type of singing bird and the name of a wharf in London's Docklands?

25 Which unit is used to measure the size of horses?

26 Of which food product is Spain's Manchego a variety?

27 In 1985, which Welsh singer and TV presenter had a UK top ten hit single with 'Walking In The Air'?

28 Found after the name of a UK company that can sell shares to the public, what do the initials plc stand for?

29 'Should auld acquaintance be forgot and never brought to mind' is the opening line of which song?

30 Which British comedian was born Michael Pennington in the Lancashire town of St Helens in 1971?

31 Who is the Roman equivalent of the Greek god Poseidon?

32 Which England footballer is the father of twins Georgie John and Summer Rose?

33 In which decade of the twentieth century was BBC2 launched?

34 With which European country are the dishes known as tapas most closely associated?

35 By what name is Jeanne Poisson, the official mistress of Louis XV of France, most commonly known?

36 In 1901, which monarch succeeded Queen Victoria on the British throne?

37 Completed in 1964, what popular name is given to the National Sports Centre in South London?

38 In the 1998 film comedy *Shakespeare in Love*, which British actress played the character of Queen Elizabeth?

39 Which British actor played Robert McCall in the TV series *The Equalizer*?

40 Bengal and Siberian are varieties of which animal?

41 Who was the lead singer with the 1960s and 70s pop group, the Four Seasons?

42 Which US president, who served from 1953 to 1961, was nicknamed 'Ike'?

43 Which actor played the title role in the 1996 film *The People vs Larry Flynt*?

44 In 2000, the BBC's main evening news bulletin moved from 9pm to what time?

45 The Californian rock singer Maria McKee had her only UK number one hit in 1990 with which love song?

46 A precursor of the EU, what did the initials EEC stand for?

47 Who was the first British sovereign of the House of Hanover?

48 From 1714 to 1837, the British monarch also ruled which state in northern Germany?

49 Which twentieth-century British prime minister was a bachelor with a passion for classical music and yachting?

50 In 1924, who became Britain's first Labour prime minister?

————————————— **SET 15** —————————————

1 In which Dickens novel does the 'ever so 'umble' clerk Uriah Heep appear?

2 Which Hollywood actress did actor Freddie Prinze Junior marry in 2002?

3 *Take It Like a Man* was the title of the 1995 autobiography of which 1980s pop singer?

4 Which Jacobean playwright's works include *The White Devil* and *The Duchess of Malfi*?

5 In 1984, which British theatre legend married singer Sarah Brightman?

6 The English singer Phil Oakey was the lead singer of which 1980s synthpop band?

7 The artist Vincent van Gogh was born in which country?

8 In the 1962 film *Lawrence of Arabia*, which Egyptian-born actor played the character Sherif Ali?

9 In Edmond Rostand's play *Cyrano de Bergerac*, what is Cyrano's distinguishing physical feature?

10 Which small, soft sweet is shaped like a baby?

11 Skiers Maria Walliser and Vreni Schneider represented which country at the Olympics?

12 Which religious leader uses the ancient title 'Pontifex Maximus'?

13 Since 1997, Jonny Wilkinson has played rugby for which UK club?

14 Which Welsh pop star sang the soaring vocals on the soundtrack to the 2001 film *A Beautiful Mind*?

15 *Football My Arse!* and *Celebrities My Arse!* are books written by which actor, star of TV's *The Royle Family*?

16 The cities of Manchester and Salford are encircled by which motorway?

17 In 1954, which US singer and actor had a UK hit with the song 'That's Amore'?

18 What is the British name for the board game that is known as checkers in the US?

19 In the *Tom and Jerry* cartoons what type of animal was Spike?

20 Which Norwegian composer wrote incidental music for Ibsen's play *Peer Gynt*?

21 Wentworth Golf Club is found in which English county?

22 In 2003, Shami Chakrabarti became the Director of which UK human rights organization?

23 By what name was John Lydon known when he was lead singer with the Sex Pistols?

24 In which century did the medieval outbreak of plague known as the Black Death first reach Britain?

25 Who was the first monarch of the House of Normandy to rule England?

26 Australian singer Darren Hayes was a member of which pop group?

27 Which Midlands ska band had a number one hit in 1981 with the single 'Ghost Town'?

28 In the US TV show *Malcolm in the Middle*, what is the first name of Malcolm's mother, played by Jane Kaczmarek?

29 Hunter's stew or bigos is a national dish of which country in eastern Europe?

30 With which European capital city did the Duke of Wellington's favourite horse share a name?

31 In popular parlance, a collection of useless and unwanted articles is often called 'flotsam and . . .' what?

32 Which emperor of Ethiopia, who died in 1975, is revered by the Rastafarian religious sect?

33 Which current affairs broadcaster was married to the writer Bel Mooney?

34 In 2006, which US pop singer divorced her husband Nick Lachey?

35 In which form of dance was Sir Kenneth MacMillan a celebrated choreographer?

36 Who directed the films *Truly, Madly, Deeply* and *The English Patient*?

37 Which legendary US singer had a number one hit in the 1950s with the song 'Stranger In Paradise'?

38 In the 1978 Clint Eastwood film *Every Which Way But Loose*, what type of ape is Clyde?

39 Which slang-word for the British refers to the limes once issued by sailors to prevent scurvy?

40 In which sport are the Scottish Rocks, Chester Jets and Sheffield Sharks leading British teams?

41 In European history, in which revolution was a ten-day week proposed?

42 Which English actor plays the role of Harry Potter in the film series of the same name?

43 The medical abbreviation ENT refers to which three parts of the body?

44 Which former country in Eastern Europe operated a secret police organization called the Stasi?

45 Which British prime minister was responsible for establishing the National Lottery in 1994?

46 Which prime minister said 'I have nothing to offer but blood, toil, tears and sweat' in a speech in May 1940?

47 In 2005, which European country elected a prime minister called Socrates?

48 In which city was the actress Elizabeth Taylor born?

49 Marie Curie was the first woman to be awarded which prestigious prize?

50 Which famed US military academy founded in 1802 is based on the Hudson River?

SET 16
---

1 What is the common name given to the fruit of the oak tree?

2 Which 1984 film featured miniature green monsters who tore through the small town of Kingston Falls?

3 The stage musical *Tommy* is set to music by which British rock band?

4 Which Broadway musical composer won an Academy Award for his song 'Sooner Or Later', from the film *Dick Tracy*?

5 Which legendary children's TV series was originally a French show called *Le Manège Enchanté*?

6 In television, what does the abbreviation BBC stand for?

7 In butchery, 'porterhouse' is a cut of which meat?

8 Which English king succeeded to the throne in 1483 at the age of 12?

9 Used as a greeting, in which language does *shalom* mean 'peace'?

10 Which Polish-born scientist discovered the element radium with her French husband Pierre?

11 In 1928, which Disney cartoon was the first to appear with both animation and sound?

12 The British Royal Arms depicts a lion together with which mythical beast?

13 In 2006, which member of the Royal Family purchased a 192-acre estate in Carmarthenshire?

14 'Sweet Caroline' and 'Forever In Blue Jeans' were 1970s hits for which US singer-songwriter?

15 Which US actor played the voice of Charlie in both the TV and film versions of *Charlie's Angels*?

16 In which Shakespeare play does Petruchio win a bet that his wife is the most docile?

17 Which 1970s and 80s glam-rock band's members include Gene Simmons and Paul Stanley?

18 Which two-word Latin phrase means 'a great work of literature' or 'an author's greatest work'?

19 Which US female singer had a UK hit in 1991 with 'When You Tell Me That You Love Me'?

20 Which British band released the 1973 album *Dark Side of the Moon*?

21 Konrad Bartelski and Martin Bell competed for Britain at which sport in the Winter Olympics?

22 First produced in Switzerland, by what name is the thin transparent wrapping material used in decoration known?

23 Which Texan rock trio had UK chart hits in the 1980s with 'Gimme All Your Lovin'' and 'Sharp Dressed Man'?

24 In which Yorkshire city is the 25,000-seat athletics arena called the Don Valley Stadium?

25 With which athletics field event is Fatima Whitbread most closely associated?

26 In the US, who gives the State of the Union address every January?

27 Which actress played the title role in the TV series *The Amazing Mrs Pritchard*?

28 Which US entertainer, once married to Gracie Allen, was famous for his ever-present cigars?

29 In 1977, which female Spanish duet had their only UK number one hit with the single 'Yes Sir, I Can Boogie'?

30 Which Poet Laureate wrote detective novels under the pseudonym Nicholas Blake?

31 Daniel arap Moi was the president of which African country from 1978 to 2002?

32 Which TV character in *The Simpsons* shares a name with the ancient Greek author of *The Odyssey*?

33 Which girl group had hits in the 1980s with 'Venus' and 'Love In The First Degree'?

34 Afrikaans is the first language of which Hollywood actress, who starred in the title role in the 2005 movie *Æon Flux*?

35 What was the codename for the Allied invasion of Normandy in June 1944?

36 Lady Jane Grey was declared queen following the death of which English monarch in 1553?

37 Who was the first host of the US version of the TV programme *The Weakest Link*?

38 With which sport is Switzerland's Roger Federer most closely associated?

39 Which two-word Latin phrase literally means 'according to the rate'?

40 In the 1968 film musical *Oliver!*, which character was played by Welsh comedian and singer Harry Secombe?

41 Bill McLaren was a respected commentator for over fifty years in which sport?

42 From which European country does the Bratwurst sausage originate?

43 Brigitte Bardot, Catherine Deneuve and Laetitia Casta have all modelled as which female symbol of the French republic?

44 When applied to wine, what does the term 'brut' mean?

45 In Terry Pratchett's novel *The Amazing Maurice and his Educated Rodents*, what type of animal is Maurice?

46 Which French soldier and saint was burned at the stake in Rouen in 1431?

47 What type of sports club is the 'Royal and Ancient of St Andrews'?

48 The society called the Sealed Knot was formed to re-enact battles from which war?

49 The fashion designer Jil Sander was born in which European country?

50 Which British actor originally narrated the TV cartoon series *Roobarb*?

--- SET 17 ---

1 Coined by Sir Thomas More in 1516, the name of which fictional place of perfection translates from Greek as 'no place'?

2 The Royal Liver Building is a feature of which UK city?

3 Who succeeded Richard III as king after defeating him at the Battle of Bosworth Field in 1485?

4 In nursing, what do the initials SRN stand for?

5 In 1968, Valerie Solanis shot which pop artist?

6 Which tropical tree provides the very light wood commonly used for making model aeroplanes?

7 Which department of London's Metropolitan Police has been known by the rhyming slang nickname of the 'Sweeney'?

8 The presenter Chris Evans made his name on which early morning TV show?

9 Which twentieth-century English comedian was famous for the catchphrases 'No Missus' and 'Titter ye not!'

10 Which tree particularly suffers from the ravages of a disease named for its first sighting in the Netherlands?

11 The words of which song, composed in 1814, is Francis Scott Key credited with writing?

12 In 2006, which heiress had her début at London Fashion Week spoiled when she was hit by fur protesters' flour bombs?

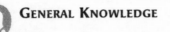

13 What nationality is the golfer José Maria Olazabal?

14 With which instrument was the Italian composer and musician Antonio Vivaldi particularly associated?

15 In which decade did Prince Charles and Lady Diana Spencer get married?

16 Which UK overseas territory is indicated by the abbreviation IOM?

17 Which Dutch duo hit the top of the UK pop charts in 1993 with 'No Limit'?

18 In November 1994, which former *Blue Peter* presenter was involved in the first National Lottery TV draw?

19 In which sport are Turnberry and Troon major championship venues in Scotland?

20 Which Yorkshire town is the setting for the TV sitcom *Last of the Summer Wine*?

21 Samuel Pepys was a confidant to two kings, Charles II and which other monarch?

22 In painting, which two primary colours, when mixed together, form purple?

23 Which Canadian-born film actress rose to fame as Julia in the TV drama series *Party of Five*?

24 Which shipping company owned the ill-fated *Titanic*?

25 Which musical features the songs 'I Get A Kick Out Of You' and 'You're The Top'?

26 In 2006, which celebrated English playwright and actor appeared in the Samuel Beckett play *Krapp's Last Tape*?

27 In 1967, in which boat did Donald Campbell attempt the water speed record on Coniston Water?

28 Which attribute of a person is generally changed by the legal procedure known as a deed poll?

29 Which French chemist developed the process known as pasteurization?

30 In 1955, which mutual defence treaty was signed in Poland by countries of the Soviet bloc?

31 In which decade of the twentieth century was the Eurovision Song Contest first held?

32 'Native New Yorker' and 'Use It Up And Wear It Out' were big disco hits for which US group?

33 What type of battles were the Battles of Britain, fought against Germany in the summer of 1940?

34 Which metal, with the symbol Pb, was used to make water pipes in ancient Rome?

35 In which 1986 film musical did a giant, man-eating plant called Audrey II immortalize the phrase, 'Feed me, Seymour'?

36 International rugby is played at Ellis Park in which South African city?

37 How many points does a pentagram have?

38 Médoc is a red wine from which European country?

39 Which cold dessert derives its name from the Italian for 'cooked cream'?

40 Which host of *Mastermind* began presenting *Today* on Radio 4 in 1987?

41 Which notorious eighteenth-century highwayman is thought to have made a legendary epic ride from London to York?

42 The All England Lawn Tennis and Croquet Club is better known as which tennis club?

43 What is the highest rank of the British hereditary peerage in the UK?

44 Credited to Watson and Crick, in which century was DNA discovered?

45 Which country's Rugby Union team is known as the Pumas?

46 In the TV quiz show hosted by Dermot Murnaghan, what are the quiz experts collectively called?

47 Mr Bun the Baker and Mr Bones the Butcher are characters depicted in which traditional children's card game?

48 Which salad based on apples, celery and walnuts was named after a New York hotel?

49 Russia's Alexei Nemov is an Olympic Gold medallist in which sport?

50 In Roman numerals, what letter is used to represent ten?

————————— **SET 18** —————————

1 Mozzarella is a type of cheese that originated in which European country?

2 Which meat pie originated in the Leicestershire town of Melton Mowbray?

3 In 1980, the song 'Call Me' was a UK number one hit for which US band?

4 The martial art of Kung Fu originated in which Asian country?

5 In the 1994 Oscar-winning film *The Adventures of Priscilla, Queen of the Desert*, what was Priscilla?

6 Britain entered the First World War when Germany invaded which neutral country?

7 Which German battleship sank HMS *Hood* during the Second World War?

8 Which Canadian city, in British Columbia, is due to host the 2010 Winter Olympic Games?

9 How many months are there in the year?

10 How many furlongs are there in one mile?

11 Who was the first actor to play Dr Who?

12 Which Radio 1 DJ's father was the Bishop of Peterborough?

13 Born in 1929, Arnold Palmer was a legendary figure in the history of which sport?

14 Which pastime, originating in Japan, has a name meaning 'empty orchestra'?

15 In which European city is the Gare du Nord located?

16 In mathematics, how many degrees are there in a circle?

17 Born in 1925, which TV presenter and artist created the original design for the *Blue Peter* badge?

18 *Vin* is the French word for which drink?

19 What was the name of musician Ziggy Marley's famous father?

20 Which metallic element, used as a nuclear fuel, has the chemical symbol Pu?

21 In which country was the twentieth-century painter Francis Bacon born?

22 The 1987 Steve Martin film *Roxanne* was inspired by which French play by Edmond Rostand?

23 Which London theatre was the location for a top-rating, Sunday night, TV variety show in the 1950s and 60s?

24 From which Italian theatre tradition is the English character of Mr Punch believed to derive?

25 The borough of Blaenau Gwent is located in which country of the UK?

26 With which sport was Nigel Benn most closely associated?

27 Often used to show when an aircraft is expected to land, what do the initials ETA stand for?

28 Complete the title of the 1971 Disney film starring Angela Lansbury, *Bedknobs and . . .* what?

29 In November 2006, which former *Baywatch* star filed for divorce after only four months of marriage?

30 In 2003, Hu Jintao succeeded Jiang Zemin as president of which country?

31 Which French World Heritage Site is a rocky island off the Normandy coast topped by a medieval abbey?

32 Which world chess champion defeated Nigel Short in 1993 and announced his retirement in 2005?

33 The journalist Alistair Cooke was most famous for his radio series entitled, *Letter from . . .* where?

34 Which TV comedy drama features the characters Frank, 'Lip' and Debbie Gallagher?

35 In UK company law, what do the initials EGM stand for?

36 *Bullitt*, *The Great Escape* and *The Towering Inferno* were hit films for which US actor?

37 In 1973, which flat cap-wearing singer-songwriter hit the top of the UK singles chart with 'Get Down'?

38 In 1977, which British pop band had their first UK number one hit with the single 'So You Win Again'?

39 Which political and spiritual leader is known as the 'Father of India'?

40 Who starred as a lone horseman dressed as a preacher in the 1985 film *Pale Rider*?

41 Which form of London public transport was pioneered by George Shillibeer in 1829?

42 In the Highway Code, which background colour is used in a school bus sign usually displayed in the rear window?

43 By which nickname was William Joyce, the propaganda broadcaster from Nazi Germany during the Second World War, better known?

44 In 2002, which Scottish manager took the helm at Everton Football Club?

45 Who is actress Bridget Fonda's Oscar-winning aunt?

46 In 1963, which Conservative cabinet minister resigned because of a scandal involving a Russian spy?

47 In Britain, pillar boxes are traditionally which colour?

48 Which wartime engineer designed the so-called 'bouncing-bombs' used in the 'Dambusters' raid?

49 In 2003, which TV presenter, known for birdwatching, received the OBE for his services to Wildlife Conservation?

50 On which river does the city of Bath stand?

-------------------- **SET 19** --------------------

1 In 2005, which English dramatist won the Nobel Prize for Literature?

2 In 1997, which French Canadian driver won the Formula 1 world championship?

3 From which material was the children's storybook character Pinocchio made?

4 Which British soul singer is the host of the Radio 2 show *Beverley's Gospel Nights*?

5 Which seventeenth-century English architect designed the Banqueting House in Whitehall?

6 The TV drama series *Silent Witness* originally starred which actress as pathologist Sam Ryan?

7 Of what is pomology the study?

8 In which decade of the twentieth century did India gain independence from Britain?

9 The red, pink or white houseplant properly termed *Impatiens*, is popularly known by what name?

10 Which alcoholic drink is sometimes referred to as 'The Green Fairy'?

11 Of what is an oenophile a connoisseur?

12 What name is given to a hat with a flat top that is worn at graduation ceremonies?

13 In 1983, which US illusionist famously made the Statue of Liberty disappear?

14 In UK politics, in which decade did the 'Gang of Four' form the SDP?

15 The 1953 film *From Here to Eternity* was set in which US state?

16 Which famous physicist wrote *A Brief History of Time*?

17 Originally created to stir up trouble in the Smurf village, what is the name of the blonde female Smurf?

18 Szechuan cuisine originated in which Asian country?

19 Who was the original lead singer of the Australian band INXS?

20 In US history, what was the name of the 'underground' organization that helped slaves escape from the South?

21 Joséphine de Beauharnais was the first wife of which French leader?

22 Which Russian word, meaning 'openness', was given to the policy of more liberal government initiated by Gorbachev?

23 What name is given to a carved Hallowe'en pumpkin?

24 The duck-billed platypus is native to which country?

25 Linda Lee Danvers is the alter ego of which superheroine?

26 Britain's Nathan Robertson and Gail Emms are leading competitors in which sport?

27 In the northern hemisphere, in which month of the year does the spring equinox fall?

28 The Huguenots were sixteenth-century Protestants from which country?

29 Under the current constitution, how many terms can the President of the US serve?

30 Fugu fish is a delicacy in which Asian country?

31 Which European city was host to the second modern Olympic Games, held in 1900?

32 Which US actor, star of *Taxi Driver* and *GoodFellas*, produced the musical *We Will Rock You*?

33 When England won the 2003 Rugby World Cup, who was their coach?

34 The most popular names for kings in British history have been Henry and which other name?

35 Which US female singer had a UK chart hit in 1989 with 'If I Could Turn Back Time'?

36 Which English city, famous for its medicinal waters, was called Aquae Sulis by the Romans?

37 Traditionally, LPs, 7-inch and 12-inch singles are made out of which material?

38 Which 1997 film featured unemployed men in the North of England who set up as strippers?

39 Which female TV presenter co-hosted the children's show *SM:TV Live* with Ant and Dec?

40 In medicine, the prefix 'haemo' refers to which part of the body?

41 Which Premiership football club moved to the Riverside Stadium in 1995?

42 Which nationality is TV presenter and model Abi Titmuss?

43 In June 1987, which UK prime minister was re-elected for a third term?

44 In the US, on the 4th of which month does Independence Day fall?

45 'All children, except one, grow up' is the opening line of which novel by J. M. Barrie?

46 In the 1986 film *Withnail & I*, which actor plays the character Withnail?

47 In 1999, which Irish boyband had a UK number one hit with the single 'You Needed Me'?

48 In the 1990s TV sitcom *Absolutely Fabulous*, which comedy actress played the part of Edina's mother?

49 Twitchers is a name associated with practitioners of which hobby?

50 An igloo is a dwelling that is typically made from which substance?

SET 20
---

1 Which Liverpudlian wrote the screenplay for the TV drama *Boys from The Black Stuff*?

2 The comic singer of the early twentieth-century music halls, Sir Harry Laude, came from which British country?

3 Which British actress played the character Iris in the 2006 film comedy *The Holiday*?

4 In terms of area, what is the largest state of the USA?

5 The cones of which climbing plant are used in brewing beer?

6 The Japanese cultivation of miniature trees is most commonly known as what?

7 Which university crew infamously sank during the 1978 Boat Race?

8 *Little Girl Lost* was the title of the 1990 autobiography of which US actress?

9 Born André Friedmann, Robert Capa was most closely associated with which branch of the arts?

10 Flamboyant Welsh star Gavin Henson plays which sport at an international level?

11 In 2003, which TV comedian starred as the title character in the spoof Bond film *Johnny English*?

12 In the First World War, which term was used by soldiers to describe the ground between two opposing army trenches?

13 Named after its place of origin, what type of sweet food is demerara?

14 Which US city is known as the 'City of Brotherly Love'?

15 Published in 1960, the quote, 'Remember it's a sin to kill a mockingbird' comes from which Harper Lee novel?

16 Which three initial letters from the Latin for 'which was to be proved' are usually put at the end of a mathematical proof?

17 Which Bank of England note has a densely coloured red triangle as its recognition symbol for the partially sighted?

18 Of which country did Bertie Ahern become prime minister in 1997?

19 In which year was Tony Blair elected Labour Party leader?

20 In art, navy is a shade of which primary colour?

21 Of which country was Mary Robinson president from 1990 to 1997?

22 Which P. G. Wodehouse character did Ian Carmichael play on British television in the 1960s?

23 Neil Tennant and Chris Lowe together formed which 1980s pop duo?

24 In the Christian religion, what name is given to the Sunday before Easter?

25 In geometry, a decagon is a shape with how many sides?

26 In French, the drink 'café au lait' is 'coffee with . . .' what?

27 Which day of the week is named after the Roman god Saturn?

28 In 1985, which band recorded their first UK number one hit 'You Spin Me Round (Like A Record)'?

29 Which former Lord Chancellor to Henry VIII was tried and executed in 1535?

30 In December 2005, which British singer-songwriter celebrated his civil partnership with David Furnish?

31 Which nineteenth-century German politician was known as the 'Iron Chancellor'?

32 In 1998, in which region did Chek Lap Kok replace Kai Tak as the international airport?

33 What name, from the Spanish for 'bleeding', is given to the Spanish punch of red wine, sugar, fruit and iced soda?

34 Which cartoon character's catchphrases were 'Drat! Drat and double drat!' and 'Muttley, do something!'?

35 In C. S. Lewis's *Chronicles of Narnia*, what type of creature is Aslan?

36 Which 1952 novel, by Mary Norton, is about a group of tiny people who live under the floorboards of an old house?

37 How many touch judges usually officiate in a game of Rugby League?

38 Dutchman Johan Cruyff was a star player in which sport?

39 Which popular Christmas song features a 'one-horse open sleigh'?

40 On which of the Channel Islands did the British author Gerald Durrell open a zoo in 1959?

41 In England, by which name is a pub lunch consisting of Cheddar cheese, bread, pickles and onion better known?

42 Stromboli, a volcanic island in the Mediterranean Sea, belongs to which European country?

43 During the US Prohibition, what name was given to illegal drinking clubs?

44 Who played the title role in the 2001 film *Mike Bassett: England Manager*?

45 Which was the first of Ian Fleming's James Bond novels?

46 In the UK, who was the long-time host of the 1950s TV panel game, *What's My Line?*?

47 In the Mr Men series of books and cartoons, what colour is Little Miss Sunshine?

48 Where in the body would you find the metacarpus?

49 What is the common name of the whale that is sometimes known as the white whale?

50 Which TV presenter was the mother of Bob Geldof's children Peaches, Fifi and Pixie?

─────────────── **SET 21** ───────────────

1 In the 1993 film *The Fugitive*, which US actor played the character of Dr Richard Kimble?

2 What name do the Germans use for mulled wine?

3 In 1974, former dancer Isabel Perón became the first female president of which country?

4 What colour are the petals of the alpine flower, edelweiss?

5 'Boz' was the pseudonym used by which celebrated Victorian novelist for some of his early works?

6 In which 1999 film comedy does Hugh Grant star as a man who is marrying the daughter of a mafia boss?

7 What is the name of the blackcurrant-flavoured liqueur added to dry white wine to make the drink known as Kir?

8 The town of Timbuktu is in which African country?

9 By which nickname is English drummer Peter Edward Baker better known?

10 Partly set in Newcastle, which 1990s TV drama followed a group of friends from the 1960s to the 1990s?

11 Which vegetable, also known as the Sugar Snap Pea, literally means 'eat everything' in French?

12 In which book of the Bible do the Ten Commandments appear?

13 In the children's TV cartoon *Count Duckula* what was the name of the character who had her arm permanently in a sling?

14 The bark of which oak tree is traditionally used to seal wine bottles?

15 In 1903 the French sportsman Maurice Garin became the first winner of which famous cycle race?

16 How many horns did the dinosaur known as Triceratops have?

17 In the 1970s TV sitcom *Some Mothers Do 'Ave 'Em*, whose catchphrase was, 'Ooh Betty'?

18 Which famous scientist said, 'Science without religion is lame, religion without science is blind'?

19 In 2006, *Fear of Fanny* was a TV drama about which TV cook?

20 Which Scottish civil engineer is credited with the design of Waterloo, Southwark, and London Bridges?

21 In which US city was the record label 'Motown Records' established?

22 In which limb of the body are the hamstring muscles found?

23 Which Radio 2 DJ's show features the items 'Factoids' and 'Ask Elvis'?

24 The young of which animal group are known as fledglings?

25 In the NATO phonetic alphabet, the name of which sport represents the letter 'G'?

26 To which royal house did King Charles I belong?

27 Which gas is the second lightest element, after hydrogen?

28 Which TV presenter is the daughter of the former *Sunday Express* editor Eve Pollard?

29 During a 2001 Japanese tour, which British girl group did Siobhan Donaghy leave?

30 Which Hollywood actor provided the voice of the baby, Mikey, in the 1989 film *Look Who's Talking*?

31 Which West End musical, which opened in 2006, is based on the songs of Boney M?

32 Which US actress won an Oscar for her role opposite Jack Nicholson in the 1997 film *As Good As It Gets*?

33 What is the collective noun for a group of crows?

34 With which sport is the Gumball 3000 Rally most closely associated?

35 Published in 1903, which novel by Erskine Childers involved a German invasion of Britain?

36 Seve Ballesteros was a leading figure in which sport?

37 Which sport is played by the Pittsburgh Penguins and the Toronto Maple Leafs?

38 From which European country does Fontina cheese come?

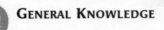

39 In US history, which president was known as Father Abraham?

40 In 2001, who was appointed US Secretary of Defense?

41 *Narcissus pseudonarcissus* is the scientific name for which popular garden flower?

42 Which 1990s TV sitcom featured Rik Mayall and Adrian Edmondson as the two repellent bachelors Richie and Eddie?

43 What was the stage name of the regular scorekeeper on the TV comedy game show *Shooting Stars*?

44 In degrees Celsius, which temperature represents the freezing point of water?

45 The TV drama *Pennies From Heaven* was written by which British writer?

46 In which 1979 film do Meryl Streep and Dustin Hoffman star as divorced parents fighting for custody of their son?

47 Which English artistic duo first made their names in the 1960s and 70s by posing as living sculptures?

48 What nationality was the playwright Anton Chekhov?

49 Which band had UK chart hits in the 1970s with 'Under The Moon Of Love' and 'Three Steps To Heaven'?

50 Which Hammersmith eatery, famous in its own right, is also known as the restaurant that launched Jamie Oliver's career?

SET 22
---

1 Which Asian country was once known as Siam?

2 Which drink, highly flavoured with wormwood, was made illegal in France in 1915?

3 A first wedding anniversary is traditionally associated with which material?

4 In 1999, which Italian trio had their first UK number one hit with the single 'Blue (Da Ba Dee)'?

5 With a name similar to Hollywood, which British film studios opened in Buckinghamshire in 1936?

6 Which actor turned singer had a hit with 'Crocodile Shoes' in 1994?

7 In 1973, Carl XVI Gustaf became king of which European country?

8 Which British actress and *Carry On* star was born Barbara Ann Deeks?

9 What name is given to a person who doesn't eat meat?

10 In a motor vehicle what do the initials 'ABS' stand for?

11 Which word, describing retail offers, was coined from the initial letters of the phrase 'buy one get one free'?

12 In which field is the Turner Prize awarded?

13 The 1997 film *Fierce Creatures*, starring Michael Palin and Jamie Lee Curtis, was the follow-up to which 1988 comedy?

14 Native to Africa, what is the fastest land animal?

15 What is the national flower of England?

16 Which male singing voice comes between a tenor and a bass?

17 On the set of which film did Tom Cruise and Nicole Kidman meet?

18 Axminster and Wilton are well-known names in which type of household floor covering?

19 Which Irish golfer won the 2006 European Order of Merit?

20 Which English actor played George Smiley in TV's *Tinker, Tailor, Soldier, Spy* and *Smiley's People*?

21 The 2004 Morgan Spurlock film about the fast food industry is entitled *Super Size . . .* what?

22 What is the name of the hunchback in Victor Hugo's novel *The Hunchback of Notre Dame*?

23 Which Australian supermodel appeared with Hugh Grant in the 1994 film *Sirens*?

24 Tartare sauce is the traditional accompaniment to eat with what food?

25 In France, the Tomb of the Unknown Soldier lies under which Parisian monument?

26 The 'horn of plenty' is a type of which edible fungus?

27 Which king of England was the father of King Charles I?

28 As well as the first successful powered aircraft, the Wright brothers managed a factory making which transport devices?

29 A popular bar snack, what is the common name for the groundnut?

30 In TV's *The Simpsons*, which character owns the Springfield nuclear power station where Homer works?

31 In 1956, in which Central European country was an uprising quashed by the Soviet Union?

32 Chianti is a type of wine produced in which country?

33 Which actor played Captain James T. Kirk in the TV series *Star Trek*?

34 Kim Clijsters and Justine Henin-Hardenne are Belgian competitors in which sport?

35 Frankie Dettori is a famous name in which sport?

36 The stage musical *Taboo* is based on the life of which 1980s British pop sensation?

37 In which country is the medal known as the Iron Cross awarded?

38 In 2001 who became Secretary of State for Culture, Media and Sport?

39 Which country in the Middle East has 'the Hashemite Kingdom' as part of its official name?

40 According to the 2006 *Michelin Guide*, which Berkshire village had two of the top three restaurants in the UK?

41 The French port of Marseille is on the coastline of which sea?

42 Born in 1955, which US actor has worked with the child stars Miko Hughes and Haley Joel Osment on film?

43 'Wood' and 'field' are species of which rodent?

44 Which ancient British tribe in East Anglia was ruled by Queen Boudicca?

45 In the French language, the word *père* refers to which member of the family?

46 Roquefort cheese originated in which European country?

47 Which British actor played politician Alan Clark in the TV adaptation, *The Alan Clark Diaries*?

48 In theatre tradition, what colour is the backstage room where actors can relax when not performing?

49 *Mr and Mrs Andrews* and *The Watering Place* are paintings by which eighteenth-century English artist?

50 In 2006, US actor Jesse Metcalfe was dating a member of which British girl group?

--------- SET 23 ---------

1 Which model village was built near Birkenhead in 1888 by W. H. Lever for workers at his soap factory?

2 Pope Benedict XVI was born Joseph Ratzinger in which country?

3 What is the official language of Egypt?

4 A BBC TV adaptation of which Charles Dickens novel won the Best Drama Serial BAFTA in 2006?

5 What colour is the animated character Betty Boop's hair?

6 What is the common name for the gas sometimes called marsh or swamp gas?

7 Which English golfer won his first US Masters title in 1989?

8 What was the nationality of gymnast Sawao Kato who won eight Olympic gold medals in the 1960s and 70s?

9 The musical *My Fair Lady* was an adaptation of which George Bernard Shaw play?

10 Ailsa Craig, Golden Sunrise and Money Maker are varieties of which fruit?

11 Which BBC radio station, once known as the 'Home Service', broadcasts on 92 to 95 FM?

12 Which measure of a person's typing speed is commonly abbreviated to WPM?

13 What was the screen name of the US film star born as Frederick Austerlitz?

14 Which Mancunian singer had a 1988 UK hit single with 'Everyday Is Like Sunday'?

15 Bronze is an alloy traditionally composed of copper and which other metal?

16 Which metallic element, with the chemical symbol Li, is the lightest known metal?

17 Malariology is the scientific study of which disease?

18 In 1970, which country won football's FIFA World Cup competition for the third time?

19 Which US pop singer had 2006 hits with 'Stupid Girls' and 'Who Knew'?

20 At which racecourse are the 1,000 and 2,000 Guineas horse races run each year?

21 Which variety of bean is traditionally used in a can of baked beans?

22 With which type of cuisine is a side order of poppadums most commonly associated?

23 The National Horseracing Museum is situated next to which major racecourse?

24 Which celebrated darts commentator also wrote the children's TV series *Jossy's Giants*?

25 In the Enid Blyton books, Noddy's car was mainly red and which other colour?

26 Zara Phillips is the daughter of which of the Queen's children?

27 In which decade was the US supermodel and actress Jerry Hall born?

28 Arborio is a type of rice originating in which European country?

29 In 1991, a dead shark floating in a tank of formaldehyde brought which British artist into the spotlight?

30 What was the name of the research ship used by underwater explorer Jacques Cousteau?

31 Clarence House is the official London residence of which of the Queen's children?

32 The carambola fruit is known more commonly by which name?

33 What was the surname of Hungarian brothers László and György, credited with inventing the modern ballpoint pen?

34 What nationality was the composer Giuseppe Verdi?

35 In 2006, which band, put together by Simon Cowell, features a group of six young choristers?

36 What is the name of magician Paul Daniels's long-term assistant, whom he married in 1988?

37 Liquorice Pomfret cakes take their name from which English town?

38 In the Netherlands, what kind of alcoholic drink is genever?

39 In a standard deck of playing cards, what colour are Hearts?

40 Which Greek Cypriot archbishop and statesman was president of the Republic of Cyprus from 1959 to 1977?

41 Which comedian co-presented the TV show *Your Face or Mine* with June Sarpong?

42 In the 1967 Disney film *The Jungle Book*, what is the name of the boy who is led out of the jungle to safety?

43 In a 2006 *Radio Times* poll of terrifying personalities, which chef was voted to be TV's Scariest Star?

44 What is the title of the novel by Katie Price that was published in 2006 and set in the world of glamour modelling?

45 In 1989, which European city was re-united by the destruction of a dividing wall?

46 In 2005, Dr Angela Merkel became the head of government of which European country?

47 According to the proverb, what is Tuesday's child full of?

48 Which 1980s TV cartoon featured the characters Cyril Sneer and Bert Raccoon?

49 Which type of triangle has no sides of equal length?

50 What nationality was the author Leo Tolstoy?

──────────────── **SET 24** ────────────────

1   Which US car company was founded on a farm near Dearborn, Michigan in 1903?

2   In 1925, which Irish playwright and critic won the Nobel Prize for Literature?

3   Phil Redmond created which long-running TV series that featured the character Tucker Jenkins?

4   In which sport have Oscar de la Hoya and Floyd Mayweather been world champions?

5   Chile Pine is an alternative name for which coniferous tree with branches covered with stiff sharp leaves?

6   What colour are the berries on mistletoe?

7   Which veteran TV comedy actor published his autobiography in 2005 entitled *If I Don't Write It Nobody Else Will*?

8   Which branch of medical science deals with old age and its diseases?

9   Double Gloucester is a variety of which dairy food?

10   In which northern UK city is the musical *Blood Brothers* set?

11   Which former Monty Python member wrote a series of books about Erik the Viking?

12   What name is given to the person who assists a golfer during a match by carrying their clubs?

13   Leonardo, Donatello, Michaelangelo and Raphael are members of which children's TV cartoon crime-busting group?

14   According to the idiom, which colour is one in if in debt, or overdrawn?

15   Taoism is an ancient system of beliefs that originated in which country?

16   Taramasalata is a dish that originated in which European country?

17   Which Yorkshire city has a professional Rugby League team called the Bulls?

18   Which TV personality's catchphrase is 'Nice to see you, to see you nice'?

19   Which element, with the chemical symbol Ca, is the most abundant metallic element in the human body?

20 The Kerry Blue Terrier breed of dog originated in which European country?

21 The BBC Three programme *The House of Tiny Tearaways* features which female clinical psychologist?

22 RTE is a national TV channel in which European country?

23 What colour are the famous Lipizzaner stallions that perform with the Spanish Riding School of Vienna?

24 Which TV cartoon featured the characters Cut Throat Jake and Tom the Cabin Boy?

25 On a compass, which direction is directly opposite South?

26 Which drink is most closely associated with the annual German 'Oktoberfest'?

27 In February 2003, which England footballer became the youngest player to represent his country?

28 In 1957, which US singer and actor had UK charts hits with 'Banana Boat Song (Day-O)' and 'Island In The Sun'?

29 Which patriotic British song by Thomas Arne, to words by James Thomson, was first performed in 1740?

30 Which TV music-hall series, with an audience in period costume, ran from 1953 to 1983?

31 The explorer Christopher Columbus was born in which Italian city?

32 Along with Pinot Noir and Pinot Meunier, which other grape is permitted in making true Champagne?

33 Which US president is reported to have said 'Honey, I forgot to duck' after an assassination attempt in 1981?

34 Which country is known to its inhabitants as 'Hellas'?

35 Which Tour de France winner's autobiography is entitled *It's Not About the Bike: My Journey Back to Life*?

36 Which Australian pop star released 1980s singles 'Got To Be Certain' and 'Je Ne Sais Pas Pourquoi'?

37 Sometimes seen on bottles of beer, what do the initials IPA stand for?

38 In the 1980s, which female TV personality co-wrote with Bettina Luxon *Your Hand (An Illustrated Guide To Palmistry)*?

39 What is the name of ventriloquist Roger DeCourcey's puppet bear?

40 Which British TV comedian and chat show host had his only UK number one hit in 1968 with the single 'I Pretend'?

41 Which former US tennis player was known as 'Superbrat'?

42 In *The Importance of Being Earnest*, in which female fashion accessory is one of the characters found as a baby?

43 Which celebrity couple released a 'his and her' perfume range in August 2006?

44 In the nursery rhyme, who '. . . sat in a corner, eating his Christmas pie'?

45 Diplodocus, Velociraptor and Iguanodon were varieties of which extinct creature?

46 Which actor played the title character in the 2002 TV adaptation of the novel *Goodbye Mr Chips*?

47 The phrase 'alter ego' comes from which language?

48 Which mime artist was the only person to speak in Mel Brooks's *Silent Movie*?

49 In which county can the Jodrell Bank radio telescope be found?

50 Which US singer's only UK chart success was the 1979 number one hit 'Ring My Bell'?

SET 25

1 Which is the brightest planet in our solar system and is the easiest to spot with the naked eye from Earth?

2 In the 1970s, which British prime minister was known as 'Big Jim' or 'Sunny Jim'?

3 In which country was the singer and actress Olivia Newton-John born?

4 Which French actress played the lead role in the classic 1967 film *Belle de Jour*?

5   Which of the Brontë sisters was originally known by the pen name Acton Bell?

6   Which weaving term is used for the crosswise thread that interlaces with the 'warp'?

7   Which nickname was given to the specially designed vehicle to enable the Pope to travel safely amongst crowds?

8   Which US country singer's songs include 'By The Time I Get To Phoenix' and 'Rhinestone Cowboy'?

9   Which member of the Royal Family has enjoyed a lengthy relationship with England rugby player Mike Tindall?

10 In 1969, Neil Armstrong and which other member of *Apollo 11* walked on the Moon?

11 Which historian presented the 2006 TV series *The Power of Art*?

12 With which sport was Ferenc Puskas, who died in 2006, most associated?

13 Which spider takes its name from the Italian town of Taranto?

14 Which poultry is traditionally eaten at the Thanksgiving Day feast in the USA?

15 First opening in 1973, which cult stage musical features the characters Columbia, Magenta and Janet?

16 Which European national rugby team plays its home matches at the Flaminio Stadium?

17 From which European country did the South-east Asian country Laos gain independence in the 1950s?

18 In November 2006, which star of *Desperate Housewives* revealed that she was dating film director Stephen Kay?

19 Who led the Labour Party to a landslide election victory in 1945?

20 The Gilbert and Sullivan operetta *Iolanthe* features which magical creatures?

21 With which sport is Colin Montgomerie most closely associated?

22 In the 1970s, which Communist Chinese leader's image did pop artist Andy Warhol use to create a series of prints?

23 Which Andrew Lloyd Webber musical tells the story of the tragic, silent movie star Norma Desmond?

24 Dutchwoman Inge De Bruijn is a multi-Olympic gold medallist in which sport?

25 Who played the title role in the 1964 film *Zorba the Greek*?

26 Which organization has the motto, 'Nation Shall Speak Peace Unto Nation'?

27 Odontology is the science dealing with which part of the body?

28 In the UK, ASH is the acronym for which health pressure group?

29 King Bhumibol has been sovereign of which South-east Asian country since 1946?

30 How many sides does the geometrical shape called a nonagon have?

31 Which Oscar-winning actress married fellow actor Ryan Philippe in 1999?

32 Which king married Catherine of Braganza in 1662?

33 In 1492, Christopher Columbus set sail with three ships; the *Pinta*, the *Santa Maria*, and which other?

34 In which 1997 film did Leonardo DiCaprio and Kate Winslet share a kiss?

35 Jeremy Vine took over the 12–2pm Radio 2 slot from which veteran DJ in 2003?

36 In November 2006, from the top of which 443-foot-high London attraction did daredevil Gary Connery jump?

37 In the Looney Tunes cartoons, what is the name of the cat who is always trying to catch Tweety Pie?

38 Which classic children's storytelling TV show was first shown in 1965?

39 In which sport would an 'iron' and a 'sand wedge' be used?

40 Which Scots poet wrote the verse 'A Red Red Rose'?

41 Which Latin phrase, meaning 'from the books of', is sometimes used on bookplate labels to identify the owner of a book?

42 Which ingredient is poured onto the top of an Irish coffee drink?

43 Mandarin, Tufted and Ruddy are three types of which water bird?

44 Which Asian city will host the 2008 Olympic Games?

45 In the 2002 film *Scooby-Doo*, which US actress played Daphne?

46 Brine is water that is saturated with which mineral?

47 What nationality was the great seventeenth-century painter Rembrandt?

48 In 1967, which singer had both a hit single and a hit album with 'Matthew And Son'?

49 Leading UK collector of contemporary art, Charles Saatchi, is married to which cookery goddess?

50 What is the first name of broadcaster David Dimbleby's younger brother?

SET 26

1 Which new London bridge opened and closed in the year 2000?

2 What four-letter word is given to an endorsement on a passport that allows the holder to enter or leave a country?

3 Photographer Anne Geddes collaborated with which French Canadian singer on her book *Miracle*?

4 In 2006, who succeeded Sue Lawley as presenter of Radio 4's *Desert Island Discs*?

5 Doon Mackichan, Fiona Allen and Sally Phillips were the original stars of which TV comedy show?

6 In darts, what is Phil Taylor's nickname?

7 In the Middle East, Beirut is the capital city of which country?

8 Which literary cookbook by Nigella Lawson was subtitled 'The Pleasures and Principles of Good Food'?

9 In which city does the Dow Jones Index measure stock market movements?

10 Which US pop singer starred with Rupert Everett in the 2000 romantic comedy film *The Next Best Thing*?

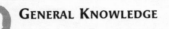
11 Which US state was an independent republic from 1836 to 1845, when it became the 28th state?

12 Which female warrior wearing a helmet and carrying a shield and trident appears on UK coins?

13 Which Roman emperor built a palace known as Domus Aurea, or the 'Golden House', after a great fire in Rome?

14 Which musical instrument is most closely associated with actor and musician Dudley Moore?

15 Which 1980s TV series, based on a book by Evelyn Waugh, featured the characters Sebastian Flyte and Charles Ryder?

16 From which country did Mozambique gain independence in 1975?

17 Plays called *Ghosts* and *The Master Builder* were the work of which Norwegian playwright?

18 Which female cookery writer's works include *A Book of Middle Eastern Food* and *The Book of Jewish Food*?

19 Which antibiotic, discovered in 1928, was the first to be used by doctors?

20 Which former Radio 1 DJ married dance music artist Fatboy Slim in 1999?

21 In 1905, which famous physicist published the equation $E=mc^2$?

22 Which type of hairdressing establishment has given its name to close-harmony, male, singing quartets?

23 Which Russian composer wrote the ballet *Sleeping Beauty*?

24 Which British actor played Arthur Parker in the 1970s Dennis Potter TV series *Pennies from Heaven*?

25 Popular in Canada, which modern sport was adapted from the competitive Native American game called baggataway?

26 In which country was the composer Sergei Rachmaninov born?

27 Which European country occupied Ethiopia from 1936 to 1941?

28 Which TV comic is best known for the series, bearing his surname, in which he played the brother of Hattie Jacques?

29 The term 'malapropism', for a confusion of words, is derived from a character in a play by which author?

30 In which cathedral was Archbishop Thomas à Becket murdered by Henry II's knights?

31 In the natural world, to which continent is the hairy frog indigenous?

32 The Seikan Tunnel is located in which country?

33 Manzanilla is a variety of which fortified wine?

34 In 1993, which of the Nobel Prizes was won by the American Toni Morrison?

35 The 'Cod War' was a 1970s confrontation that took place between Britain and which country?

36 In which European country did the Advent calendar originate?

37 The Suffragette political movement campaigned to give women the right to do what?

38 Which famous conspiracy of 1605 was led by Robert Catesby?

39 With which Oasis song did Mike Flowers Pops have a UK number two hit in 1995?

40 In tableware, what is a demitasse?

41 The Giant Panda is native to which Asian country?

42 In 2004, which US female singer had a UK number one hit with the single 'Everytime'?

43 Which US city's initials can precede the words 'confidential' and 'story' to form the titles of two hit films?

44 Panama has a land border with Colombia and which other country in Central America?

45 Which nationality was the seventeenth-century philosopher Thomas Hobbes?

46 The George Bush Intercontinental Airport serves which Texan city?

47 Which actor played the title role in the TV series *Quincy*?

48 Who released the album *Confessions on a Dance Floor* in 2005?

49 Which TV presenter's novels include *The Maid of Buttermere* and *A Time to Dance*?

50 In a series of sketches with Harry Enfield, which friend of Kevin the Teenager does Kathy Burke play?

———————————————————— SET 27 ————————————————————

1 Which code name was given to the 1991 US-led UN operation to liberate Kuwait from Iraq?

2 In 1982, which member of the Royal Family was asked for a cigarette by a bedroom intruder?

3 The UK pop legend Sir Cliff Richard also produces wine at his home in which country?

4 In 2006, which US wannabe rapper claimed to be 'America's most hated man' following his marriage breakdown?

5 Eamonn Andrews, Leslie Crowther and Michael Aspel all presented which long-running children's TV show?

6 What is the name given to the Celtic pattern worn by distinguished clans and military forces?

7 In a leap year, which month has twenty-nine days instead of twenty-eight?

8 'Night And Day' and 'Let's Do It' are both songs by which US songwriter?

9 Which Scandinavian nationality shares its name with the sweet yeasted pastries often eaten for breakfast?

10 In Greek mythology, what name is given to the three-headed dog who guards the gates of Hades?

11 Which animated TV series features the characters of Peter Griffin, Glenn Quagmire and Cleveland Brown?

12 In which Scottish city is Queen Street railway station located?

13 In Australia and New Zealand, on the 25th of which month is ANZAC Day commemorated?

14 Which US rock star released the 1975 album *Born To Run*?

15 Which US vocalist had UK chart hits with 'War' and 'Contact'?

16 With which sport is the name Andy Murray most associated?

17 Which cheese is used to make a traditional Greek salad?

18 With which sport is the name Scott Harrison most associated?

19 In rugby, which European country won the 2006 Six Nations Championship?

20 The 2004 film *House of Flying Daggers* was set in which country?

21 Which Formula 1 motor racing circuit has corners called Tabac, Casino and La Rascasse?

22 In which 2003 film did Julia Roberts star as a 1950s art professor?

23 The Teddy Bear is named after which US president?

24 Which English admiral led the first English expedition to sail around the world?

25 In 1984, which city hosted the Olympic Games where runner Zola Budd famously had a collision with Mary Decker?

26 Which 1980 Abba hit begins with the line, 'I don't wanna talk, about the things we've gone through'?

27 The amphibian found in Britain with the scientific name *Bufo bufo*, is the Common . . . what?

28 Which toy consists of a figure in a box that jumps out when the lid is opened?

29 From which country did Barbados gain independence in 1966?

30 Which previously rare girl's name was popularized by J. M. Barrie in his 1904 play *Peter Pan*?

31 Which sort of instrument would normally be made by a horologist?

32 What name is given to the Bibles purchased by a Christian organization and placed in hotel rooms?

33 In the seventeenth century, which French philosopher wrote *Meditations on First Philosophy*?

34 Which British city failed to win the bid to host the 2000 Summer Olympics?

35 Which French wine-producing region includes Chablis, Beaujolais and Nuits-St-Georges?

36 With which sport is the name Nigel Mansell most closely associated?

37 Which football club did Steve McClaren manage prior to his appointment as England manager in 2006?

38 Johnny Borrell is the lead singer with which chart-topping UK band?

39 A Mancunian is a native or inhabitant of which UK city?

40 With which wind instrument is Sir James Galway most closely associated?

41 How many strings does a violin have?

42 Which artificial red flower is worn in Britain for Remembrance Sunday?

43 From which fruit is the traditional West Country drink 'scrumpy' made?

44 Which word can be a short name for the given name Edward and a child's word for a donkey?

45 In 1620, which ship took the Pilgrim Fathers from Plymouth to what is now the US?

46 Which twentieth-century US president was known by his initials LBJ?

47 In which Chinese city is the Yuyuan Garden located?

48 Which British prime minister was the first to be born during the present Queen's reign?

49 Which 1937 Disney movie contained the line, 'Magic Mirror, on the wall, who is the fairest one of all'?

50 In Greek mythology, which hero led the Argonauts to capture the Golden Fleece?

—————————————— SET 28 ——————————————

1 'Ol' Man River', from the musical *Showboat*, is a song about which great US river?

2 Who was chancellor of West Germany from 1982 to 1990 and of a reunified Germany from 1990 to 1998?

3 In 1935, which American children's author wrote the book *Little House on the Prairie*?

4 With which John Lennon song did Roxy Music have a UK number one hit single in 1981?

5 Which year of the 1960s was dubbed the 'Summer of Love'?

6 Which term describes the triangular or wedge-shaped writing system used in ancient Persia and Mesopotamia?

7 In the 1960s, the so-called Red Guard was a revolutionary youth movement in which Communist country?

8 Which Buckinghamshire house was the base of British codebreakers during the Second World War?

9 Under the 2006 Formula 1 points system, how many points does the driver finishing second in a Grand Prix race receive?

10 What colour precedes the words 'Grape', 'Lace' and 'Sabbath' to make the names of three different musical bands?

11 Which celebrated director made the films *Spartacus*, *A Clockwork Orange* and *Eyes Wide Shut*?

12 What is the common name for the contagious disease 'infectious parotitis', which frequently affects young people?

13 Which British athlete won the Olympic gold medal for the 800m in 1980?

14 The island of Lesbos is part of which European country?

15 Which clover-like plant was used by St Patrick, the patron saint of Ireland, to illustrate the doctrine of the Trinity?

16 Who is the youngest child of Queen Elizabeth II and the Duke of Edinburgh?

17 The French cheese Camembert originated in which northern region of France?

18 The ballet *The Nutcracker* is set during which holiday season?

19 Which classical composer wrote *The Magic Flute*?

20 Prosecco is a light sparkling wine from which European country?

21 Which late 1980s TV series starred Gary Cole as the late night phone-in DJ, Jack 'Nighthawk' Killian?

22 Which creator of the hit TV comedy *Seinfeld* now stars in his own TV show, *Curb Your Enthusiasm*?

23 Born in 2002, Levon Roan is the son of actor Ethan Hawke and which Hollywood actress?

24 Apart from tennis, which other sport features in the full title of the All England Club based at Wimbledon?

25 Which rock band had UK number one hits in 1972 with the songs 'Take Me Bak 'Ome' and 'Mama Weer All Crazee Now'?

26 In 2004, José Luis Rodriguez Zapatero became prime minister of which European country?

27 According to the Highway Code, the traffic warning sign for a school crossing patrol shows how many children?

28 Which English music band took its name from a phrase in a French magazine meaning 'fast fashion'?

29 Which borough of New York City is the only one to be located on the mainland?

30 In the 1950s, what was the name of singer Bill Haley's backing group?

31 *Totally Frank* is the autobiography of which England soccer player?

32 In 2006, the 75th anniversary of which working dogs was celebrated in the UK?

33 According to a 1964 hit song by The Animals, in which US city was 'The House Of The Rising Sun'?

34 At the Battle of Trafalgar, Lord Nelson defeated the combined fleets of Spain and which other country?

35 Along with the Senate, which other body makes up the United States Congress?

36 In 1712, which engineer developed the first practical steam engine?

37 With which genre of music was the legendary US singer Johnny Cash most closely associated?

38   Which member of the Royal Family distributes special coins to a selected group of poor people on Maundy Thursday?

39   Which US musician's UK chart hits include 'Living In America' and 'Get Up Offa That Thing'?

40   During the Second World War, which country's secret police were known as the Gestapo?

41   Home to the Grand National, Aintree racecourse is in which UK city?

42   From which language does the name of the Saluki dog come?

43   In the TV series *Thunderbirds*, who was Lady Penelope's chauffeur and loyal assistant?

44   In which winter sport is the 'Silver Broom' awarded?

45   In which country of the UK is the Royal Mint situated?

46   Which 2002 Martin Scorsese film had the tagline: 'America was Born in the Streets'?

47   In which month of the year is Thanksgiving celebrated in Canada?

48   By what name is London's Central Criminal Court more commonly known?

49   In May 2006, which country voted for independence from its union with Serbia?

50   Who directed the 1988 film *The Last Temptation of Christ*?

SET 29

1   From which Asian country does the martial art Kendo originate?

2   In which European country is the wine Frascati produced?

3   In which year did Queen Elizabeth II come to the throne?

4   Who was president of the European Commission from 1985 to 1994?

5   In 2006, which stage musical overtook *Cats* as the world's longest-running?

6   Of which Mediterranean island country was Dom Mintoff formerly prime minister?

7 In 1962, which British actor first played the lead role in the TV series *The Saint*?

8 Who is the lead singer of the US metal band Limp Bizkit?

9 'When Will I See You Again' and 'Year of Decision' were 1970s hits for which US girl group?

10 A Balinese is a native of which Indonesian island?

11 The French cheese 'chèvre' is made from the milk of which animal?

12 Which comedian sang lead vocals on The Wonder Stuff's 1991 number one UK hit single, 'Dizzy'?

13 Which US rock star was born John Francis Bongiovi Jr?

14 Crown Princess Victoria is heir to the throne of which northern European country?

15 Who was the last Stuart monarch to rule England?

16 Sir Simon Rattle became principal conductor of which Midland city's orchestra in 1980?

17 The Battle of El Alamein was fought during which war?

18 In music, what name is given to a group of eight musicians or a piece of music written for such a group?

19 Traditionally in the UK, how many years of marriage constitute a pearl wedding anniversary?

20 The Transantarctic Mountains are situated on which continent?

21 Cricket bats are traditionally made from the wood of which tree?

22 Photographer and environmentalist Ansel Adams is most closely associated with photographing which US National Park?

23 What is the principal ingredient of the Middle Eastern delicacy falafel?

24 One of the Seven Wonders of the Ancient World, the lighthouse called the Pharos was in which port?

25 The Gilbert and Sullivan comic opera *The Gondoliers* is set in which city?

26 Which German footballer won FIFA's Golden Shoe award for the top scorer at the 2006 World Cup?

27 In music, a sextet is a composition for how many performers?

28 In the seventeenth century, William Penn founded which US state?

29 Jimmy Porter is the main character in which groundbreaking 1956 play by John Osborne?

30 Which musical features the songs 'Angel Of Music' and 'Music Of The Night'?

31 The dance called the samba developed in which South American country?

32 In 1994, with which Labour politician is Tony Blair alleged to have made a pact at the Granita Restaurant in London?

33 On which temperature scale is 212 degrees the boiling point for water?

34 Which international organization was founded in 1971 to heighten environmental awareness, often through direct action?

35 Maxton Gig are the first names of which actor, once linked with ex-Spice Girl Mel B?

36 Fettuccine is a variety of which food product?

37 Which type of American country music takes its name from the nickname of the state of Kentucky?

38 Which Yorkshire-born author wrote the 1947 play, *An Inspector Calls*?

39 Which chef, a host of TV's *Masterchef*, has also had a hit TV series called *Rhodes around Britain*?

40 In which sport is American Justin Gatlin a leading competitor?

41 Which fruit juice is mixed with Champagne to make a Buck's Fizz cocktail?

42 In 2001, Reese Witherspoon starred as law student Elle Woods in which film?

43 The 2006 feature film *The Last King of Scotland* is based on events in the life of which African dictator?

44 Which month is named after Janus, the Roman God of doors and gates?

45 On a standard UK Monopoly board, how many railway stations are there?

46 In which 1980 film did Anthony Hopkins play the role of a Victorian surgeon named Dr Frederick Treves?

47 Which word, from the Latin for 'year', is used for a plant that lives only for a year?

48 The Strait of Magellan connects the Pacific with which other ocean?

49 From which European country did Algeria gain independence in 1962?

50 Which 1989 film featured an inventor who accidentally shrunk his children and their friends?

─────────────── **SET 30** ───────────────

1 In 1970, which Second World War US General was portrayed by actor George C. Scott in an Oscar-winning film?

2 In 1974 George Foreman and which other boxer fought in the 'Rumble in the Jungle'?

3 Of which country did Mary McAleese become president in 1997?

4 Who played the title character in the 2001 film *Bridget Jones's Diary*?

5 Which London-born Hollywood director said: 'Television has brought back murder into the home – where it belongs'?

6 What name was popularly given to Schubert's Symphony No. 8 after his death?

7 What name is given by hillwalkers to Scottish mountains of more than 3,000 feet in height?

8 Australian singer Peter Andre is married to which model?

9 On which Scottish island did St Columba establish a monastery in AD 563?

10 What is the name of the channel that separates the southern coast of England and northern France?

11 Which Brummie stand-up comedian had a UK hit single with 'Funky Moped/Magic Roundabout' in 1975?

12 The four March sisters, Meg, Jo, Beth and Amy, first feature in which Louisa M. Alcott novel published in 1868?

13 Occurring on 31 October, what name is traditionally given to All Saints' Eve?

14 In 2006, the official BBC Children In Need single 'Downtown' was sung by which former Spice Girl?

15 Which US president said on air, 'I have signed legislation to outlaw Russia for ever. We begin bombing in five minutes'?

16 Which element, with the chemical symbol Cl, and is widely used to purify water?

17 Who became British prime minister following the resignation of Harold Wilson in 1976?

18 The Vinson Massif is the highest mountain on which continent?

19 In 1964, which British pop band had their first UK number one hit with the single 'Do Wah Diddy Diddy'?

20 According to the legend, which nationality was William Tell?

21 Which then Home Secretary is credited with the creation of the Metropolitan Police in 1829?

22 With which instrument is musician Jools Holland most closely associated?

23 Iraq's invasion of which neighbouring country led to the Gulf War of 1991?

24 Cu is the chemical symbol for which reddish-orange metal?

25 What is the name of Tony Benn's son, who became Secretary of State for International Development in 2003?

26 Which Hollywood actress was married to actor Mickey Rooney, band leader Artie Shaw and Frank Sinatra?

27 After which city in southern France is Salade Niçoise named?

28 The process invented by Henry Bessemer in the nineteenth century converted pig iron into which metal?

29 In 1975, Andrew Lloyd Webber collaborated with which playwright on the unsuccessful musical *Jeeves*?

30 In 2001, an outbreak of which agricultural disease led to a European ban on British farm products?

31 Which part of the body is affected by the medical condition conjunctivitis?

32 With which other gas does hydrogen combine to make water?

33 Topping the charts in late 1970, what was US soul singer Freda Payne's only UK number one hit single?

34 In 1958, which film actor married the actress Joanne Woodward?

35 According to the Old Testament, what sign did God give to Noah to show that the Earth would not be flooded again?

36 Since 1947, which Scandinavian country has provided the annual Trafalgar Square Christmas tree?

37 Which professional football team is nicknamed the Posh?

38 Which TV drama series starring Trevor Eve features a team of murder detectives working on 'cold cases'?

39 In which European country did the cheese Brie originate?

40 Which UK singer's backing group was called the Attractions?

41 In Rudyard Kipling's *The Jungle Book*, what type of animal is Shere Khan?

42 Which metal, with the chemical symbol Ni, is used in the making of coins?

43 Now preserved at Portsmouth, what was Lord Nelson's flagship at the Battle of Trafalgar?

44 A dish of peaches, ice cream and raspberry sauce is named after which Australian opera singer?

45 Which England player won the Golden Shoe award for scoring most goals at the 1986 World Cup in Mexico?

46 Rhinitis is an inflammation of the mucous membrane that lines which part of the body?

47 Used in Indian cookery, gram flour is derived from which pulse?

48 Which world champion darts player is nicknamed 'The Power'?

49 Which famous ship, docked in Greenwich, has a name meaning 'short shirt'?

50 Used to make a type of oil, which palm tree produces copra?

SET 31

1 Andrology is the study of health and disease in which gender?

2 In 1933, which colour poppies were created to symbolize peace?

3 How many legs does a hexapod have?

4 In which country is the city of Dijon?

5 In the 2002 film of the same name, what is 'Seabiscuit'?

6 Which colourful children's TV programme did Geoffrey Hayes present from 1973 to 1992?

7 Which opera by Georges Bizet is set in Seville, Spain?

8 In which decade did the Falklands War take place?

9 In the animated 1973 Disney film, what type of animal was Robin Hood?

10 Which English monarch was crowned King of France in Paris in 1431?

11 Supermodel Cindy Crawford married which Hollywood heartthrob in 1991?

12 In the comic strip, which Italian dish is Garfield's favourite food?

13 On which evening of the week does the Queen traditionally meet her serving Prime Minister?

14 How many frames are there in one game of tenpin bowling?

15 England's longest-running independent student magazine, *Isis*, was established at which university?

16 The twin stars for which the Gemini constellation is named are Castor and which other?

17 The 2006 film *Starter for Ten* is based on which TV quiz show?

18 In the Shakespeare play *A Midsummer Night's Dream*, who is the King of the Fairies?

19 Along with egg and fish, what is the main ingredient of the breakfast dish kedgeree?

20 Which actor played the title character in the 1992 film biopic *Malcolm X*?

21 Which 1987 sci-fi film had the tagline, 'Part man. Part machine. All cop'?

22 According to Thomas Edison, 'Genius is one per cent inspiration, ninety nine per cent . . .' What?

23 The Cape Cod peninsula in Massachusetts extends into which ocean?

24 What are the offspring of a bear called?

25 The German Bratwurst is a type of which meaty food item?

26 The egg dish known as frittata originated in which European country?

27 'My Coo-Ca-Choo' and 'Jealous Mind' were 1970s hits for which glam rocker?

28 'Puffing Billy' and the *Rocket* were early steam-powered types of which form of transport?

29 Enya, who topped the charts in 1988, was a member of which 1980s folk-rock group?

30 Who succeeded Lyndon B. Johnson as US president?

31 Which small, two-wheeled vehicle pulled by one or two men is common in many parts of Asia?

32 In 1642 the Battle of Edgehill was the first battle in which conflict?

33 Which English comedian was born in the Liverpool suburb of Knotty Ash?

34 Nichiren is a branch of Buddhism that was founded in the thirteenth century in which Asian country?

35 Which word, referring to an area of light winds around the Equator, is now used for a state of depression?

36 Which southern US state is famous for the dish, Gumbo?

37 Which Jacobean playwright's works include *The Alchemist* and *Volpone*?

38 Which twentieth-century prime minister was known as 'The Welsh Wizard'?

39 Which Spanish actress starred with Nicholas Cage in the 2001 film *Captain Corelli's Mandolin*?

40 What is the name of John Cleese's ex-wife, who co-wrote *Fawlty Towers* with him?

41 In the UK, what is model and TV personality Jordan's real name?

42 Who reached number two in the UK singles charts in 1984 with 'Ghostbusters'?

43 With which Kurt Weill song did Bobby Darin have a UK number one hit in September 1959?

44 Which nationality was the philosopher René Descartes?

45 In which country of the UK is the area of Fife located?

46 Which US actor directed and starred in the 2006 film *The Good Shepherd*?

47 'Love means never having to say you're sorry' was the tagline for which 1970 film, starring Ryan O'Neal?

48 The 1980s pop singer Sonia came from which UK city?

49 Which British band had UK number one hits in the 1960s with the instrumental songs 'Kon Tiki' and 'Wonderful Land'?

50 The adjective 'Kantian' relates to the work of which German philosopher?

SET 32

1 Which Italian screen legend posed semi-nude for the 2007 Pirelli Calendar at the age of seventy-one?

2 Malcolm Fraser was Prime Minister of which country from 1975 to 1983?

3 The phrase 'bric-a-brac' comes from which language?

4 Which rigid airship, first flown in 1900, was named after the German count who designed it?

5 The actor Johnny Depp had a tattoo on his arm surgically altered when his relationship with which actress broke up?

6 What is the name of Jamie Oliver's wife?

7 What was the surname of the pioneering aviator brothers Orville and Wilbur?

8 Which island group was the only British territory to come under German occupation during the Second World War?

9 In which TV sitcom did John Inman first play Mr Wilberforce Clayborne Humphries?

10 The Gorbals, once notorious for its terrible slums, is a district of which Scottish city?

11 Which US rap star got his artist name from the observation 'Ladies Love Cool James'?

12 Who played 'Wolfie' in the 1970s BBC sitcom *Citizen Smith*?

13 The dingo is a wild dog found in which country?

14 In which country is the Mason-Dixon Line a traditional separation of North and South?

15 In May 2006, who was appointed Foreign Secretary by Tony Blair?

16 In which sport did the St Louis Cardinals play the Detroit Tigers in the 2006 World Series?

17 Jomo Kenyatta was president of which African country from 1964 to 1978?

18 From which country does the bread 'ciabatta' originally come?

19 At which Welsh castle was Prince Charles invested as Prince of Wales in 1969?

20 Which seventeenth-century poem by John Milton tells the story of Adam and Eve's expulsion from the Garden of Eden?

21 What nationality was the composer Benjamin Britten?

22 At sea level, Mach 1 is the speed of what?

23 In Russia, the word 'babushka' describes which member of the family?

24 The great Renaissance artist Michelangelo was born in Caprese, a small town near which Italian city?

25 Which US animated TV series features the city of 'New New York'?

26 In 2006, which city hosted the Australian Formula 1 Grand Prix?

27 What nationality was the nineteenth-century painter Paul Cézanne?

28 Who was leader of the Conservative Party for the 2005 General Election?

29 Sir Stanley Matthews played for Stoke City and which other football league club?

30 After 45 years of trying, which northern European country won the Eurovision Song Contest for the first time in 2006?

31 Which TV illusionist published his book *Tricks of the Mind* in 2006?

32 In 1973, which US Secretary of State was jointly awarded the Nobel Peace Prize?

33 In the UK, what is the name of the trade union to which most professional actors belong?

34 Anna Anderson Manahan famously claimed to be which member of the Russian royal family?

35 In Britain, what is the legal age at which alcohol can be bought in a pub, supermarket or off-licence?

36 Invented by Christopher Cockerell in 1959, what is a vehicle that travels over land or water on a cushion of air?

37 Which Icelandic singer had a UK chart hit in 1995 with 'It's Oh So Quiet'?

38 Yarra Valley and Coonawarra are wine-producing areas in which country?

39 Samuel Preston is the lead singer of which British band?

40 Which Liverpudlian band had UK chart hits in the 1990s with 'Female Of The Species' and 'Avenging Angels'?

41 Which of Henry VIII's wives was the mother of Edward VI?

42 Who played Terry, Arthur Daley's Minder, in the hit TV series of the same name?

43 Which Crimean War battle has given its name to a woollen hat fitted closely over the head and neck?

44 According to the New Testament of the Bible, Jesus miraculously turned water into what?

45 Benjamin Barker was the real name of which infamous Fleet Street barber?

46 Meaning 'Blues', which country's national football team is nicknamed the 'Azzurri'?

47 What was the first name of Henry VIII's father?

48 What French name is given to the tall white hat worn by chefs?

49 Which Portuguese explorer sailed around the Cape of Good Hope in 1497 and reached India the following year?

50 What substance has the chemical formula CO_2?

 SET 33

1 John Motson is a respected commentator in which sport?

2 Which of the four Gospel authors is the patron saint of doctors?

3 Which hit 1994 stage show was based on the Irish 'stepdance'?

4 Which broadcaster, son of the legendary Richard Dimbleby, took over as chairman of TV's *Question Time* in 1994?

5 *The Edge of Reason* is the follow-up title to which Helen Fielding novel?

6 In the animated Disney film *The Little Mermaid*, what is the name of the crab?

7 Who is the father of Nicole Appleton's son, Gene Appleton Gallagher?

8 Which group had a hit in 1983 with the song 'Red Red Wine'?

9 In 1917, which organization, abbreviated to WAAC, was formed to offer women jobs during wartime?

10 On the throne from 1830 to 1837, which monarch preceded Queen Victoria?

11 In the TV cartoon series *Henry's Cat*, what colour was Henry's cat?

12 In which city were the Olympics of ancient Greece held?

13 In the Disney cartoons, what type of animals were Chip and Dale?

14 Which one-legged pirate is the main villain in Robert Louis Stevenson's classic *Treasure Island*?

15 Which fashionable London department store was started in 1813, by Benjamin Harvey?

16 In global politics, what does the abbreviation WTO stand for?

17 Of what type of plant is the prickly pear a variety?

18 Of what is conchology the study?

19 In the 1958 film thriller *Vertigo*, which legendary US actor played Detective John Scottie Ferguson?

20 In *The Flintstones*, what was the name of Fred and Wilma's daughter?

21 Which French dish consists of an upside-down apple tart made with caramelized apples?

22 The people known as Inuits were once commonly known by what name?

23 Lois Maxwell and Samantha Bond have both played which role in James Bond films?

24 Founded in 1980, the trade union and opposition movement Solidarity was started in which country?

25 In which UK city is Marylebone Station located?

26 In which sport is the Harry Vardon trophy awarded?

27 Who was charged with the assassination of John F. Kennedy in November 1963?

28 What type of mythical creature is Roald Dahl's BFG?

29 BALPA is an acronym for which professional association?

30 Released in 1962, what was the title of the Beatles first single?

31 Which colour follows the word 'Deacon' to make the name of a hit 1980s pop band?

32 From which fruit is the alcoholic drink cider made?

33 Which animal product is an ingredient of the traditional confection known as Lardy cake?

34 Which English king defeated the French at the Battle of Crécy in 1346?

35 What is the common name for the green vegetable, with edible seed pods, sometimes known as a 'stick bean'?

36 What specific name, from the Greek for nerve, is given to the study and treatment of diseases of the nervous system?

37 In cookery, vinaigrette is often known as 'French . . .' what?

38 The three symbols on the flag of the former Soviet Union were a star, a hammer and which other implement?

39 The Mercalli scale is used to measure the intensity of which natural phenomenon?

40 What is the common name for *Euphorbia pulcherrima*, the houseplant with large red bracts that is popular at Christmas?

41 In which Charlie Chaplin film did the child star Jackie Coogan become world famous?

42 The hit Broadway song 'New York, New York' is from which Leonard Bernstein musical?

43 In which country did the foodstuff 'capellini' originate?

44 The Babington Plot of 1586 was a plan to assassinate which English monarch?

45 In the 1960s, which US dramatist wrote the plays *Who's Afraid of Virginia Woolf?* and *A Delicate Balance*?

46 In which sport is France's Amélie Mauresmo a leading competitor?

47 Later a successful British film staring Anthony Hopkins, Kazuo Ishiguro won the 1989 Booker Prize with which novel?

48 In August 2006, England footballer Ashley Cole moved from Arsenal to which London club?

49 Nicaragua shares a border with Costa Rica and which other Central American country?

50 Which important Roman road ran from London to Wroxeter near Shrewsbury?

---------------------- **SET 34** ----------------------

1　In 1987, which US pop star had a UK number one hit with the single 'Who's That Girl'?

2　By what name are the official free-fall display team for the Parachute Regiment and the Army known as?

3　The word 'mug', originally referring to a drinking cup with a handle, has also come to mean which part of the body?

4　In Shakespeare's *Hamlet*, which character said, 'Good morrow. 'Tis St Valentine's Day'?

5　Lilongwe is the capital of which south-east African country?

6　Which Scottish architect and designer designed the Glasgow School of Art?

7　In which sport is Belgium's Christophe Soumillon a leading competitor?

8　What is the principal ingredient of the Greek dish taramasalata?

9　In which UK country does the cairn terrier dog breed originate?

10　By what name are the top eight American universities collectively known?

11　Which critically acclaimed US filmmaker appeared in the TV series *Alias* as McKenas Cole?

12　In 1976, who became the first native of the state of Georgia to be elected President of the United States?

13　What is the first line in English of the Christmas carol often referred to by its Latin name, 'Adeste Fideles'?

14　In which religion is Rosh Hashana the festival of the New Year?

15　In which London venue is the 'Last Night of the Proms' traditionally held?

16　In 2006, which former *Baywatch* star shut down her online gaming website just four months after it launched?

17　In 2002, All Saints' Natalie Appleton married Liam Howlett, a member of which UK dance group?

18　In 1752, Britain replaced the Julian calendar with which other?

19 Which German baroque composer did Beethoven refer to as 'the immortal god of harmony'?

20 Who captained England in the 1966 World Cup final?

21 With which country's cuisine is the snack known as a samosa most closely associated?

22 On daytime TV, Tim Wonnacott presents which antiques show?

23 Which TV fashion presenter was born Sarah-Jane Woodall?

24 The Bollywood actress Aishwarya Rai won which international beauty competition in 1994?

25 Which metal, with the chemical symbol Al, is the most abundant metallic element in the Earth's crust?

26 Which Russian breed of dog is also known as 'the Russian Wolfhound'?

27 How many times has Kenneth Clarke contested the leadership of the Conservative Party?

28 Which US pop star was born in Kentwood, Louisiana in 1981?

29 Who succeeded Edward Heath as leader of the Conservative Party in 1975?

30 Which film star and singer played Clayton Farlow in the TV series *Dallas*?

31 Which US singer and actor famously said, 'You're not drunk if you can lie on the floor without holding on'?

32 Born in 1954, which actor played Chon Wang opposite Owen Wilson in the film *Shanghai Noon*?

33 What is the common name for the garbanzo, a nut-like pulse widely used in Middle-Eastern stews and casseroles?

34 Which children's TV cartoon series featured the characters 'Not-Now', 'Go-to-Bed' and 'Comb-Your-Hair'?

35 In Beatrix Potter's books what kind of creature is Mrs Tiggywinkle?

36 Soave is a dry white wine from which European country?

37 El Al is the national airline of which country?

38 Which features of a tree trunk's cross section are studied by a dendrochronologist?

39 Goa is a state in which Asian country?

40 Which channel port in Kent shares its name with a species of sole?

41 On which continent did the order known as the 'Whirling Dervishes' originate?

42 Which ballet, composed by Tchaikovsky, features 'Aurora's Wedding'?

43 Which veteran DJ and TV personality presented both the first and the last editions of *Top of the Pops*?

44 In 2005, which US pop star married music executive Jordan Bratman?

45 Which actor played the Fonz in the TV series *Happy Days*?

46 Which type of wireless communication is named after a tenth-century king of Denmark?

47 In 1997, at what game was the former world champion Garry Kasparov defeated by a computer called Deep Blue?

48 In the children's book *The Wind in the Willows*, what is the name of the ancestral home of Mr Toad?

49 In which east Asian country did the martial art of Tae Kwon Do originate?

50 Lord's Cricket Ground is located in which UK city?

SET 35
---

1 Billie Piper married which red-haired TV presenter in 2001?

2 In which West Indian dance does the dancer bend backwards under a horizontal bar that is progressively lowered?

3 Chorizo sausages are traditionally made with the meat of which animal?

4 In becoming a QC, barristers are said to 'take . . .' which fine material?

5 Which word connects a small lizard with an ability to change colour, and a changeable or inconstant person?

6 Fraser Island, the largest sand island in the world, is part of which country?

7 In the 1989 film version of *Henry V* directed by Kenneth Branagh, who plays the title role?

8 The Polonaise is a slow stately dance that originated in which country?

9 Which 1954 film musical tells the story of Adam, the eldest of seven brothers, marrying Milly?

10 The 'Glimmer Twins' is a nickname for Mick Jagger and which other member of the Rolling Stones?

11 Which British playwright wrote *Chicken Soup with Barley* and *Chips with Everything*?

12 Which musical term, of Italian origin, is used to describe separate, short detached notes?

13 The dessert bread Panettone comes from which European country?

14 Which English playwright of the 1940s had West End hits with *The Winslow Boy* and *The Browning Version*?

15 In the children's TV show *Balamory*, what is the name of the nursery schoolteacher?

16 According to legend, which character 'peeped' out of his window at Lady Godiva while she rode naked through Coventry?

17 Which Belgian cyclist won the Tour de France five times between 1969 and 1974?

18 Beginning in 1983, which TV comedy drama starred Timothy Spall, Jimmy Nail and Kevin Whately as British workmen abroad?

19 The city of Salzburg is in which country?

20 In the 1922 film *Nosferatu, a Symphony of Horrors*, what type of horror creature was Nosferatu?

21 In the USA, in which decade was MTV launched?

22 Which cigar-smoking US comic was the husband and partner of the comedienne Gracie Allen?

23 What name is given to the process in which water vapour becomes liquid water?

24 The stage musical *Gypsy* depicts the real life rise to fame of which Burlesque star?

25 In the 2006 film *Hollywoodland*, which award-winning US actor starred as the actor George Reeves?

26 The three brothers Barry, Robin and Maurice Gibb formed which pop group in the 1960s?

27 In South America, Caracas is the capital city of which country?

28 Since 1957, which acronym has been given to the series of machines used to pick the numbers for the Premium Bond draw?

29 Kirkwall is the largest town in which group of Scottish islands?

30 In 2005, Private Johnson Beharry became the first living soldier since 1969 to be awarded which decoration for valour?

31 Who was the father of Alexander the Great?

32 In 1306, who was crowned King of Scotland?

33 Which French ocean explorer and filmmaker invented the aqua-lung?

34 In 1975, who became King of Spain?

35 In February 2006, Stephen Harper became prime minister of which country?

36 Which Australian comedian created, and plays the part of, housewife-superstar Dame Edna Everage?

37 Which composer wrote the music for the 1957 hit musical *West Side Story*?

38 Which winter sport has a boundary known as the hog line?

39 In 1997, which member of the rock group Oasis married actress Patsy Kensit?

40 Which government department, responsible for justice, has the abbreviation DCA?

41 What do Americans call a dinner jacket?

42 What type of reptile is the iguana?

43 Which BBC TV makeover show was first fronted by fashion experts Trinny Woodall and Susannah Constantine?

44 Which city is the capital of Serbia?

45 In which year did the Battle of Hastings take place?

46 Which *Dallas* TV soap character was famously dubbed 'the poison dwarf' by Terry Wogan?

47 Which US First Lady chaired the committee that drafted the Universal Declaration of Human Rights?

48 A Laotian is a native of which country in South-east Asia?

49 In 1975, which two Hollywood superstars remarried, sixteen months after getting divorced?

50 Of which Caribbean country was 'Papa Doc' Duvalier president from 1957 to 1971?

—————————— SET 36 ——————————

1 In 1969, Golda Meir became prime minister of which Middle East country?

2 Which British scientist was famously inspired by a falling apple?

3 The name of the English theatre manager Richard D'Oyly Carte is particularly associated with the work of which duo?

4 Which Comic Relief single was a number one hit for comedy duo Hale and Pace and the Stonkers in 1991?

5 Conservative Party leader David Cameron attended which leading public school?

6 Which boxer retired in 1956 as the undefeated Heavyweight Champion of the World?

7 Which future US president was born in Hope, Arkansas, in 1946?

8 Which Australian singer is known for his infamous jungle-penned song 'Insania'?

9 Brent, Barnacle and Greylag are all types of which large bird?

10 In 1773, in which US city was the so-called 'Tea Party' held in protest at British taxation?

11 Which wizard was an important adviser to the legendary English King, Arthur?

12 The abbreviation LW stands for which radio frequency range?

13 Meaning 'butterflies' in Italian, what name is given to 'bow-tie' shaped pasta?

14 Which Broadway musical is based on the play *Green Grow the Lilacs* by Lynn Riggs?

15 When Harold Wilson became British Prime Minister in 1964, which Conservative Party incumbent did he take over from?

16 Which comic actor played Terry in the TV sitcom *Terry and June*?

17 On being bombed in 1940, which Royal said, 'I'm glad we have been bombed. I feel I can look the East End in the face'?

18 In motor racing what name is given to the advantageous starting position on the inside of the front row?

19 In the eighth century, Offa ruled which Anglo-Saxon kingdom?

20 Launched in 1934, which record-breaking British ocean liner is now a tourist attraction at Long Beach, California?

21 Which British bird of prey is also called the fish hawk because of its favoured prey?

22 Model Katie Price is married to which London-born, Australian pop star?

23 Dolcelatte is a milder version of which other blue-veined Italian cheese?

24 In the TV series *Marion and Geoff*, which comic actor played the taxi driver Keith Barret?

25 'D.I.S.C.O.' and 'Hands Up (Give Me Your Heart)' were Top 10 1980s hits for which French vocal duo?

26 In 1991, *Use Your Illusion II* became a number one album in the UK for which US rock band?

27 Who played Lord Peter Wimsey in the BBC drama during the 1970s?

28 In 1957, the French existentialist writer Albert Camus won which prestigious Prize for Literature?

29 With which same song have Norman Greenbaum, Doctor and the Medics and Gareth Gates all had a UK number one hit?

30 Piri-Piri is an African word for which hot and spicy vegetable?

31 Noted for the production of lager, in which European country is the city of Pilsen located?

32 In TV's *Only Fools and Horses* who moved into the flat with Del and Rodney after their granddad died?

33 In 1974, who succeeded Richard Nixon as President of the USA?

34 Henry VII and Elizabeth I were members of which English royal dynasty?

35 Hastings Banda was the president of which country in south-east Africa from 1966 to 1994?

36 In the Beano comic, what was the name of Dennis the Menace's pet pig?

37 In TV's *The A-Team* what army rank was John 'Hannibal' Smith?

38 In which 1967 film musical did Tommy Steele play the role of Arthur Kipps?

39 In the board game Pictionary, by which method does the player identify a topic to his teammates?

40 What is the name of Elvis Presley's daughter?

41 In the title of the orchestral piece by Vaughan Williams which bird is 'Ascending'?

42 Roger McGough is part of a group of poets associated with which UK city?

43 Born in 1813, what was the first name of the great German opera composer Wagner?

44 In which country did the boxer breed of dog originate?

45 What distance was Roger Bannister running when he famously broke a four-minute record?

46 In Greek mythology, of what is Eros the god?

47 Mick Hucknall is the lead singer of which pop group?

48 In addition to directing and producing, US dancer Bob Fosse was famed in which other field?

49 In which ocean are the Volcano Islands located?

50 Which wine has types called Fino and Amontillado?

--- SET 37 ---

1 British band The Feeling's bass guitarist Richard Jones is married to which UK pop princess?

2 The character Miss Hannigan runs an orphanage in which hit Broadway musical?

3 Which sailor character features in one of the stories of the Arabian Nights?

4 In 1989, who was chancellor of West Germany when the Berlin Wall came down?

5 With which sport is Goran Ivanisevic most closely associated?

6 Which ex-pub singer turned opera star's first album *The Voice* was released in 2000?

7 How many ancient wonders of the world are there?

8 In the sporting world, what does the abbreviation FA stand for?

9 Which tree produces the seed from which chocolate is made?

10 The Classic horse race the Derby is run at which English racecourse?

11 Which medieval heraldic symbol, depicting a lily or iris, was adopted by the kings of France?

12 Fusilli is a spiral-shaped variety of which food product?

13 Toronto and Vancouver are cities located in which country?

14 Which British government department is sometimes known by the abbreviation FCO?

15 From which South American country did Paddington Bear come?

16 In 1964, which French philosopher declined the Nobel Prize for Literature?

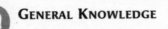

17 Hampton Court Palace was given to Henry VIII by which English cardinal?

18 What name is given to the traditional Venetian one-oared, flat-bottomed boat mainly used by tourists?

19 St Apollonia is the patron saint of people suffering from what painful complaint?

20 In 2001, Belgian doctor Jacques Rogge was elected president of which international sports organization?

21 In 2006, which Rugby League team won both the Grand Final and the Challenge Cup?

22 What colour is the children's TV and film character Stuart Little?

23 With which indoor sport was Alex 'Hurricane' Higgins principally associated?

24 Which novel by John Wyndham featured man-eating plants trying to take over the world?

25 The Koi is an ornamental Japanese variety of which deep-bodied freshwater fish?

26 From which European country does feta cheese originally come?

27 Which Berkshire racecourse traditionally holds a 'Royal' meeting every June?

28 Pop singer Alecia Moore is better known by which stage name?

29 In which Australian city is the WACA cricket ground located?

30 The 'Flying Scotsman' train service ran non-stop between London and which other major city?

31 Which US author wrote the horror tales 'The Telltale Heart' and 'The Pit and the Pendulum'?

32 Which 2000 Tom Hanks film is mainly set on a deserted island?

33 The Wallaroo is a large, stocky variety of which Australian animal?

34 Which British comedian and actor published his book of *Flanimals* in 2004?

35 Publicly voted the greatest painting in Britain in 2005, *The Fighting Téméraire* is by which artist?

36 With which sport is Steve Davis most closely associated?

37 Which city in French Guiana shares its name with a type of pepper?

38 What type of animal is the title character in the children's TV series *Arthur*?

39 Traditionally, which UK country celebrates Hogmanay?

40 Pop star Kylie Minogue came to fame in which Australian TV soap?

41 In 1968, which Czech leader's reforms led to the Soviet occupation of Czechoslovakia?

42 In 1963, which Conservative politician renounced his earldom before becoming prime minister?

43 Which screen legend founded the Sundance Institute?

44 What nationality is Heath Ledger, the actor and star of *Brokeback Mountain*?

45 What was the first name of journalist Carol Thatcher's father?

46 In the TV cartoon series *He-Man and the Masters of the Universe*, what was the name of He-Man's alias?

47 The French writer Victor Hugo spent the majority of his years of exile living on which Channel Island?

48 In the *Superman* films, what colour is Superman's cape?

49 In the traditional children's song about London church bells, what do the bells of St Clements say?

50 Who played the character John Shaft in the 2000 remake of the film *Shaft*?

SET 38

1 What does a manometer measure?

2 In the *Dr Who* TV spin-off *Torchwood*, which character does John Barrowman play?

3 Complete the title of the steamy book by Jilly Cooper, *The Man Who Made Husbands . . . what?*

4 With which field of the arts is David Bailey most closely associated?

5 Which well-known song and poem contain the lines, 'Be it ever so humble, there's no place like home . . .'?

6 Addis Ababa is the capital city of which African country?

7 In the US, in which sport is Wilt 'the Stilt' Chamberlain regarded as an all-time great?

8 The Republic of Moldova is bordered on the west by Romania and on the north, east and south by which country?

9 What nationality is ballerina Sylvie Guillem?

10 With which sport is the name Josh Lewsey most associated?

11 Which 1960s musical film, starring Richard Harris, told the story of King Arthur and his court?

12 Which Amendment to the United States Constitution addresses the rights of freedom of speech and freedom of religion?

13 During her time with the Spice Girls, what was Melanie Chisholm's nickname?

14 Which insects are referred to collectively as an 'army'?

15 In Roman Catholicism, when a new Pope is elected, what colour smoke emerges from the chimney of the Sistine Chapel?

16 Which Italian phrase, meaning 'the sweet life', was the title of a 1960 film by Federico Fellini?

17 Whom did US photographer Linda Eastman marry in 1969?

18 Which American tennis star won the men's singles title at the 2003 US Open?

19 What was the first name of Margaret Thatcher's husband?

20 Prospero and Caliban are both characters in which Shakespeare play?

21 How many centimetres are there in a decimetre?

22 The Isles of Scilly are situated twenty-eight miles off the south-west coast of which English county?

23 Which musical is subtitled 'The American Tribal Love-Rock Musical'?

24 On TV's *Strictly Come Dancing* who is the only female judge?

25 Exmoor, Welsh Mountain and Shetland are varieties of which member of the horse family?

26 By which name, meaning 'from the beginning' in Latin, are the native people of Australia known?

27 Which of golf's major championships is always held at Augusta National Golf Club?

28 In the 1999 film *An Ideal Husband*, which English actor starred as Lord Arthur Goring?

29 Sparkling wine from which country would feature the word 'frizzante' on the label?

30 Pathologist Kay Scarpetta is the main character in a series of books by which popular author?

31 Which play by Tennessee Williams features the character of Blanche DuBois?

32 The arrangement of neighbours keeping an eye on each other's property is known as a 'Neighbourhood . . .' what?

33 Which actor, and former husband of Angharad Rees, is best known for appearing as Ben Carrington in TV's *Dynasty*?

34 Darcey Bussell is a famous name in which of the performing arts?

35 Henrietta Maria of France was the wife of which English king?

36 Inspired by comic strips of warplanes, the 1963 painting called *Whaam!*, was by which American artist?

37 In the late 1960s, former US President Bill Clinton spent two years studying at which UK university?

38 In the 1970s TV crime drama *Kojak*, which American actor played the lead role?

39 Actor Joaquin Phoenix is the brother of which tragically shortlived star?

40 In November 2006, which TV executive resigned as Chairman of the BBC?

41 Cardinal Wolsey was the Lord Chancellor to which king of England?

42 By which acronym is the independent regulator, the Office of Communications, better known?

43 Tony Hawk is a famous name in which extreme sport?

44 In palaeontology, was the Triceratops a herbivore or a carnivore?

45 Charlie Fairhead, Megan Roach and 'Duffy' have been regular characters in which TV medical drama?

46 In what does the waiter known as a sommelier specialize?

47 Dermatology is the study of which part of the body?

48 In the original arcade game, what type of creature was 'Donkey Kong'?

49 During which war was the 1980s TV series *Tenko* set?

50 To which section of the orchestra does the clarinet belong?

SET 39

1 In 1998, Mikka Hakkinen was World Champion in which motor sport?

2 In 1975, which British silent film legend received a knighthood in his mid eighties?

3 Which children's animated TV character lived 'in the top left-hand corner of Wales'?

4 Orvieto is a light white wine from which country?

5 Which famous British music festival did Michael Eavis establish?

6 Which collective name is given to the gaseous elements helium, neon, argon, krypton, xenon and radon?

7 Which sign of the zodiac is also known as 'the virgin'?

8 Which American composer's film soundtracks have included *Candyman*, *The Hours* and *The Truman Show*?

9 What does the Scottish Gaelic word 'loch' mean?

10 Which Jamaican reggae singer was born Orville Richard Burrell in 1968?

11 Which classic 1970s TV sitcom featured a hard-nosed warder called Mr Mackay?

12 In British history, how many kings have been called Henry?

13 With which bird is the name of the American, Colonel Sanders, most closely associated?

14 In the world of transport, what do the initials HGV stand for?

15 Which German general of the Second World War was known as the 'Desert Fox'?

16 Kelly Rowland is a singer in which chart-topping US girl group?

17 Which dance style, involving jumping up and down on the spot, was popular with 1970s punk rock fans?

18 What name is given to the clarified butter used in Indian cooking?

19 The bird sometimes known as the Yaffle is usually called the 'Green . . .' what?

20 On TV's *The Apprentice* which two words does Sir Alan Sugar use to dismiss losing hopefuls?

21 In 2003, which TV star published a book entitled *I Don't Mean to Be Rude, But . . .*?

22 Which veteran US singer-songwriter had hits with 'Walk On The Wild Side' and 'Perfect Day'?

23 Barley wine is a very strong type of which alcoholic drink?

24 In the 1968 horror film *Rosemary's Baby*, which American actress had her first leading role as Rosemary Woodhouse?

25 With nine victories, which jockey holds the record for most wins in the Epsom Derby?

26 What is the first name of Prince William's younger brother?

27 What name, meaning 'cherry' in German, is given to the clear distilled liqueur that is often added to fondues?

28 To ignore or snub someone is to 'give them the cold . . .' what?

29 Which Monty Python stage musical is based on the tale of King Arthur and his Knights' quest for the Holy Grail?

30 The famous Bodleian Library is the main research library of which university?

31 Lisa Left Eye Lopes was a member of which US girl group?

32 Which Grand Slam tennis championship is played at Flushing Meadows?

33 Originally distilled in Kentucky, 'bourbon' is a name given to a type of which alcoholic spirit?

34 Raspberry ripple, mint choc chip and rum and raisin are traditional flavours of which frozen dessert?

35 In Formula 1, which famous motor racing circuit stages the United States Grand Prix?

36 What name is given to a male alligator?

37 Balsamic vinegar comes from which European country?

38 Which 2006 road trip comedy film featured a family taking their daughter to a beauty pageant in their VW bus?

39 Which comic-book hero did George Reeves play in the 1950s on TV?

40 Which army marching tune was used in the film *The Bridge on the River Kwai*?

41 Ben Elton wrote the lyrics for which Andrew Lloyd Webber musical?

42 What name is given to the rich, coarse, typically green, felt-like woollen material used to cover a snooker table?

43 Chekov, Uhura and McCoy were characters in which TV sci-fi show?

44 The town of Calais is located in which European country?

45 Which London band had UK chart hits in the late 1970s with 'Cool For Cats' and 'Up The Junction'?

46 How many centimetres are there in one metre?

47 Who was Oliver Hardy's on-screen comic partner?

48 Kim Campbell became the first female prime minister of which country in 1993?

49 After which port city in southern France is the French national anthem named?

50 Which US city, the capital of Tennessee, is regarded as the centre of the country music industry?

--- **SET 40** ---

1 Which American supermodel was formerly married to singing star, Billy Joel?

2 What is the profession of the Australian Gemma Ward?

3 Which common English vegetable has three types known as 'white', 'red' and 'savoy'?

4 Which leading Yorkshire Rugby League team is nicknamed the Rhinos?

5 Which flightless bird has given its name to people born in New Zealand?

6 The 2005 film *Memoirs of a Geisha* was set in which Asian country?

7 With which track and field event is athlete Ashia Hansen most associated?

8 In Ireland, camogie is a women's version of which stick-and-ball game?

9 Which French footballer holds the record since 1958 for scoring the most goals at a World Cup finals tournament?

10 In the field of education, what does TEFL stand for?

11 Which BBC TV presenter won the women's singles in the 1976 French Open tennis championships?

12 Which band had a number one hit single in 1994 with the song 'Doop'?

13 In which year were women over the age of 30 first awarded the right to vote in England?

14 In a story from *The Arabian Nights*, how many thieves does Ali Baba encounter?

15 'Royal Rumble', 'Summerslam' and 'King of the Ring' are events associated with which TV sport?

16 With which genre of music was the US singer Jim Reeves most associated?

17 Which Anglo-American band had UK hits in the 1970s with 'Breakfast In America' and 'The Logical Song'?

18 Which of Shakespeare's title characters takes on the title Thane of Cawdor?

19 What nationality is opera star José Carreras?

20 In Greek legend, which river in Hades produced the waters that made the souls of the dead forget their life on earth?

21 In the Noël Coward comic song, the only people to go out in the midday sun are Mad Dogs and . . . what?

22 What form of transport is the setting for Cole Porter's musical *Anything Goes*?

23 Galapagos, Fairy, and Adélie are species of which flightless bird?

24 In the ancient world, by what name was the Dardanelles Strait known?

25 Who served as US Secretary of State from 2001 to 2005?

26 The haddock is related to which other popular food fish?

27 What name is given to the large peninsula in southern Greece, connected to central Greece by the Isthmus of Corinth?

28 Perrier Award-winning comedian Chris Collins is better known by which name?

29 The adjective 'feline' describes which type of animal?

30 Who was the British monarch throughout the First World War?

31 In 1936, from which London building were the first regular high definition BBC TV broadcasts made?

32 In 1991, which Italian tenor sang in the rain in London's Hyde Park, to an audience of 100,000?

33 On 5 November children traditionally ask for a 'penny for the . . .' what?

34 In Canada, what is the profession of a 'Mountie'?

35 Which 1950s singer inspired the Don McLean song 'American Pie'?

36 The UK grouse-shooting season traditionally opens on the 12th of which month?

37 Which traditional playground game requires nimble footwork to hop across a numerical grid?

38 On which temperature scale is zero degrees the freezing point of water?

39 Which leading playwright's works include *Jumpers, Heroes* and *Rock'n' Roll*?

40 In the Austin Powers film trilogy, what does Powers claim is his 'middle name'?

41 Which Welsh actress played Gladys Pugh in the TV sitcom *Hi-De-Hi!*?

42 In the natural world, is an octopus classified as a squid or a mollusc?

43 What was the name of the band formed by former Beatle, Paul McCartney, in 1971?

44 The 'Sally Army' is an abbreviation of the name of which international evangelical organization?

45 In which country is the town of Leerdam, where Leerdammer cheese originated?

46 The Basenji is a breed of which domesticated animal?

47 The coconut grows on which sort of tree?

48 Which twentieth-century artist famously said, 'In the future everybody will be world famous for fifteen minutes'?

49 In 2006, which Tory politician selected Benny Hill's song 'Ernie' as one of his choices on *Desert Island Discs*?

50 Which night of the Promenade Concerts or 'Proms', held at the Albert Hall, is marked by the singing of patriotic songs?

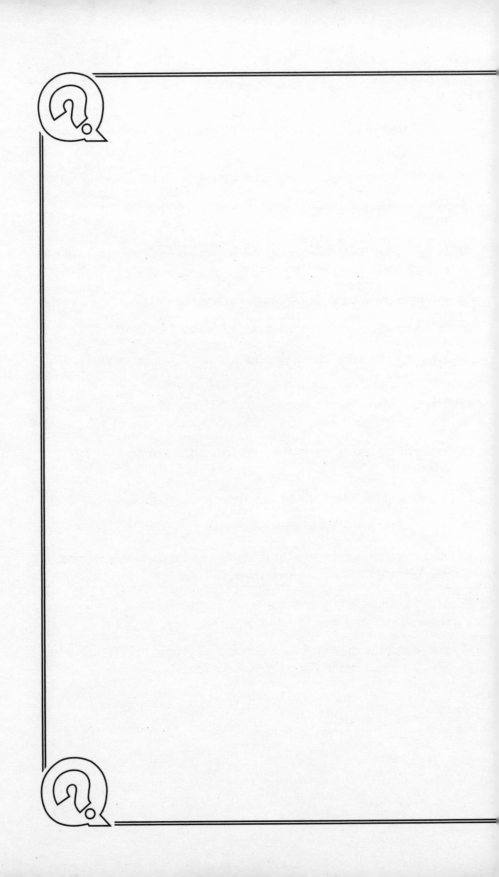

Part 3
Specialist Subjects

I N ROUND three of the studio show – Do or Die –
contestants are offered a choice of eight subjects on
which to answer questions. The subjects on offer change
week by week. You can use this section to find your
strengths and weaknesses in forty different subject
categories.

───── *SET 1* WORDS AND LANGUAGES ─────

1 'Strong as an ox' and 'brave as a lion' are both examples of which figure of speech?

2 Ergophobia is an abnormal dislike of what?

3 In the French language, the word *reine* refers to which royal figure?

4 A vexillologist is an expert in what?

5 Taken from the words 'smoking' and 'flirting', what new word describes outdoor socializing where smoking bans operate?

6 In teenage language, what is the word 'peeps' short for?

7 In the French language, the word *jupe* denotes which item of female clothing?

8 Relating to eyesight, which term describes the inability to perceive differences between some or all colours?

9 Which word comes from the French meaning 'born', and is used when citing a married woman's maiden name?

10 Which word that rhymes with 'bump' describes a dance phenomenon that began on the streets of south central, LA in 2005?

11 Meaning 'joy of living', the expression 'joie de vivre' comes from which language?

12 What is the name for a sentence that contains all twenty-six letters of the alphabet?

13 The word 'graffiti' originated in which modern European language?

14 The adjective 'nosocomial' describes which type of institution?

15 In the US, which name is commonly used to refer to a seaside promenade made of wooden planks?

16 Who, in 1961, became the first American driver to win the Formula 1 world motor racing championship?

17 What is the English equivalent of the French word *qui*?

18 In which language is a housewife known as a *Hausfrau*?

19 Which two-word French phrase is used to describe a bathroom directly connected to a bedroom?

20 Which word means a pronounceable name made up of a series of initial letters or parts of words?

21 Which Latin phrase, meaning 'bountiful mother', is sometimes used to refer to a person's old school or university?

22 What name is traditionally given to the small balls of camphor used to protect stored clothes from insect damage?

23 In martial arts terminology, the word Ninja originated in which language?

24 The action known as defenestration involves throwing someone out of which part of a building?

25 The word 'armada', used in English for a large number of ships, comes from which European language?

26 The word 'Neanderthal' originated in which European language?

27 A coven is the collective noun traditionally used for a group of what?

28 Which reading disorder takes its name from the Greek language and means 'difficulty with words'?

29 What name, derived from the Spanish for 'little war', is given to a member of a group taking part in irregular warfare?

30 In the stock exchange, the name of which animal describes a market in which share prices fall over a prolonged period?

31 Which word connects the time when something is most powerful or successful, and the point in the sky directly overhead?

32 Which popular alcoholic spirit has a name which means 'little water' or 'dear water' in Russian?

33 What word, which is a blend of the words 'smoke' and 'fog', is given to a type of haze or air pollution?

34 What word, a blend of the words 'breakfast' and 'lunch', is given to a late morning meal?

35 Used in emails and texts, what does the abbreviation 'FYI' stand for?

36 Which word from the Spanish meaning 'fair weather' is used for something that is a source of wealth or good fortune?

37 What name connects Shakespeare's Moor of Venice and a board game involving black and white counters?

38 Which word for someone who damages property is taken from a Germanic tribe that sacked Rome in AD 455?

39 What name is given to both a bombproof shelter and a sand hazard on a golf course?

40 What does a teetotaller abstain from drinking?

41 If someone is described as 'garrulous', what do they do a lot?

42 What word, which is a blend of 'cinema' and 'complex', is given to a cinema with several separate screens?

43 When translated literally, what does the Italian word 'pizza' mean?

44 Which George Orwell novel opens with 'It was a bright cold day in April, and the clocks were striking thirteen'?

45 Which letter is represented by a single dot in Morse Code?

46 In popular parlance, a letter of which colour describes an important or especially memorable day?

47 What is the Russian word for an astronaut?

48 Which word, meaning 'children's garden' in German, is used for a type of nursery school?

49 Which name is given to a word or phrase which reads the same forwards as well as backwards?

50 Established in 1804, which British organization is also known by the abbreviation RHS?

———— SET 2 WELL-KNOWN PHRASES ————

1 According to the saying, what is the sincerest form of flattery?

2 Complete the proverb, 'A rolling stone gathers no . . .' what?

3   In a saying used for attempting an impossible task, what would be difficult to find 'in a haystack'?

4   In bodybuilding slang, exercising with weights is sometimes called 'pumping . . .' what?

5   Which two-word Latin phrase means 'in memory of'?

6   A person who makes a stand by being firm or insistent is said to be 'putting their foot . . .' in which direction?

7   Which 1987 hit movie gave rise to the expression 'bunny boiler' to describe a vengeful woman?

8   The word 'prenup' is shorthand for a legal agreement made between a couple before entering into which institution?

9   A vacation spent doing the same things as at work, is known popularly as what type of holiday?

10   A person who only has one particular talent is sometimes referred to as a 'one-trick . . .' what?

11   Someone who prevents others from using something he has no use for himself, is often called a 'dog in the . . .' what?

12   The abbreviation SW stands for which range of radio frequencies?

13   Complete the phrase: 'A rising tide lifts all . . .' what?

14   What does the Welsh phrase *Nos da* mean?

15   If a person has a grievance, they could be said to have an 'axe to . . .' what?

16   Which term for an overweight feline is used to describe a very wealthy or influential person?

17   Towers made from which material are said to be places of retreat away from the practicalities of life?

18   If someone is plain-speaking and straight to the point they are said to call a 'spade a . . .' what?

19   Which two-word term, meaning 'good faith' in Latin, is used to describe something that is real or genuine?

20   If you have the freedom to do anything or go anywhere then the world is said to be your . . . what?

21 If a person is particularly good at growing plants he is said to have 'green . . .' what?

22 Which Latin phrase is used legally to mean 'let the buyer beware'?

23 Damage or depreciation resulting from ordinary use is known as 'wear and . . .' what?

24 Which term, meaning 'blow of state' in French, is used for a sudden violent seizure of power from a government?

25 If someone is particularly diligent, they can be described as an 'eager . . .' what?

26 Metaphorically speaking, a ceiling of which material blocks progress?

27 Which three words can be added to the expression 'jack of all trades' to turn it into a negative comment?

28 Which word follows 'bone', 'dunder' and 'knuckle' to give three different insults?

29 What was the occupation of someone known as 'Jack Tar'?

30 According to the idiom, which branch can be held out to indicate a desire for peace?

31 Complete the saying: 'Blood is thicker than . . .' what?

32 In popular parlance, a continual round of hectic activity is often referred to as 'the rat . . .' what?

33 In popular slang, obstructive and time-consuming bureaucratic procedure is often known as red . . . what?

34 What name, meaning 'long chair' in French, is given to a sofa with a backrest at only one end?

35 Figuratively speaking, when it is hard to tell cause from effect, it is said to be a 'chicken and . . .' what situation?

36 Which surname is used to complete the phrase meaning an easy existence, 'Living the life of . . .'?

37 If something is hard to accept then it is said to be a 'bitter pill to . . .' what?

38 Complete the saying, 'To open a can of . . .' what?

39 If someone is from a wealthy family they are said to have been born with a silver what in their mouth?

40 In the proverb, whose wife 'must be above suspicion'?

41 Which two-word French term literally translated means 'high cookery'?

42 A person with a good memory is said to have a memory like which animal?

43 If something is excellent it can be said to be 'the best thing since sliced . . .' what?

44 Which French term that translates as 'I don't know what' is used to describe a certain indescribable quality?

45 According to the saying, which animal is 'let out of the bag' when a secret is disclosed?

46 According to the saying, if a person gets off to a successful start, he 'hits the ground . . .' what?

47 To be caught between two difficult alternatives is to be between 'The Devil and the . . .' what?

48 'Dog and Bone' is cockney rhyming slang for which piece of communication equipment?

49 Complete this famous phrase, 'Power tends to corrupt and absolute power corrupts . . .' what?

50 The Latin expression 'Veni, vidi, vici' means 'I came, I saw, I . . .' what?

SET 3 LITERATURE
---

1 In 1776, during the Industrial Revolution, which economist wrote *The Wealth of Nations*?

2 The travel books *Pole to Pole* and *Full Circle* were written by which former Monty Python member?

3 Which of Arthur Miller's plays highlighted the Salem witch trials?

4 Who wrote the poem 'The Charge of the Light Brigade'?

5 In which country did the haiku poem originate?

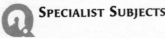

6 Which detective made his first appearance in the short story 'A Study in Scarlet'?

7 In 1513, which Italian political philosopher wrote *The Prince*?

8 In which country was the bestselling writer Bill Bryson born?

9 In Shakespeare's play *The Taming of the Shrew*, who is known as the shrew?

10 Which Ancient Greek poet wrote the epic poems *The Iliad* and *The Odyssey*?

11 Which English poet was quoted as saying 'To err is human; to forgive, divine'?

12 In 1970, which American poet and novelist wrote *I Know Why The Caged Bird Sings*?

13 In which H. G. Wells novel is there a race of beings called 'Morlocks'?

14 Which Roman poet wrote the epic poem *The Aeneid*?

15 In George Orwell's novel *Animal Farm*, what is the name of the farmer?

16 Published in 2006, *The Sound of Laughter* is the autobiography of which Bolton-born comedian?

17 Which nineteenth-century novelist worked in a London factory pasting labels on bottles of blacking at the age of twelve?

18 In English literature, the 'General Prologue' and 'The Knight's Tale' are parts of which great work?

19 In Charles Dickens's *Oliver Twist*, what is the nickname of the pick-pocket Jack Dawkins?

20 Which George Orwell novel features the nation of Oceania?

21 In the writings of J. R. R. Tolkien, hobbits live in which peaceful land in Eriador in north-western Middle-earth?

22 In Miguel de Cervantes' novel, which buildings did Don Quixote mistake for evil giants?

23 Which French author used a madeleine cake to inspire memories, in his novel *À la Recherche du Temps Perdu*?

24 Which US author wrote the novella *The Old Man and the Sea*?

25 Which town in Massachusetts is the inspiration for the Nathaniel Hawthorne book *The House of Seven Gables*?

26 Which Native American tribe leader is the subject of an epic poem by Henry Wadsworth Longfellow?

27 In 1857, who wrote the bestselling book *Missionary Travels and Researches in South Africa* about his expeditions?

28 Which American dramatist wrote *The Glass Menagerie* and *A Streetcar Named Desire*?

29 Which fictional gentleman explorer lived at No. 7 Savile Row, London?

30 Which famous Scottish poet was born in Alloway in 1759?

31 Complete the title of a play by Shakespeare, *The Merchant of* . . . what?

32 Which book, first produced in 1549, is known by the abbreviation BCP?

33 In June 2004 which former US president published his autobiography, *My Life*?

34 Originally a column in the *New York Observer*, Candace Bushnell's observations were the basis for which bestseller?

35 The 2002 novel *An Act of Treachery* was written by which female Conservative MP?

36 In the series of books by J. K. Rowling, what school does Harry Potter attend?

37 Published in 2000, which US author wrote the bestselling novel *Angels and Demons*?

38 In 1929, which German-born author wrote the First World War novel *All Quiet on the Western Front*?

39 In *Frankenstein* by Mary Shelley, what is the name of the scientist who makes a living creature from dead body parts?

40 Complete the title of the bestselling novel by Mitch Albom: *The Five People You Meet In* . . . what?

41 In a series of novels by Edgar Rice Burroughs, how is the orphaned Lord Greystoke better known?

42 With which branch of literature is Robert Frost most closely associated?

43 Anne Hathaway was the wife of which famous English playwright?

44 Which controversial author wrote the novel *Midnight's Children*?

45 What is the name of the lion in C. S. Lewis's *The Lion, The Witch and The Wardrobe*?

46 The Victorian poet Edward Lear popularized which five-line comic verse form?

47 Paris and which other city is the setting for the Charles Dickens novel, *A Tale of Two Cities*?

48 'Love makes the world go round? . . . Whisky makes it go round twice as fast', is a line from which Compton Mackenzie novel?

49 According to *The Hitchhiker`s Guide to the Galaxy*, what number is 'the answer to life, the universe and everything'?

50 Robert Louis Stevenson's novel, *The Strange Case of Dr Jekyll and Mr Hyde*, is set in which city?

———— *SET 4* **CHILDREN'S LITERATURE** ————

1 Published in 2006, what is the name of the 'official sequel' to J. M. Barrie's children's classic, *Peter Pan*?

2 Which famous French children's book by Antoine Saint-Exupéry was made into a 1974 Lerner and Loewe film musical?

3 In the nursery rhyme 'Mary Had a Little Lamb', what was the colour of the lamb's fleece?

4 What is Charlie's surname in Roald Dahl's *Charlie and the Chocolate Factory*?

5 According to the fairy tale, what did Rip Van Winkle do for twenty years?

6 'A Fairy Tale for a Land-Baby' is the subtitle of which children's novel by Charles Kingsley?

7 Complete the title of the children's novel by Frances Hodgson Burnett, *The Secret . . .* what?

8 In the nursery rhyme 'Little Boy Blue', where is the sheep?

9   To which historical date does the nursery rhyme 'Remember, Remember' allude?

10 In the children's book *Horton Hatches the Egg* by Dr Seuss, what type of creature is Horton?

11 Which famous children's book by Kenneth Grahame is about the adventures of a mole, a water-rat, a badger and a toad?

12 What was the surname of the German brothers Wilhelm and Jacob, famous for their collection of classic fairy tales?

13 What is the name of the tank engine hero in the popular series of children's books and TV programmes?

14 In the nursery rhyme 'The Muffin Man', where does the muffin man live?

15 Which English author created the children's book *The Snowman*?

16 In the fairy tale 'Little Red Riding Hood', as whom did the wolf dress up?

17 In the 1970s, Roger Hargreaves created a series of books featuring which popular children's characters?

18 Which British children's author wrote *The Gruffalo*?

19 In the famous fairy tale, which animal tried to eat 'The Three Little Pigs'?

20 In the Raymond Briggs children's book, what is the name of Fungus the Bogeyman's son?

21 In the nursery rhyme 'Yankee Doodle' what did the title character put in his hat?

22 In *Alice's Adventures in Wonderland*, what did the Cheshire Cat leave behind when he vanished?

23 Which Italian author wrote the children's story *Pinocchio*?

24 In which country is the children's book *Anne of Green Gables* set?

25 According to the nursery rhyme, what fruit did Little Jack Horner pull out of his pie?

26 In the Roald Dahl book *Charlie and the Chocolate Factory*, which child chews gum and turns into a giant blueberry?

27 How many children make up Enid Blyton's 'Famous Five'?

28 In the nursery rhyme, which garment is Wee Willie Winkie wearing when he runs through the town?

29 In which novel by Anne Fine were a class of school children entrusted with little bags of flour?

30 Which author wrote *The Just So Stories for Little Children*?

31 The 'Pushmi-Pullyu' is a rare animal in which children's book by Hugh Lofting?

32 In the children's poem by Edward Lear, which bird went to sea with a pussy-cat?

33 In the nursery rhyme, what did the Queen of Hearts make 'All on a summer's day'?

34 In the classic children's novel *Carrie's War*, to which country of the UK are Carrie and her brother evacuated?

35 Which author wrote the children's book *The Cat in the Hat*?

36 In the children's books, Paddington Bear arrives at the railway station with a suitcase, a hat, and a jar of what?

37 Which illustrator famously provided illustrations for many of Roald Dahl's books including *The BFG* and *Matilda*?

38 In *The Tale of Peter Rabbit*, from whose garden did Peter eat vegetables?

39 In the nursery rhyme 'Rub-A-Dub-Dub', the three men in the tub are the butcher, baker and who else?

40 Which member of the British royal family wrote the children's story *The Old Man of Lochnagar*?

41 Which English author wrote *The Railway Children*?

42 Complete the title of the children's song: 'One, Two, Buckle My . . .' what?

43 Which bestselling children's author wrote *Matilda*?

44 In E. B. White's children's book *Charlotte's Web*, what type of creature is Charlotte?

45 In the nursery rhyme, the old woman who 'had so many children she didn't know what to do', lived in a . . . what?

46 In the *Mr Men* series of books and cartoons, which green character has an extremely long nose?

47 In the children's story 'Jack and the Beanstalk', who shouts 'Fee! Fi! Fo! Fum!'?

48 According to the nursery rhyme, what is Tuesday's child full of?

49 Who wrote the fairy tale 'The Little Mermaid'?

50 In the *Winnie the Pooh* stories, what colour is Pooh's T-shirt?

———— SET 5 PRESS AND PUBLISHING ————

1 Which US comic strip featured the characters Dogbert and Catbert?

2 The cartoonist 'Matt' appears on the front of which daily broadsheet newspaper?

3 Which 2005 film, starring Rachel Weisz and Keanu Reeves, is based on the comic *Hellblazer*?

4 Who created the comic-book heroes Spider-Man and The Hulk?

5 In Stan Lee's comic book *Daredevil*, who is Daredevil's nemesis?

6 Which film director and food critic writes the *Sunday Times* restaurant review, 'Winner's Dinners'?

7 Which US cartoonist created the comic strip cat Garfield?

8 Which national newspaper bills itself as 'Britain's only socialist daily'?

9 In the *Beano* comic, which character was the nemesis of Walter the Softy?

10 In the comic strip *Garfield*, what is the name of Garfield's romantic interest?

11 Which superhero's alter ego worked for the *Daily Bugle* newspaper?

12 In Brad Anderson's comic strip *Marmaduke*, what type of dog is Marmaduke?

13 Which DC Comics heroine has a lie-detecting lasso and bullet-deflecting bracelets?

14 What is the name of the BBC's weekly television and radio listings magazine?

15 Which current British national daily newspaper was first published in 1986?

16 In which fictional city do the adventures of the comic-book hero Superman take place?

17 In 1981, which Australian-born businessman bought *The Times* newspaper?

18 In which comic are the characters Lord Snooty and Minnie the Minx found?

19 Which UK national newspaper, once notorious for misprints, is still sometimes jokingly referred to as the 'Grauniad'?

20 What is the main colour of the scarf and trousers worn by the cartoon bear Rupert?

21 'Footsie' is the informal name given to the 100-share index of which British financial newspaper?

22 In which European country are *La Stampa* and *La Repubblica* leading newspapers?

23 In which town did Superman's alter ego, Clark Kent, grow up?

24 England's longest-running independent student magazine, *Isis*, was established at which university?

25 Which former newspaper editor wrote the 2005 bestseller *The Insider: The Private Diaries of a Scandalous Decade*?

26 What name is given to a short biography of a recently deceased person, often published in a newspaper?

27 In which European country is *Le Monde* the leading daily newspaper?

28 Created by Pete Nash in 1985, the football comic strip *Striker* made its début in which tabloid newspaper?

29 In 2003, Rebekah Wade became the first female editor of which daily newspaper?

30 In 2004, Piers Morgan was sacked as editor of which daily national newspaper?

31 Created by Carl Giles, the *Family* comic strips appeared in which daily newspaper for over 40 years?

32 Who created the comic strip *Doonesbury*, which was first published in 1970?

33 *Premiere* is a US magazine for which branch of the arts?

34 Which book by Helen Fielding began its life as a series of articles in the *Independent* newspaper?

35 Which US magazine, published weekly in New York since 1925, is famous for its wit, journalism and cartoons?

36 In 1986, the *Sun* newspaper ran the famous headline, 'Freddie Starr ate my . . .' what?

37 The Thing, Mr Fantastic, the Human Torch and the Invisible Girl make up which comic-book superhero team?

38 In 1913, the *New York World* newspaper's Sunday supplement published the first modern version of which puzzle?

39 Which British newspaper launched a new 'Berliner' format in September 2005?

40 Founded in 1791, what is Britain's oldest national Sunday newspaper?

41 John Brownlow and Simon Donald were both founders of which British comic?

42 The *Lancet* is an authoritative magazine published for members of which profession?

43 Which Russian newspaper, with a name meaning 'truth', was the official newspaper of the Communist Party?

44 In 2006, which US designer appeared with Scarlett Johansson and Keira Knightley on the cover of *Vanity Fair* magazine?

45 In the French press, which actress is affectionately known simply as 'La Binoche'?

46 Which central London street was, for many years, the home of Britain's national press?

47 In British newspapers, what one-word term is given to the leading editorial in a newspaper?

48 Which US cartoonist created the characters Fritz the Cat and Mr Natural?

49 The showbiz column 'Bizarre' appears in which UK tabloid?

50 Wade the Duck and Roy the Rooster feature in which comic strip by Jim Davies?

—————— *SET 6* **ART AND ARTISTS** ——————

1 By what name does the English-speaking world know the Italian painter Tiziano Vecellio?

2 Which American artist was famous for artwork depicting Campbell's soup cans?

3 The Willow Tea Room, designed in 1904 by Charles Rennie Mackintosh, is in which Scottish city?

4 Which frame, usually in the form of an upright tripod, is used to support an artist's canvas?

5 Which world-famous London art school shares its name with a 1970s pop group?

6 Which British artist designed the album cover of *Sergeant Pepper's Lonely Hearts Club Band* for The Beatles?

7 In 1993, which art prize was won by Rachel Whiteread for her concrete cast of the interior of an East End London house?

8 Which important artist of the Italian Renaissance had the surname Buonarotti?

9 Which sculptor created the huge figure in Gateshead called the 'Angel of the North'?

10 In architecture, the Doric and Ionic orders are classical styles of what?

11 The Rembrandt House Museum, dedicated to the famous artist who lived there, is in which European city?

12 In which seaside town in Cornwall is there a Tate art gallery?

13 In art, vermilion is a shade of which primary colour?

14 The Elgin Marbles, originally outside the Parthenon in Athens, are now in which museum?

15 Origami is the Japanese art of folding which material into ornate shapes?

16 Which eighteenth-century Suffolk-born artist painted *The Blue Boy*?

17 Which French Impressionist artist painted a series of views in the 1900s of the Houses of Parliament?

18 Which Renaissance sculptor carved the famous marble statue of *David*?

19 The subject of a recent exhibition, painter Hans Holbein is particularly associated with which English king?

20 Which artistic style, in which the subject is reduced to basic geometric shapes, was popularized by Picasso?

21 What nationality was the painter Egon Schiele?

22 Which London museum was founded in 1856 upon Philip Henry Stanhope's plea for 'a gallery of original portraits'?

23 Known for his work with celebrities, with which field of the arts is David LaChapelle most closely associated?

24 In Western art, 'chinoiserie' is an artistic style reflecting the influence of which country?

25 The mask in the 1996 film *Scream*, was based on a painting by which artist?

26 Born in 1718, the Yorkshire cabinet-maker who gave his name to an eighteenth-century style of furniture was Thomas . . . who?

27 Opened in 1959, which US architect designed the Guggenheim Museum in New York City?

28 Which British town became famous for its herd of concrete cows designed by the artist Liz Leyh?

29 Which animal is depicted in the Landseer painting, *The Monarch of the Glen*?

30 In which of the arts was Auguste Rodin a famous name?

31 What nationality was the artist Salvador Dalí?

32 Which member of the Rolling Stones rock band is also a respected painter?

33 Renowned for his landscapes, what nationality was the painter John Constable?

34 What nationality was the seventeenth-century painter Jan Vermeer?

35 In painting, which colour is formed when red and yellow are mixed together?

36 Which internationally acclaimed British artist was born in Bradford, Yorkshire in 1937?

37 Which nun became famous as a result of her 1990s TV programmes on art?

38 Which New York art museum is commonly known by the acronym, MOMA?

39 The Queen's late cousin Patrick Lichfield was famous in which field of the arts?

40 Which London gallery of modern art is housed inside a former power station?

41 Which British photographer was married to Princess Margaret?

42 In 2006, which leading London modern art gallery installed a fifty-six-metre-long indoor slide?

43 In art, azure is a shade of which primary colour?

44 Which famous painting by Leonardo da Vinci is also known as *La Gioconda*?

45 Which modern artist won the Turner Prize with a severed cow and calf preserved in formaldehyde?

46 Which Italian word meaning 'fresh' is used for a painting on a wall, applied whilst the plaster is damp?

47 Award-winning artist Anne Geddes is best known for photographing which subjects?

48 Which Austrian artist painted *Portrait of Adele Bloch-Bauer I*, which sold for a record $135 million in June 2006?

49 Which Plymouth-based artist is famed for her flamboyant depictions of large, often scantily-dressed, cartoon women?

50 Which painter abandoned his life as a Parisian stockbroker to become an artist?

SET 7 **RELIGION**

1 In which town in south-west France did Marie Bernarde Soubirous claim to have had visions of the Virgin Mary in 1858?

2 What name did Joseph Ratzinger take when he became Pope in 2005?

3 Passover is an important festival in which religion?

4 Annually celebrated, what is the name of the Hindu 'festival of lights'?

5 What is the minimum age a Jewish boy must be to have a bar mitzvah ceremony?

6 The Taoist philosophy and religion is native to which country?

7 Opus Dei is an institution belonging to which Christian church?

8 Between 1473 and 1481, which chapel was erected in the Vatican Palace for Pope Sixtus IV?

9 Which word for a large lorry is taken from the name of a Hindu god who is carried on a huge chariot?

10 In which religion is the comb known as a 'kangha' traditionally worn?

11 Which shirt was traditionally worn as an act of penance by Christians?

12 In Christian religion, which calendar has small doors, to be opened on each of the twenty-four days leading up to Christmas?

13 Members of which religious movement commonly wear their hair in dreadlocks?

14 In the Christian religion, what name is given to the period of abstinence between Ash Wednesday and Easter Sunday?

15 Among world religions, which religion observes 'The Five Ks'?

16 Which religious order became known as the 'Grey Friars' from the colour of their habits?

17 In the Bible, the term 'Pentateuch' refers to how many books of the Old Testament?

18 Guru Nanak was the founder of which world religion?

19 Which religious order was founded by Saint Ignatius Loyola?

20 Hanukkah is an important festival in which major religion?

21 The Adi Granth is the principal sacred scripture of which religion?

22 Appearing in the Old Testament, how is the Decalogue more commonly known?

23 In the Muslim faith, worshippers say the ritual prayer facing the direction of which city?

24 In the Catholic church, what is the traditional apparel of a nun called?

25 In Buddhist teachings, how many 'Noble Truths' are there?

26 In which world religion is the festival of Yom Kippur celebrated?

27 Which saint is also known as the 'Maid of Orleans'?

28 Named for a god and considered sacred by Hindus, what type of creature is a hanuman?

29 In the New Testament, who preached the famous sermon known as the 'Sermon on the Mount'?

30 In the New Testament, how many men did Jesus originally choose to be disciples?

31 A novena is a Roman Catholic devotion consisting of special prayers or services on how many successive days?

32 Traditionally, by what name are Balthazar, Melchior and Caspar better known?

33 What is the first book of the Old Testament?

34 In which Asian country did the religion Jainism originate?

35 Joseph Smith is hailed as the founder of which church?

36 According to the Bible, which disciple of Jesus also walked on water?

37 What popular name is given to members of the Church of Jesus Christ of Latter-day Saints?

38 Which religious leader wears a piece of jewellery called 'The Fisherman's Ring'?

39 What is the name of the Archbishop of Canterbury's official London residence?

40 Isaac and Ishmael were the sons of which biblical male figure?

41 The Huguenots were sixteenth-century Protestants from which country?

42 What is the major religion of the republic of Mongolia?

43 Which British archbishop uses the signature 'Rowan Cantuar'?

44 In the Bible, who was the first king of Israel?

45 The name of which British monarch is associated with the 1611, Authorized Version of the Bible?

46 Dealing with the departure of the Israelites from Egypt, what is the second book of the Old Testament?

47 In which Italian town was the Franciscan religious order founded in 1208?

48 In the Old Testament, who is the brother of Moses and the traditional founder of the Jewish priesthood?

49 Which strict North American religious movement featured in the 1985 film *Witness*?

50 Associated with Santa Claus, who is the patron saint of children?

—— SET 8 MYTHOLOGY AND ASTROLOGY ——

1 Who is the Roman god of love, represented as a naked, winged boy with a bow and arrows?

2 Uther Pendragon was the father of which mythical British hero?

3 In folklore, what name is given to the eve of May the first, when witches are said to meet on Brocken mountain?

4 A person born on April Fool's Day would be which sign of the zodiac?

5 According to tradition, rain on St Swithin's Day, 15 July, will be followed by rain for how many days afterwards?

6 In *The Odyssey*, who did the sea nymph Calypso detain on the island of Ogygia for seven years?

7 A set of scales is the symbol for which sign of the zodiac?

8 Which day of the week has a name that is derived from the Norse goddess Frigg?

9 What was the name of the Roman goddess of the hearth, whose temple in Rome was tended by virgins?

10 In Norse mythology, what is the name of Odin's golden hall, where he feasted with those killed in battle?

11 In Greek literature, who visited the underworld to ask for his wife Eurydice to be released from the dead?

12 In Greek mythology, Pasiphaë was the wife of Minos and mother of which half-human creature?

13 Cuchulain is a hero in the mythology of which country?

14 Which day of the week is named after Thor, the Norse god of thunder?

15 Which figure in Greek mythology was given the task of obtaining the girdle of the Queen of the Amazons?

16 Which summer sign of the zodiac lies between Cancer and Virgo?

17 In Greek mythology, Penelope was the wife of which widely travelled hero?

18 The deities Osiris and Isis appear in which ancient mythology?

19 In Greek mythology, of what was Nike the goddess?

20 It is traditionally considered to be bad luck to walk under which object?

21 According to legend, which creature was slain by Saint George?

22 In Greek mythology, what type of three-headed creature is Cerberus who guards the gates of Hades?

23 Virgos have their birthdays in August and which other month of the year?

24 Which legendary race of female warriors fought against the ancient Greeks during the Trojan war?

25 Poseidon, the ancient Greek god of the sea and earthquakes, is usually depicted carrying which weapon?

26 Which legendary creature has the head and upper body of a woman and the tail of a fish?

27 In Greek mythology, who solved the riddle of the Sphinx?

28 In classical Greek mythology, what was said to be the food of the gods?

29 In Greek myth, which goddess of retribution caused Narcissus to waste away until only a small flower was left behind?

30 In Greek mythology, what was the name of the race of one-eyed giants?

31 According to Greek mythology, looking at a Gorgon would turn a person to what?

32 Pisceans have their birthdays in March and which other month of the year?

33 In Norse mythology, what name is given to the handmaidens who served the god Odin?

34 In Greek mythology by what was the sword of Damocles suspended?

35 In Greek mythology, Clytemnestra was the wife of which Greek king of Mycenae?

36 Which sign of the zodiac is traditionally represented by the Archer?

37 In Greek mythology, who was the supreme ruler of the gods?

38 In Greek mythology, who stole fire from the gods and gave it to human beings?

39 Who was the Greek god of nature, flocks and herds, from whom the word 'panic' is derived?

40 In Arthurian legend, what was the name of King Arthur's sword?

41 The Yeti, a mythical monster that inhabits the Himalaya mountains, is also known by which two-word name?

42 The Griffin is a legendary creature with the body of a lion and the head of which bird?

43 Who was the ancient Roman goddess of agriculture, plants and grain?

44 Which Greek god took the form of a goat from the waist down and had a goat's ears and horns?

45 In Greek mythology, how many muses were there?

46 Which sign of the zodiac is often depicted as a goat?

47 In Greek mythology, which hero escaped from the labyrinth with the help of King Minos's daughter, Ariadne?

48 In Greek mythology, Aphrodite was the goddess of which emotion?

49 In Greek mythology, what was the name of the ship on which Jason sailed in search of the Golden Fleece?

50 'The Dreamtime' is the mythology of which southern hemisphere people?

SET 9 TECHNOLOGY

1 In computing, which word was shortened to create the well-known term 'blog'?

2 In computer science, what does the letter 'C' stand for in the acronym CPU?

3 In 1963, who became the first woman to go into space?

4 'Qwerty' is formed by the first six letters on the top line of a standard keyboard; what is the next letter in the row?

5 Which term is used for a radio-style programme that is downloaded on to an MP3 player?

6 Authorities encourage the public to store ICE numbers on mobile phones; what does 'ICE' stand for?

7 Which three letters correspond to the number two on a standard mobile phone keypad?

8 In computer science, how many bytes are in one kilobyte?

9 By what acronym is 'radio detection and ranging' more commonly known?

10 In computer terminology, which term is indicated by the abbreviation MB?

11   What name is given to a person who uses computers to gain unauthorized access to data?

12   In 1928, which country established the Royal Flying Doctor Service?

13   In 1901, which radio pioneer became famous when he transmitted a signal across the Atlantic?

14   In computer terminology, what does the abbreviation BCC stand for?

15   Which type of wireless communication is named after a tenth-century king of Denmark?

16   The alloy of copper and zinc called pinchbeck is often used to imitate which valuable material?

17   A structure to assist space exploration, what do the initials ISS stand for?

18   A daguerreotype was an early form of which invention?

19   In 1925, the first public display of a working television was given at which London department store?

20   On a sundial, what name is given to the raised arm that casts the shadow pointing to the time?

21   For which European country is '.be' the specific domain on the internet?

22   In 1830, Edwin Beard Budding was granted a patent for which widely used piece of grass-cutting equipment?

23   The name of the computer language called Basic is an acronym for which phrase?

24   In technology, what does the abbreviation CAD stand for?

25   In photography, the term 'single-lens reflex' is commonly abbreviated to which three letters?

26   In transport technology, the term 'sat nav' is an abbreviation for what?

27   In the nineteenth century, Scottish mechanic Alexander Bain received a patent for a basic form of which office communication?

28   In 1991, scientist Tim Berners-Lee invented a method of organizing information on the internet better known as what?

29 What was the number of the Apollo mission that was the first to land men on the Moon?

30 By which name is the personal stereo cassette player invented by Japanese engineer Akio Morita in 1979 better known?

31 Businessman Bill Gates dropped out of which Ivy League university in Massachusetts?

32 Launched in June 2003, what was the name of the first UK-built spacecraft to travel to another planet?

33 In 1983, what was the name of the first American woman to travel into space?

34 Referring to television, what does the letter 'D' stand for in the abbreviation HDTV?

35 What is the name of the space telescope that was launched into orbit in 1990?

36 What nationality was liquid rocket fuel inventor Robert Goddard?

37 Which international company, founded in 1976, has a name derived from the words 'microcomputer' and 'software'?

38 In 1975, which US businessman co-founded Microsoft with Paul Allen?

39 The Hang Seng index measures share prices on which stock exchange?

40 Which scientist discovered penicillin in the 1920s?

41 In computer terminology, what does the acronym RAM stand for?

42 The process invented by Henry Bessemer in the nineteenth century converted pig iron into which metal?

43 By which abbreviation is the US computer manufacturer International Business Machines better known?

44 Which Australian businessman controls the large international media company called News Corporation?

45 Which Scottish chemist and physicist is credited with devising the vacuum flask?

46 In economic terminology, what do the initials GDP stand for?

47 Which scientist first featured on the Bank of England ten-pound note in 2000?

48 Which French execution device was originally called the 'Louisette' after its designer?

49 In which famous street in New York City is the New York Stock Exchange situated?

50 The NASA rovers called *Spirit* and *Opportunity* landed on which planet in 2004?

-------------------- *SET 10* **SCIENCE** --------------------

1 Which word did US mathematician Edward Kasner introduce for the number made up of one followed by a hundred zeroes?

2 In mathematics, Pythagoras's theorem relates to the sides of which right-angled figure?

3 In Roman numerals, which letter is used to represent one hundred?

4 In taxation terms, the word 'tithe' indicates what fraction of income?

5 Which metal is the best conductor of electricity?

6 Which Russian scientist developed conditioned reflexes in dogs that were trained to salivate on hearing a bell?

7 What is deoxyribonucleic acid better known as?

8 On a weather map what name is given to a line that shows areas with equal atmospheric pressure?

9 What quantity is represented by the mathematical symbol that appears to be a figure eight on its side?

10 In imperial measurements, how many pints make up a quart?

11 Which type of wispy or feathery high cloud derives its name from the Latin for 'curl'?

12 The group of seven stars that form the Plough are in which constellation?

13 What name is given to the distance from the centre of a circle to the circumference?

14 In the northern hemisphere, the longest day falls in which month?

15 Which gas is required for the process of aerobic respiration?

16 A dodecahedron is a solid figure with how many faces?

17 What name is given to a mixture of two or more different metals?

18 In mathematics, how many degrees are there in a right angle?

19 How many centimetres are there in a metre?

20 Which metallic element, common in bananas, has the chemical symbol 'K'?

21 The Centigrade scale is an alternative name for which temperature scale?

22 The 1969 *Apollo 11* mission to the moon included Neil Armstrong, Buzz Aldrin, and which other astronaut?

23 What name is commonly given to the gas called nitrous oxide, due to its euphoric effects when inhaled?

24 According to legend, which Greek scientist jumped out of his bath and ran naked through the streets shouting 'Eureka!'?

25 Which Russian chemist devised the periodic table?

26 Which type of radiation is abbreviated as UV?

27 In electronics, what do the letters in the abbreviation LED stand for?

28 Which metal, used in some types of thermometers, is sometimes called 'quicksilver'?

29 What is the common name for the mineral with the chemical name sodium chloride?

30 On which temperature scale is thirty-two degrees the freezing point for water?

31 Which element, with the chemical symbol Kr, is one of the noble gases?

32 In geometry, how many right angles does a square have?

33 An anemometer is an instrument that measures the speed of what?

34 What is the name of the bitter compound found in the bark of the cinchona tree, used as an anti-malarial drug?

35　By which acronym is the US space agency better known?

36　Which female scientist is the only woman to have won two Nobel prizes in two different categories?

37　In mathematics, what is the cube root of eight?

38　In the periodic table, which chemical element has an atomic number of one?

39　Among gemstones, which is the only one to be composed of a single element?

40　Used as a raising agent in cooking, baking soda is also known as sodium . . . what?

41　Which temperature scale takes its name from an eighteenth-century Swedish astronomer?

42　In Einstein's famous equation, $E=mc^2$, which letter is the symbol for the speed of light?

43　Which month is named after Mars, the Roman god of war?

44　Brass is an alloy of copper and which other metal?

45　As is the chemical symbol for which poisonous element?

46　What was the name of the world's first cloned sheep?

47　The Richter scale is used to measure the magnitude of what?

48　In geometry, how many faces does a cube have?

49　Which word, meaning 'equal night' in Latin, is used for when day and night are of equal length?

50　In science, for what does the abbreviation RNA stand?

―――――――― *SET 11* **HUMAN SCIENCE** ――――――――

1　What bodily function is also called sternutation?

2　What is the common name for the eye condition hypermetropia?

3　In medicine, what is the alternative name for tetanus?

4　In human biology, which sex has two X chromosomes?

5 In human biology, in which limb is the fibula bone found?

6 In medicine, which letter is used for the most common blood group?

7 Born in 1856, which psychiatrist proposed the existence of three forces called the id, ego and superego?

8 By which two-word name is the projection of cartilage at the front of a male neck known?

9 What name is given to the hormone which regulates the amount of glucose in the blood?

10 The human heart consists of how many chambers?

11 How is the habit of somnambulism better known?

12 The cerebrum is part of which organ in the human body?

13 What is the largest internal organ in the human body?

14 Which 'H' is the part of the brain which controls body temperature and sleep patterns?

15 In human anatomy, the medulla oblongata connects the base of the brain to the upper end of which other body part?

16 The cosmetic surgery procedure called brachioplasty involves operations on which part of the body?

17 A dermatologist specializes in which part of the human body?

18 To which vital organ does the optic nerve carry information from the eye?

19 Osteoporosis affects which part of the human body?

20 If a person is suffering from laryngitis, what part of the anatomy is inflamed?

21 Rickets is a medical disorder brought on by a deficiency of which vitamin?

22 In which part of the human body are the metatarsal bones located?

23 In the 1950s, Jonas Salk discovered a vaccine for which disease?

24 The word 'hepatic' refers to which of the body's internal organs?

25 How many ribs does a human being usually have?

26 Which part of the body is studied by a phrenologist?

27 In the human body, what is sometimes referred to as a 'fang'?

28 Rhinology is a branch of medicine concerned with which part of the body?

29 In human physiology, the term 'astigmatism' refers to a condition affecting which sense?

30 Found in the human body, what is the common name for the sternum?

31 In which part of the human body is the tympanic membrane found?

32 In the health profession, what do the initials GP stand for?

33 Malaria is contracted from the bite of which insect?

34 What is the name of the coloured part of the eye that surrounds the pupil?

35 In which limb of the body is the funnybone located?

36 In medicine, which organ of the body is affected by Wolff-Parkinson-White (WPW) syndrome?

37 In which part of the human body is the labyrinth?

38 In 1953, the double-helix structure of which substance was discovered by Crick and Watson?

39 The interior of which organ of the body is examined by means of an ophthalmoscope?

40 Found in the human body in front of the knee joint, what is the common name for the patella?

41 In medical terms and relating to sleep, what does the abbreviation REM stand for?

42 In medicine, haematology is especially concerned with which aspect of the human body?

43 What is the common name for rubeola, an infectious viral disease causing fever, typically occurring in childhood?

44 In 1980, the World Health Organization announced that which fatal disease had been globally eradicated?

45 A heliophobic person is sensitive to which natural phenomenon?

46 What is the name of the largest bone in the human body?

47 Normal vision is informally expressed as which numerical measure?

48 In medicine, what is an Ishihara test used to specifically determine?

49 From what do graphologists believe they can identify human characteristics?

50 Which colour blood cells contain haemoglobin to carry oxygen to the cells?

———————————— SET 12 **ANIMALS** ————————————

1 In a circus, how many riders does a liberty horse have?

2 What breed of dog was the famous TV and film character Lassie?

3 Bedlington, Skye and Cairn are all breeds of what type of dog?

4 Hippophobia is an irrational fear of which animal?

5 In the animal world, which specific part of its anatomy does a leopard use to maintain balance?

6 Which country's ambassador introduced pelicans to London's St James's Park as a gift to Charles II?

7 Arctic, Bat-eared and Fennec are varieties of which member of the dog family?

8 Which lizard is famously known for its ability to change colour?

9 In the natural world, to which bird does the word 'keelie' refer?

10 In 1985 and 1986, which English greyhound won a world record thirty-two consecutive races?

11 Which pet animal is informally referred to as a 'moggy'?

12 In the animal world, what colour is the adult female blackbird?

13 To which class of animals do insects, spiders and crustaceans all belong?

14 In the animal world, 'cob' is the name given to the male of which bird?

15 A quokka is a kind of wallaby native to which country?

16 Which spotted, dog-like animal is well known for producing a loud laugh or cackle?

17 Which type of gazelle is a national and sporting emblem of South Africa?

18 Which Indonesian island gives its name to the largest species of lizard?

19 Males of which animal over five years old are called 'harts'?

20 In horse riding, what is the metal mouthpiece attached to a bridle called?

21 By which name is a young sheep known?

22 To which animal family does the jackal belong?

23 Used in road safety information campaigns, what sort of animal was Tufty Fluffytail?

24 Used to measure the height of a horse, how many inches are there in a hand?

25 The world's largest spider is named after which biblical character?

26 Introduced to Britain from Asia, the muntjac and the sika are types of which large mammal?

27 Which black-and-white wading bird is the symbol of the RSPB?

28 The adjective 'porcine' describes which type of animal?

29 What name is given to an adult female black bear?

30 On which Mediterranean rock are the famous monkeys, known as the Barbary apes, to be found?

31 Which aquatic British mammal feeds mainly on fish and has the scientific name *Lutra lutra*?

32 The rhea is a large flightless bird native to which continent?

33 In the dog world, which is the largest breed of poodle?

34 What is a young goose called?

35 Which other name is often given to the common viper, Britain's only poisonous snake?

36 The dalmatian dog shares its name with the inhabitants of a region of which European country?

37 What does the 'T' stand for in the name of the dinosaur that is abbreviated to T-Rex?

38 What is a male rabbit called?

39 What name is given to a young cow that hasn't given birth to a calf?

40 In the comic strip, what type of animal is the character Garfield?

41 What type of creature is a 'Bombay Duck'?

42 What is the only bird that can fly backwards?

43 What are the offspring of a goat called?

44 Which missing appendage is the distinguishing feature of a Manx cat?

45 What is the name given to a female peacock?

46 What is the name given to animals that only eat plants?

47 Which breed of dog is named after a saint who established hospices near two Alpine passes?

48 In which US TV series did a Jack Russell terrier called Moose play a dog called Eddie?

49 To which family of mammals do the llama and alpaca belong?

50 In the animal world, what is a Camberwell Beauty?

——————— SET 13 **THE WORLD OF MUSIC** ———————

1 Which instrument is most closely associated with the English jazz musician, Courtney Pine?

2 Which US jazz musician and bandleader made one of his last recordings at the Abbey Road studio in 1944?

3 Played with the hand in Indian music, the tabla is which specific type of musical instrument?

4 How many strings are there on a viola?

5   With which instrument is the jazz musician Jamie Cullum particularly associated?

6   Zildjian is a name associated with drumsticks and which other percussion instrument?

7   Jazz trumpeter John Birks Gillespie earned which nickname for his clowning around?

8   By which nickname was the jazz composer Edward Kennedy Ellington better known?

9   Which percussion instrument's name means 'bell play' in German?

10   What is the largest bowed instrument in the string family?

11   The name of which percussion instrument literally means 'wood sound' in Greek?

12   Which title was given to the leading jazz musician William Basie as a nickname?

13   Which style of syncopated jazz piano music, heard in the film *The Sting*, was developed by Scott Joplin around 1900?

14   Which jazz singer was known by the nickname 'Lady Day'?

15   Which instrument in the percussion family takes its name from its own shape?

16   In the 1840s, who invented the saxophone?

17   The balalaika is a stringed musical instrument originating in which country?

18   With which instrument is the jazz musician Sonny Rollins particularly associated?

19   Which large musical instrument has up to forty-seven strings?

20   Stradivarius is a name most closely associated with which musical instrument?

21   Which legendary US jazz saxophonist was known by the nickname 'Bird'?

22   To which section of the orchestra does the cor anglais belong?

23 In 1924, which US composer wrote the jazz-classical work for piano and orchestra, *Rhapsody In Blue*?

24 Fats Waller was a famous jazz musician most commonly associated with which instrument?

25 To which section of the orchestra does the cello belong?

26 Which musical instrument featured prominently on the soundtrack of the film classic, *The Third Man*?

27 Taking its name from the Italian for 'small', what is the highest pitched of all woodwind instruments?

28 Which legendary jazz trumpeter had a huge 1959 hit album with *Kind of Blue*?

29 On a traditional piano, what colour are the ebony keys?

30 The tuba belongs to which instrumental family?

31 Which legendary jazz singer's life was portrayed by Diana Ross in the film *Lady Sings the Blues*?

32 With which instrument is the jazz legend John Coltrane most closely associated?

33 A sarangi is a stringed instrument from which Asian country?

34 A violin bow is traditionally made using the tail hair of which animal?

35 Which Yorkshire city is home to an international piano competition held every three years?

36 Which German composer wrote the popular song 'Mack The Knife'?

37 With which instrument is the jazz musician Acker Bilk most closely associated?

38 Which US jazz trumpeter was nicknamed 'Satchmo'?

39 With which instrument was the American jazz musician Thelonious Monk particularly associated?

40 The songs 'Chattanooga Choo Choo' and 'Moonlight Serenade' were recordings by which famed 1940s bandleader?

41 With which musical instrument was Stéphane Grappelli particularly associated?

42 In 1958, which female US jazz singer had a big hit with the song 'Fever'?

43 Meaning 'very soft', the abbreviation 'pp' on sheet music stands for which Italian term?

44 Which machine is used by musicians to measure tempo?

45 Which US vocalist partnered Bob Hope in the comedy *Road To* series of films?

46 Louis Armstrong is most closely associated with which genre of music?

47 Which US jazz singer and bandleader will always be associated with the song 'Minnie The Moocher'?

48 The tam tam is part of which section of the orchestra?

49 How many keys are there on a standard upright piano?

50 Which jazz instrument was Dizzy Gillespie famous for playing?

SET 14 CLASSICAL AND OPERA

1 The comic opera *La Cenerentola*, by Rossini, is based on which popular fairy tale?

2 Whose Eighth Symphony is known as the 'Unfinished'?

3 The aria 'La donna è mobile' comes from which opera by Verdi?

4 Which Gilbert and Sullivan operetta features the characters Dick Deadeye and Little Buttercup?

5 The musical *Miss Saigon* is an adaptation of which of Puccini's operas?

6 Which nineteenth-century German composer had a wife called Clara who was a leading concert pianist?

7 Which composer's *Fantasia on British Sea Songs* is regularly played at the Last Night of the Proms?

8 Which nineteenth-century operatic soprano was known as the 'Swedish Nightingale'?

9 In music, what nationality is the twentieth-century composer Arthur Bliss?

10 Which English composer's series of five orchestral marches is entitled 'Pomp and Circumstance'?

11 In music notation, how many minims are there in a semibreve?

12 The German composer George Frideric Handel is buried in which London church?

13 Who composed the operas *Tosca* and *Turandot*?

14 Which oratorio by Handel features the famous 'Hallelujah Chorus'?

15 Which opera by Verdi features the 'Anvil Chorus'?

16 In which century did the English opera composer Henry Purcell die?

17 In which opera by Bizet does Escamillo sing the 'Toreador Song'?

18 Which word, derived from the Italian for 'book', is used for the text of an opera or other long vocal work?

19 Which two-word term, literally meaning 'first lady' in Italian, is used for the chief female singer in an opera?

20 Which Tchaikovsky overture, celebrating the Russian victory over Napoleon, often features bells and cannons?

21 In opera, what term is used for the lowest category of female voice?

22 Which classical composer gives his name to an important piano competition held every four years in Moscow?

23 What is the nationality of the opera singer Dame Joan Sutherland?

24 The title of which operetta by Johann Strauss the Younger translates into English as 'The Bat'?

25 What was the name of the Ravel ballet music used by Torvill and Dean in a famous 1984 ice dance routine?

26 Which German composer wrote 'The Ring Cycle'?

27 What nationality was the classical composer Giacomo Puccini?

28 Under what name did José Carreras, Plácido Domingo and Luciano Pavarotti perform together during the 1990s?

29 Israel Baline was the original name of which American composer?

30 Benjamin Britten's 1953 opera *Gloriana* was about which English monarch?

31 Which nineteenth-century German composer wrote the overture *The Hebrides,* often known as 'Fingal's Cave'?

32 Which Italian composer wrote the opera *William Tell*?

33 Which classical composer's most famous works includes *The Four Seasons*?

34 In which Middle-Eastern country is the Verdi opera *Aida* set?

35 *Fidelio* is the only major opera by which German composer?

36 Which Russian composer wrote the ballet *The Nutcracker*?

37 In the popular piece of music by Johann Sebastian Bach, on what string was the Air played?

38 What nationality was the classical composer Maurice Ravel?

39 Which Gilbert and Sullivan comic opera is set in a Cornish seaport?

40 Which Russian composer's Sixth Symphony is known as the 'Pathetic' or 'Pathétique'?

41 In 1749, which composer wrote the piece entitled *Music for the Royal Fireworks*?

42 Which Czech composer's most famous works include the symphony 'From the New World'?

43 With which musical instrument is the composer Sergei Rachmaninov most closely associated?

44 What nationality is opera singer Plácido Domingo?

45 In which country was the classical composer Frederick Delius born?

46 The 'Waltz King' Johann Strauss was born in which European city in 1804?

47 Which Polish composer lived with the French author George Sand for about ten years?

48 Who wrote the opera *The Flying Dutchman*?

49 Which composer wrote the orchestral suite known as *The Planets*?

50 Which Italian composer wrote the romantic opera *Madam Butterfly*?

——————— *SET 15* **TOP OF THE POPS** ———————

1 According to the title of the Four Tops' 1988 Top 10 hit, in which Mexican resort was the 'Loco' in?

2 *Warning* and *American Idiot* were Top 10 albums in the UK for which US rock group?

3 Which soul singer's first Top 20 hit in the UK was 'My Girl' in 1965?

4 In 2006, 'Why Won't You Give Me Your Love' and 'Valerie' were UK top ten hits for which Liverpool five-piece?

5 In November 2006, which Irish boyband topped the UK singles charts with 'The Rose'?

6 Which 1965 Beatles chart-topper did John Lennon describe as, 'one of the earliest heavy metal records made'?

7 'Waterloo' was Abba's first British number one hit single; what was their second?

8 Which British band had a number one hit in 1963 with the song 'Glad All Over'?

9 In 1984, which British band had a UK number one hit with 'The Reflex'?

10 In 1982, which Guyanese-born singer-songwriter had a UK number one hit with the single 'I Don't Wanna Dance'?

11 Which Irish band had a UK number one hit in 1979 with the song 'I Don't Like Mondays'?

12 Which UK soul singer had 1990s hits with 'Give Me A Little More Time' and 'Walk On By'?

13 Which US boyband had major 1990s hits with the singles 'Quit Playing Games (With My Heart)' and 'Larger Than Life'?

14 In 1992, Snap! had a UK number one hit with the single 'Rhythm Is A . . .' what?

15 In 1982, which pop group, of Eurovision Song Contest fame, had a number one hit with the single 'Land Of Make Believe'?

16 In 1996, which US trio had a UK number one hit with the single 'Ready Or Not'?

17 In 1997, which band had their second UK number one hit with the song 'Beetlebum'?

18 The songs 'Bad' and 'Dirty Diana' were 1980s hits for which US pop star?

19 Which Beatles song has been a UK chart-topper for Joe Cocker, Wet Wet Wet and Sam & Mark?

20 In 1991, which heavy metal band had a UK number one hit with the single 'Bring Your Daughter . . . To The Slaughter'?

21 Complete the title of the 2004 chart-topping album from U2, *How To Dismantle . . .* what?

22 Which British reggae band had 1980s hits with 'Rat In Mi Kitchen' and 'Sing Our Own Song'?

23 Which US pop star had UK hits in the 1980s with the songs 'Crazy For You' and 'Borderline'?

24 The Fun Lovin' Criminals' 1999 hit 'Love Unlimited' is a tribute to which legendary soul singer?

25 Which British rock band had 1960s hits with 'Itchycoo Park' and 'Lazy Sunday'?

26 In 1987, Firm had a UK number one hit with 'Star Trekkin'', parodying the characters of which TV series?

27 Which Geordie singer-songwriter has had UK chart hit singles with 'Englishman In New York' and 'Fields Of Gold'?

28 'Superstition', 'Living For The City' and 'Sir Duke' were UK chart hits in the 1970s for which US singer-songwriter?

29 Irishman Feargal Sharkey is famous for being the lead singer with which hit-making punk band of the 1970s and 80s?

30 Little Richard had a 1958 hit with 'Good Golly Miss . . .' what?

31 Which Scottish band won a BRIT award for their bestselling album *The Man Who*?

32 Which hit song by U2 begins with the line, 'I have climbed the highest mountains, I have run through the fields'?

33 Which 'grunge' band had the hit single 'Smells Like Teen Spirit'?

34 Which 1970s disco group had hits with 'Go West' and 'YMCA'?

35 Which ex-Beatle had a chart hit in 1987 with 'Got My Mind Set On You'?

36 'Fairytale Of New York' and 'Dirty Old Town' were hits for which rock band?

37 The 1968 UK chart hit by the Foundations was called 'Build Me Up . . .' what?

38 In 1984, which US singer had a UK hit with 'Private Dancer'?

39 Which British band released the chart-topping 1985 album *Brothers In Arms*?

40 Which US pop group had their first UK number one hit in 1966 with the single 'Good Vibrations'?

41 Which 1990 love song by Roxette begins, 'Lay a whisper on my pillow, leave the winter on the ground'?

42 In 1954, 'Three Coins In The Fountain' became which US singing legend's first UK number one hit single?

43 What was the title of the theme tune of the 1997 film *Titanic*?

44 Which former *Neighbours* heartthrob sang the 1989 hit 'Too Many Broken Hearts'?

45 'You're The One That I Want' and 'Summer Nights' were hit singles from which 1978 film musical?

46 In 1978, with which Dionne Warwick single did UK punk band the Stranglers also have a hit?

47 Which female trio had big hits in the 1990s with the singles 'Waterfalls' and 'No Scrubs'?

48 Which cockney duo had UK top ten hits in the 1980s with 'Rabbit' and 'Ain't No Pleasing You'?

49 Which US rapper had posthumous UK chart hits with 'Changes' and 'Ghetto Gospel'?

50 In 2006, the hit single 'Patience' launched the revival of which 1990s boyband?

———————————— SET 16 **POP STARS** ————————————

1 In 1999, which former Spice Girl released an album entitled
    Schizophonic?

2 Which US pop singer collaborated with the Black Eyed Peas on their
    UK number one hit 'Where Is The Love'?

3 In 2006, the President of Venezuela opened a military air base for a
    concert by which Colombian pop star?

4 'Tutti Frutti', 'Lucille' and 'Good Golly Miss Molly' were all hits for
    which US singer and pianist?

5 In 1997, which US singer-songwriter had a UK number one hit with the
    single 'Professional Widow'?

6 Which US singer was born Anna Mae Bullock in 1939?

7 By what name was the legendary American singer and songwriter
    Charles Hardin Holley better known?

8 Which nationality is the singer Joni Mitchell?

9 Which Beatle had solo UK hits with the songs 'Woman' and '(Just Like)
    Starting Over'?

10 In 1981, which US pop star had his first solo UK number one hit with
    the single 'One Day In Your Life'?

11 In 1968, which British pop singer had a UK number one hit with the
    losing Eurovision single, 'Congratulations'?

12 In 2005, which US singer and actress secured her second UK number
    one hit with the single 'Get Right'?

13 In 1981, which Welsh singer had a UK number one hit with the single
    'Green Door'?

14 In 1981, which bestselling Spanish singer had a UK number one hit
    with the single 'Begin The Beguine'?

15 In 1995, which US pop star had a UK number one hit with the single
    'You Are Not Alone'?

16 In 1962, which yodelling pop singer had UK number one hits with the
    songs 'I Remember You' and 'Lovesick Blues'?

17 In 1960, which British singer had his only UK number one hit with the single 'Tell Laura I Love Her'?

18 In 1999, which US rock singer had his only UK number one hit with the single 'Fly Away'?

19 In 1982, Irene Cara had her only UK number one hit with which single that was also the title of a film musical?

20 In 2000, which US pop star had a UK number one hit with the single 'Born To Make You Happy'?

21 Which US singer is remembered for her 1962 Christmas hit single 'Rockin' Around The Christmas Tree'?

22 In 1978, the song 'Do Ya Think I'm Sexy' was a UK number one hit for which British rock singer?

23 Which British singer had 1980s hits with the songs 'In The Air Tonight' and 'Two Hearts'?

24 In 1973, which US singer and entertainer had a UK number one hit with 'The Twelfth Of Never'?

25 Which Australian pop singer had 1990s hits with 'Step Back In Time' and 'What Do I Have To Do'?

26 Which US female artist had hits in the 1990s with 'All I Wanna Do' and 'If It Makes You Happy'?

27 Which Australian pop star had a début album entitled *Left of the Middle*?

28 In 2005, which female singer had hits with the singles 'Other Side Of The World' and 'Suddenly I See'?

29 By what nickname is the US singer and musican Richard Melville Hall better known?

30 Which red-headed Liverpudlian had a UK number one hit in 1989 with 'You'll Never Stop Me From Loving You'?

31 Which US singer had UK Top 10 hits in the 1980s with 'We Didn't Start The Fire' and 'Tell Her About It'?

32 In 1987, which US pop star had a UK number one hit with 'La Isla Bonita'?

33 Which pop star of the 1960s, and later TV actor, was originally called Terence Nelhams?

34 'Big Yellow Taxi' was an international hit in 1970 for which female, US folk singer?

35 'If Not For You' and 'Banks Of The Ohio' were UK Top 10 hits in 1971 for which female vocalist?

36 The 1984 UK hit single 'Eat It' by Weird Al Yankovic was a parody of which Michael Jackson song?

37 Which Trinidad-born singer had a UK chart hit in 1976 with 'Love Really Hurts Without You'?

38 Elvis Presley is better known by which royal nickname?

39 Which female vocalist had UK chart hits with 'All Woman' and 'All Around The World'?

40 Which Liverpudlian singer-turned-TV personality had a UK number one hit in 1964 with the single 'You're My World'?

41 Which British singer had a big UK hit with 'Addicted To Love' in 1986?

42 In 1990, who had a UK hit with the song 'U Can't Touch This'?

43 Which US female singer sang with Meat Loaf on the 1981 UK chart hit 'Dead Ringer For Love'?

44 Which UK female vocalist of the 1980s is nicknamed 'Alf'?

45 Which Irish singer-songwriter's songs include 'Missing You' and 'Tender Hands'?

46 Which English singer had 1980s hits with 'Together Forever' and 'She Wants To Dance With Me'?

47 Name the female vocalist in the band 'Garbage'.

48 Released in 2005, which female singer's first pop album was entitled *Tissues and Issues*?

49 Which TV talent show winner had a UK number one hit in 2005 with a cover of the single 'Against All Odds'?

50 Which US pop singer had her first UK number one hit in 1985 with the single 'Saving All My Love For You'?

———————— *SET 17* **CLASSIC ROCK** ————————

1 'Paradise City' and 'November Rain' were top ten hits in the UK for which US rock group?

2 James Hetfield is the lead singer of which US rock band?

3 Actress Liv Tyler is the daughter of the lead singer of which American rock band?

4 The rock drummer Zak Starkey, who played with The Who on their 2006 World Tour, is the son of which former Beatle?

5 In 2004, which Irish rock band had a UK number one hit with the single 'Vertigo'?

6 In 1971, which rock band had their first UK number one hit with the single 'Coz I Luv You'?

7 In 1964, which British rock band had a UK number one hit with the single 'Little Red Rooster'?

8 In 1986, which Swedish rock group had a UK number one hit with the single 'The Final Countdown'?

9 In 1984, which British rock band had a major UK hit with 'I Want To Break Free'?

10 In 1981, the rock band Queen teamed up with which UK singer-songwriter for the UK number one hit 'Under Pressure'?

11 In 2000, which British rock band had a UK number one hit with the single 'Go Let It Out'?

12 In 1965, which English band had a UK number one hit with the single 'Tired Of Waiting For You'?

13 What nationality are the rock band Orson?

14 The songs 'Whatever You Want' and 'Rockin' All Over The World' were Top 10 chart hits for which veteran band?

15 Which UK rock group had UK Top 10 hits in the 1980s with 'Is This Love' and 'Here I Go Again'?

16 Which rock band had UK chart hits in the 1970s with 'Won't Get Fooled Again' and 'Who Are You'?

17 Which band released the 1973 UK chart hit 'I Wish It Could Be Christmas Everyday'?

18 Which band had UK chart hits in the 1960s with 'Wild Thing' and 'With A Girl Like You'?

19 Which US soft-rock band had chart hits in the 1980s with 'Africa' and 'Hold The Line'?

20 In 1969, the band Steppenwolf had a UK hit with 'Born To Be . . .' what?

21 Which rock band took its name from a British agriculturalist who invented the seed drill?

22 Which Anglo-American rock group had UK Top 10 hits in the 1980s with 'Little Lies' and 'Everywhere'?

23 With which song have the Righteous Brothers, Gareth Gates and Robson and Jerome all had a UK number one hit single?

24 Which Scottish band had UK chart hits in the 1980s with 'Belfast Child' and 'Alive and Kicking'?

25 Which hit song did the band Survivor record for the 1982 film *Rocky III*?

26 Which US singer with The Doors rock band is buried at Père Lachaise Cemetery in Paris?

27 Which English rock guitarist was born Eric Clapp in 1945?

28 Who was lead singer with the Irish rock group Thin Lizzy?

29 Vincent Furnier is the real name of which US rock star?

30 With which instrument was the rock musician Duane Allman particularly associated?

31 Which British 'Prince of Darkness' famously bit the head off a bat whilst performing live on stage?

32 Which 1980s New York soft-rock band was led by the London-born guitarist and songwriter Mick Jones?

33 Steve Tyler is the lead singer of which US rock band?

34 Which 1960s rock supergroup was founded by Eric Clapton, Ginger Baker and Jack Bruce?

35 Which US rock band had 1980s hits with the singles 'Livin' On A Prayer' and 'You Give Love A Bad Name'?

36 David Lee Roth was the frontman with which US rock band of the 1980s?

37 Which US rock star is commonly known as 'The Boss'?

38 'De Do Do Do, De Da Da Da' was a 1980 UK hit single for which rock trio?

39 Which US rock band released the album *August and Everything After* in the 1990s?

40 Which 1983 UK number one hit for Bonnie Tyler contains the line 'Every now and then I fall apart'?

41 Which Australia-based rock band released the hit album *Back In Black* in 1980?

42 The rock opera *Tommy* was written by which English rock musician?

43 Chris Martin is lead singer of which internationally famous English rock band?

44 Which US rock star had his only UK number one hit in 1970 with the single 'Voodoo Chile'?

45 Jack and Meg White are members of which US rock band?

46 Which UK rock 'n' roll band had a number one hit in 1974 with 'Tiger Feet'?

47 Which New York rock band had a UK number one hit in 1985 with the single 'I Want To Know What Love Is'?

48 Which 1970s rock band had UK number one hits in 1972 with 'Telegram Sam' and 'Metal Guru'?

49 Which British rock band secured the UK Christmas number one slot in 1979 with the single 'Another Brick In The Wall'?

50 Justin Hawkins was the lead singer of which British rock band?

—————— SET 18 **FASHION AND DESIGN** ——————

1　Who was the first African-American model to appear on the cover of *Sports Illustrated*'s swimsuit edition?

2　What nationality is the fashion designer Christian Lacroix?

3　In 1981, who designed Princess Diana's wedding dress?

4　A hacking jacket or coat would traditionally be worn for which activity?

5　From which language does the fashion term 'bustier' derive?

6　Which style of overcoat sleeve is named after a British commander of the Crimean War?

7　With which profession is the name Charles Worthington most closely associated?

8　Stella McCartney designed the dress for which pop star's wedding in 2000?

9　Which punk hairstyle takes its look and name from a Native American tribe?

10　A suit jacket which has overlapping fronts in order to give double thickness is known by which name?

11　Fashion designer Diane Von Fürstenberg is most closely associated with which style of dress she created in the 1970s?

12　Which clothing item was named after a nineteenth-century British Earl, James Thomas Brudenell, who fought in the Crimean War?

13　Which German supermodel played Brumhilda in the 2004 film, *Ella Enchanted*?

14　The 2006 film *The Devil Wears Prada* is rumoured to be based on the antics of which real-life magazine editor?

15　DJ is an abbreviation for which male item of clothing that would be worn on a formal evening occasion?

16　Famous for its knitwear, the fashion house Missoni is based in which country?

17　On which part of the body would you wear a homburg?

18　Of which textile fibre is the fabric gingham traditionally made?

19   In the 1970s, which top British fashion designer opened the shop 'Let It Rock' with her partner Malcolm McLaren?

20   Which four-letter word is the name of the traditional Dutch wooden shoe?

21   Meaning 'Like Some Boys', what is the French name of the fashion label set up by Rei Kawakubo?

22   In the 1950s, on which part of the body would a winkle-picker have been worn?

23   Jean-Paul Gaultier designed the costumes for which 1997 sci-fi film starring Bruce Willis?

24   In 2006, which former First Lady of the Philippines launched her own fashion label?

25   On which part of his body would a Scotsman normally wear a tam o'shanter?

26   Which British designer set up the fashion label 'Red or Dead' with his wife, Geraldine?

27   Which French fashion designer, who launched the Rive Gauche boutiques, was born in Algeria in 1936?

28   In 1969, which fashion store, founded by Barbara Hulanicki, opened in Kensington High Street?

29   By what nickname was French fashion icon Gabrielle Bonheur Chanel more commonly known?

30   Which fabric is made from the fibre in the stems of flax?

31   Which South American cloak is made of a piece of cloth like a blanket with a slit in the middle for the head?

32   Which fashion model was named 'The Face of 1966' by the *Daily Express*?

33   Immediately after the Second World War, which French fashion designer created the 'New Look'?

34   Vera Wang designed the wedding dress of which famous footballer's wife in 1999?

35   What does the 'NY' stand for in the name of the fashion label 'DKNY'?

36   The 'bunad' is a traditional costume in which country?

37 Popular in the 1920s, 'Oxford bags' were a form of which garment?

38 A brand of which undergarment was once famously advertised using the slogan 'Hello boys'?

39 In which country was the supermodel Linda Evangelista born?

40 Chelsea, Wellington and Cowboy are all types of what?

41 What nationality was the glassmaker and interior decorator Louis Comfort Tiffany?

42 Who famously wore a dress held together with safety pins to the premiere of the movie *Four Weddings and a Funeral*?

43 What nationality was the fashion designer Gianni Versace?

44 Which Australian supermodel is known as 'The Body'?

45 Which two-word French fashion term literally translated means 'high fashion'?

46 Which two-piece swimsuit shares its name with a Pacific atoll where atom bombs were tested?

47 In which Asian country is the 'hanbok' the traditional dress?

48 In 2006, which US heiress opened Julien Macdonald's London Fashion Week show wearing diamonds worth £2 million?

49 Complete the name of the influential Italian fashion-designing duo, 'Dolce & . . .' what?

50 In 1964, who founded the Habitat chain of furniture stores?

——————— *SET 19* **WORLD GEOGRAPHY** ———————

1 Which feat of civil engineering in Egypt is associated with the name of Ferdinand de Lesseps?

2 In North America, which topographical feature is known as 'the Rockies'?

3 How many stars are there on the national flag of Germany?

4 Which mountainous coastal region in County Galway, Ireland, has given its name to a hardy breed of pony?

5 On which continent is the Republic of Cameroon located?

6 Guernesiaise is the local dialect of which Channel Island?

7 Inner Mongolia is an autonomous region of which Asian country?

8 What is the only US state whose name begins with the letter 'P'?

9 Which geological fault caused the San Francisco earthquake of 1989?

10 In which country is the Roman road known as the Appian Way?

11 Which African mountain range creates a border between the Mediterranean Sea and the Sahara Desert?

12 Which European country is officially known as the Hellenic Republic?

13 From 1842 to 1997, Hong Kong was a colony of which country?

14 Which French-speaking Canadian city is built around the slopes of Mount Royal?

15 In which European city is Trinity College, founded by Elizabeth I in 1592?

16 On an Ordnance Survey map, what do the letters 'PH' stand for?

17 What name is given to the imaginary line around the earth at 0 degrees latitude?

18 Two branches of which tree appear on the flag of the United Nations?

19 Benelux is a collective name for Belgium, The Netherlands and which other country?

20 On which river does the city of New Orleans lie?

21 The Caribbean group of islands called Guadeloupe is an overseas region of which country?

22 What is the name given to an area of wetland that is flooded by sea water at high tides?

23 Which area, south-west of Johannesburg in South Africa, has a name which is an acronym of 'South Western Township'?

24 Which desert has its highest point at the summit of Mount Koussi?

25 Speleology is the scientific study of which geographical feature?

26 In which US state is Cape Canaveral, a launching site for space travel?

27 What name is given to the mainly Dutch-speaking northernmost region of Belgium?

28 Catalonia is a region in which European country?

29 In the Commonwealth, Waitangi Day is the national day of which country?

30 Which country is the northernmost of the three Baltic states?

31 The Tokyo Tower is a building located in which Asian country?

32 Which UK shipping forecast area shares its name with a bay off the north coast of Spain and the west coast of France?

33 Which archipelago in the South Atlantic is also known as Las Malvinas?

34 Noted for its desert plant life, the Joshua Tree National Park is situated in which US state?

35 Liliuokalani was the last reigning queen of which island group, annexed by the US in 1893?

36 Bangladesh shares a land border with Myanmar, formerly Burma, and which other Asian country?

37 Which British dependency is situated near the southern tip of the Iberian peninsula?

38 Reportedly in 1790, on which Pacific island did mutineers from HMS *Bounty* settle?

39 The diamond-mining centre of Kimberley is in which African country?

40 Which Venetian explorer coined the name 'Cathay' for north China?

41 Which Greek city was European Capital of Culture for 2006?

42 Galileo Galilei is the name of an international airport in which country?

43 The French national flag is made up of bands of blue, white and which other colour?

44 What is the official language of Venezuela?

45 The 38th parallel of latitude roughly forms the boundary between South Korea and which other country?

46 Equal to one hundred piastres, what is the main unit of currency in Egypt?

47 In China, what colour is traditionally worn by a person in mourning?

48 Which of the Channel Islands, situated in the English Channel, is the largest?

49 In which Asian country is Urayasu, the site of a Disney theme park that opened in 1983?

50 What colour is the circle on the Japanese flag?

———— SET 20 WATERS OF THE WORLD ————

1 The Victoria Falls are on the border of Zimbabwe and which other country?

2 The Kiel Canal in north-west Germany connects the North Sea with which other sea?

3 In Canada, the city of London is situated on which river?

4 In North America, the St Lawrence Seaway links the Great Lakes with which ocean?

5 The Tay is the longest river in which country of the UK?

6 What is the name of the longest river in Ireland?

7 What is the name of the gate at the Tower of London that leads onto the Thames?

8 In which sea does the island of Dominica lie?

9 The International Date Line runs north to south through which ocean?

10 Which river flows through Florence in Italy?

11 Which is the largest island in the Mediterranean Sea?

12 The Cook Strait divides the North and South islands of which Commonwealth country?

13 The geographic North Pole is located in which ocean?

14 The Dead Sea is located on the border between Israel and which other country?

15 In which ocean do the islands of Madeira lie?

16 Which sea, a branch of the Mediterranean, lies between Italy and Croatia?

17 The river Rhône flows through Switzerland and which other country?

18 Which freshwater lake, in Northern Ireland, is the largest in the British Isles?

19 In which sea are the Turks and Caicos islands found?

20 The largest lake in Africa is named after which British monarch?

21 The river Danube rises in the Black Forest mountains of which European country?

22 In which ocean does the island of Zanzibar lie?

23 How are the US Horseshoe Falls and American Falls better known?

24 On which river does the city of Baghdad stand?

25 What is the name of the largest lake in Scotland?

26 Which major African river has branches called the 'Blue' and the 'White'?

27 The Rio Grande river forms much of the border between the US State of Texas and which other country?

28 In which European country is the river Somme located?

29 Llyn Tegid, also known as Bala Lake, is the largest natural lake in which country of the UK?

30 Which sea lies between the east coast of Britain and the north European mainland?

31 The area called the Camargue is formed by the delta of which French river?

32 Which river is the longest in England?

33 The Orange River is the longest river in which African country?

34 Which large salt lake is known in Russian as the Kaspiyskoye More?

35 In which mountainous European country does the Rhine river have its source?

36 Lakes Superior, Michigan, Huron, Erie and Ontario are collectively known by which name?

37 Through which Asian country does the Yangtze river flow?

38 The Sahara Desert is bounded on the west by which ocean?

39 Goat Island lies in the middle of which North American waterfalls?

40 The Strait of Gibraltar connects the Atlantic Ocean with which sea?

41 The largest lake in Central Europe, Lake Balaton, is situated in which country?

42 Which lake, in the Lake District, is the largest in England?

43 Lake Titicaca is located in which continent?

44 Which strait, named after a Portuguese explorer, separates Tierra del Fuego island from mainland South America?

45 In which ocean is the area known as the Bermuda Triangle?

46 In which Australian city would you find Bondi Beach?

47 Russia, Ukraine and Bulgaria all have coastlines on which sea?

48 In which Irish county are the Lakes of Killarney found?

49 The Aral Sea is situated on the border between Kazakhstan and which other country?

50 Which lake, lying between France and Switzerland, is known in German as 'Genfersee'?

──────── *SET 21* **TOWNS AND CITIES** ────────

1 In which city would you find the landmark St Stephen's Tower, which houses Big Ben?

2 Baden-Baden is a famous spa town located in which European country?

3 Which capital city is known to its inhabitants as Moskva?

4 Which Australian town is known by the slang name 'the Alice'?

5 From a city in which European country does the New York area of Harlem take its name?

6 Firenze is the local name for which Italian city?

7 A Varsovian is a native of which Polish city?

8 Which US city, a shortening of 'Motor Town', is known as 'Motown'?

9 Heian-kyō , Miyako, and Saikyo are former names of which city, once capital of Japan?

10 Monrovia, the capital city of Liberia, is named after which US president?

11 The meat-exporting city of Fray Bentos is in which South American country?

12 Which is the most northern capital city in Europe?

13 Which US city, once known as New Amsterdam, was renamed after its capture by British forces in 1664?

14 Which city in Turkey was once known as Constantinople?

15 In which Middle-Eastern city is the Wailing Wall found?

16 What new name was given to the city of Saigon after its surrender to North Vietnamese troops in 1975?

17 Which Norwegian city was once known as Christiania?

18 Which Russian city was known as Stalingrad from 1925 to 1961?

19 Marrakech is a city in which North African country?

20 Which Australian city is known as the 'city of churches'?

21 The Spanish city Malaga is situated on which sea?

22 Which Central European capital city is known in its native country as Praha?

23 The city of Helsingør, the setting for Shakespeare's *Hamlet*, is situated in which European country?

24 Christchurch and Dunedin are cities in which Commonwealth country?

25 The cities of Antwerp and Bruges are located in which European country?

26 Which European capital city is served by the port of Piraeus?

27 In which country is the city of Cork found?

28 In which European capital is the Arc de Triomphe found?

29 Mumbai is the official name of which Indian city?

30 Radio City Music Hall is in which US city?

31 In which Indian city did Mother Teresa found the Missionaries of Charity religious order?

32 The Anne Frank House is a famous museum in which capital city?

33 A bronze statue of which charging animal is situated in New York's financial district?

34 Which Polish port city was once known as Danzig?

35 Cologne is the oldest major city in which country?

36 In which Italian city would you find Marco Polo airport?

37 The German parliament building known as the Reichstag is in which city?

38 On which of the Great Lakes does the city of Chicago lie?

39 In which European country is the town and ski resort of Chamonix?

40 St Stephen's Cathedral and the Hofburg Palace are located in which European capital city?

41 Kabul is the capital of which Asian country?

42 The Inca ruin Machu Picchu is located in which South American country?

43 Alice Springs is a town located in which country?

44 Which capital city in Latin America is the highest in the world?

45 The area of Kowloon is part of which Asian city?

46 Which city in the Far East was founded in the nineteenth century by Sir Thomas Stamford Raffles?

47 Lake Havasu City, Arizona, is now home to which historic English bridge?

48 Which city, on the south-east coast of India, was renamed Chennai in 1996?

49 The flag of which tiny state depicts the crossed keys of Saint Peter?

50 Of which Asian nation is Kuala Lumpur the capital city?

─────────── *SET 22* **TRAVEL AND TOURISM** ───────────

1 The Notting Hill Carnival takes place in London during the last weekend of which month?

2 The city of Dubrovnik is a popular tourist destination in which country?

3 Varadero is a popular tourist destination on which Caribbean island?

4 Halkidiki is a tourist destination in which Mediterranean country?

5 A popular tourist destination, on which body of water does Portugal's Algarve coast lie?

6 Which New York park occupies over 840 acres in the middle of Manhattan Island?

7 The ancient historical site of Petra is found in which Middle-Eastern country?

8 In which South American country would you find the famous statue of Christ the Redeemer?

9 In which US city is The Metropolitan Museum of Art found?

10 The Freud Museum is found in which English city?

11 In the UK, the tourist attraction Legoland is in the same town as which royal residence?

12 Val d'Isère and Meribel are popular ski resorts in which European country?

13 Which currency is used in Greece?

14 Ben Gurion is the name of an international airport in which country?

15 Las Palmas is the main town on which of the Canary Islands?

16 Commonly found in Egypt, what form of transport is a felucca?

17 According to a 2004 English Tourist Board survey, which Kent cathedral is one of England's top twenty visitor attractions?

18 The Copacabana beach is situated in which South American city?

19 Which Caribbean island is divided into three counties, Middlesex, Surrey and Cornwall?

20 The Museum of Classical Archaeology is found in which English university city?

21 The UK National Space Centre is found in which city of the East Midlands?

22 Benidorm is a popular holiday destination in which country?

23 In California, which bridge spans San Francisco's Golden Gate Strait?

24 The beach resort of Albufeira is found in which Portuguese holiday region?

25 On which of the Spanish 'costas' is the holiday resort of Lloret de Mar found?

26 Orchard Road is the central shopping and entertainment street of which South-east Asian city?

27 Which stone circle near Salisbury Plain in Wiltshire is now a major tourist attraction?

28 Strawberry Fields is a memorial to which member of the Beatles in New York City's Central Park?

29 One of the Seven Wonders of the World, in which country is the Great Pyramid of Giza?

30 How many tunnels does the Channel Tunnel have?

31 What is the English name of the Greek holiday island of Kérkyra?

32 In which European capital is the landmark building known as the 'Gherkin'?

33 Acapulco has long been a popular tourist destination in which country?

34 In Spain, which sport takes place in the Plaza de Toros?

35 The Côte d'Azur is a famous holiday region of which country?

36 Bodrum and Marmaris are tourist resorts in which Mediterranean country?

37 Which US desert city, the largest in the state of Nevada, is famous for casinos and lavish showbiz spectaculars?

38 Kingsford Smith International Airport serves which Australian City?

39 John F. Kennedy Airport is located in which borough of New York City?

40 In which Greek city would you find the Acropolis?

41 Yosemite Falls in Yosemite National Park are in which US state?

42 In Japan, on which side of the road do cars drive?

43 By which name is the Disney attraction the Experimental Prototype Community of Tomorrow best known?

44 Siam Square is a popular shopping area in which Asian city?

45 In which African country is the 'Valley of the Kings'?

46 Which small West African country, a popular tourist destination, shares its entire land border with Senegal?

47 Which word, meaning 'shore' in Italian, is given to parts of the Mediterranean coast between Italy and France?

48 Which river valley in France is famous for the Renaissance chateaux of Chambord, Saumur and Chenonceaux?

49 Cortina d'Ampezzo is a popular winter resort in which European country?

50 Menorca is a tourist destination belonging to which country?

SET 23 WORLD HISTORY
---

1 Which natural satellite of the Earth was the first object to be visited by man in 1969?

2 On 1 January 1973, the United Kingdom became a fully fledged member of which organization?

3 John Reed's book *Ten Days That Shook the World* was an eyewitness account of which historical event?

4 Which ancient city was also known as Ilium?

5 The Hill of Tara is the historic seat of the ancient kings of which European country?

6 Until 1867, which country was under the control of military leaders called 'shoguns'?

7 Which Central American country was named the 'Rich Coast' by Christopher Columbus in 1502?

8 The ancient civilization of the Toltecs was based in the area of which modern country?

9 The Battle of the Alma and the Battle of Inkerman both occurred during which war?

10 One of the Seven Wonders of the Ancient World, in which city were the Hanging Gardens?

11 Which Roman emperor ordered the invasion of Britain in AD 43?

12 The Mau Mau uprising of the 1950s took place in which former British colony in Africa?

13 What is the name of the ancient temple in Rome that was built by Hadrian and dedicated to all the gods?

14 One of the Seven Wonders of the Ancient World, the lighthouse called the Pharos was in which port?

15 In 1671, who attempted to steal the Crown Jewels from the Tower of London?

16 What name was given to the court ceremony in Imperial China that involved three kneelings and nine prostrations?

17 In 1803, from which country did the United States buy land in the deal called the Louisiana Purchase?

18 What is the name of Tory leader David Cameron's wife?

19 Which US frontier hero, who died at the Alamo, had a long type of knife named after him?

20 The eruption of Mount Vesuvius destroyed the city of Pompeii and which other ancient city?

21 Who was the Austrian-born wife of King Louis XVI of France?

22 Dubbed 'Mother of the civil rights movement', who triggered the Montgomery Bus Boycott when she was arrested in 1955?

23 What nationality was the sixteenth-century prophet Nostradamus?

24 Who was the Soviet premier during the 1962 Cuban Missile Crisis?

25 Which supersonic aeroplane made its first flight in 1969?

26 Which Roman leader gave his name to the medical procedure known as a Caesarean section?

27 Which British band's arrival in the US in February 1964 sparked what was dubbed 'The British Invasion'?

28 The radical communist movement that ruled Cambodia from 1975 to 1979 was known as the 'Khmer . . .' what?

29 In 1975, which major UK political party chose its first female leader?

30 From 1974 to 1990, which South American country was ruled by a military government headed by General Pinochet?

31 Who succeeded Colin Powell as US Secretary of State in 2005?

32 In European history, in what year was the Berlin Wall knocked down?

33 Which Asian country was unified, with Hanoi as its capital, after the Communist North seized the South?

34 In the mid-1930s, in which Asian country did the historic six-thousand-mile trek known as the 'Long March' take place?

35 The peace treaty concluding the First World War was signed in the Hall of Mirrors in which French palace?

36 In which country did the world's first woman prime minister take office in July 1960?

37 In Second World War history, which letter of the alphabet is used before the word 'Day' in relation to 6 June 1944?

38 The original United States Declaration of Independence is on public display in which US city?

39 Zog the First was king of which Eastern European country from 1928 to 1939?

40 In 1993, which country separated into two independent republics in a process known as the 'Velvet Divorce'?

41 Which religious organization was founded by William Booth in 1865?

42 Which Scottish heroine smuggled Bonnie Prince Charlie in a boat to the Isle of Skye?

43 The Siege of Sebastopol was a major event during which nineteenth-century war?

44 Most commonly known as the 'Prohibition', The Volstead Act prohibited the sale of what type of beverage in the US?

45 In 1865, which US president was shot by an actor whilst watching a play?

46 Which Italian city was the birthplace of Casanova?

47 Which reed was used in ancient Egypt to make a form of paper?

48 From which country did Brazil gain independence in 1822?

49 In AD 330, the ancient city of Byzantium was given which new name?

50 Which nineteenth-century US business tycoon made a huge fortune from his ownership of the Standard Oil company?

———— SET 24 HISTORICAL FIGURES ————

1 Which US president, nicknamed Teddy, created the first Antitrust laws to stop private companies forming monopolies?

2 King Constantine II, who reigned from 1964 to 1973, was the last king of which European country?

3 Who was vice-president of the United States during the administration of President Clinton?

4 The Soviet Union recruited the Cold War spies Guy Burgess and Donald Maclean whilst they were at which university?

5 What was the name of Adolf Hitler's mistress during the Second World War?

6 In 1959, Cuban President Fulgencio Batista was overthrown by rebels led by which communist leader?

7 'Peace in our time' is a phrase particularly associated with which twentieth-century British prime minister?

8 Who was chancellor of West Germany from 1969 to 1974?

9 The black American political activist Malcolm Little was better known by which name?

10 Of which North African country was Anwar Sadat president from 1970 until 1981?

11 In British history, who was the only monarch from the House of Saxe-Coburg-Gotha?

12 Which future prime minister was First Lord of the Admiralty at the outbreak of the First World War?

13 Who was the female prime minister of India from 1966 to 1977, and again from 1980 to 1984?

14 What nationality was the psychoanalyst Sigmund Freud?

15 In ancient Rome, which emperor murdered his wife Octavia in order to marry Poppaea?

16 In 1974, which English earl, nicknamed 'Lucky', went missing in mysterious circumstances?

17 Dubbed 'Braveheart', what nationality was William Wallace?

18 Tenzing Norgay and which other mountaineer became the first men to reach the summit of Everest?

19 Against which invaders did the British queen Boudicca lead a revolt in AD 60?

20 The Gunpowder Plot of 1605 was a failed attempt to kill which British monarch?

21 Which ancient Greek philosopher was Aristotle's teacher and mentor?

22 In which US city was President John F. Kennedy assassinated in 1963?

23 Of which country did Georges Pompidou become president in 1969?

24 Of which East African country was Idi Amin head of state in the 1970s?

25 Iva Toguri D'Aquino, the Japanese-American broadcaster in Japan during the Second World War, was better known by what nickname?

26 Who designed the Me109 German fighter plane that rivalled the Spitfire during the Battle of Britain?

27 In which country did Che Guevara serve as Minister of Industry from 1961 to 1965?

28 Of which European country was Silvio Berlusconi first elected prime minister in 1994?

29 In 1973, which US president stated 'there can be no whitewash in the White House'?

30 The *Golden Hind* was a ship captained by which Elizabethan adventurer?

31 In antiquity, what nationality was the epic poet Homer?

32 Who was the first king of the House of Windsor?

33 For which famous event in British history is baker Thomas Farynor known?

34 Mrs Lovett was the accomplice of which infamous Fleet Street barber?

35 In 1915, which British nurse was shot for helping Allied soldiers escape from German-occupied Belgium?

36 Of which African country was P. W. Botha president from 1984 to 1989?

37 Which commander in the English Civil War was nicknamed 'Ironsides'?

38 For what occupation was Dick Turpin notorious?

39 Which notorious US outlaw was shot dead by sheriff Pat Garrett on 4 July 1881?

40 Which leading scientist refused the Presidency of Israel when it was offered to him in 1952?

41 Which king married Catherine Howard in 1540?

42 Which river did Julius Caesar cross in 49 BC, thereby giving rise to a famous proverb?

43 Who is remembered in US history for his midnight ride from Boston in 1775 to warn of approaching British troops?

44 Who was chancellor of Germany from 1998 to 2005?

45 In 1984, Mrs Thatcher referred to which future leader of the Soviet Union when she said, 'We can do business together'?

46 In 1976, which US economist, who died in 2006, was awarded the Nobel Prize for economics?

47 What is the nationality of Kofi Annan, who was appointed Secretary-General of the United Nations in 1997?

48 Pervez Musharraf seized power in which Asian country in 1999?

49 Which former senior British intelligence officer fled to Moscow in 1963, facing exposure as a Russian spy?

50 Which former British prime minister popularized the phrase 'wind of change', in a 1960 speech on the future of Africa?

—————————— *SET 25* **BRITAIN** ——————————

1 Which former British prime minister was known as the 'grey man' of politics?

2 In 1971, which Milton-Keynes-based university admitted its first students?

3 How many feet are there in one yard?

4 With which charity is Pudsey the bear associated?

5 Who was the controversial leader of the National Union of Miners during the 1984 industrial disputes?

6 1990 saw protests in the streets of London over the imposition of which unpopular tax?

7 Before decimalization, which letter of the alphabet denoted a penny in Britain?

8 In the UK, in which decade were Premium Bonds introduced?

9 In 1950, the British philosopher Bertrand Russell won which prestigious Prize for Literature?

10 MoD is an abbreviation for which UK government department?

11 The University of Strathclyde is based in which Scottish city?

12 In 2005, Prince William graduated from the University of St Andrews with an MA degree in which subject?

13 What colour are the seats in the House of Commons?

14 Eboracum was the Roman name for which northern English city?

15 A charitable organization formed in 1824, what do the initials RSPCA stand for?

16 The song 'Land Of My Fathers' is the national anthem of which UK country?

17 Douglas is the capital of which self-governing British Crown dependency?

18 Which British financial institution is known as the 'Old Lady of Threadneedle Street'?

19 British coronations traditionally take place in which building?

20 Which mythical bird is the symbol of Liverpool and is said to have given the city its name?

21 Which island off the coast of Devon is famous as a breeding ground for puffins?

22 The name of which military award is abbreviated as VC?

23 Which small island off the coast of Northumberland is also known as Holy Island?

24 The Welsh annual competitive poetry and music festival is known by what name?

25 Which Scottish city has held an international festival of music and drama every year since 1947?

26 Which British politician has the nickname 'Two Jags'?

27 Which river is crossed by The Gateshead Millennium Bridge?

28 Which British mountain range is frequently referred to as the 'backbone of England'?

29 Which canal system crosses Scotland from the North Sea to the Atlantic Ocean?

30 Which of the official residences of the Queen is the largest occupied castle in the world?

31 In the ninth century, Kenneth I was king of which country?

32 Which coin went into circulation in Britain on 9 June 1982?

33 Which writer, famous for his dictionary, was born in the Staffordshire town of Lichfield?

34 'Auld Reekie', meaning 'Old Smokey', is a nickname for which Scottish city?

35 In London, which church stands between Westminster Abbey and the Houses of Parliament?

36 In the British army, which rank comes immediately above captain?

37 In 1967, on which Lake District stretch of water did Donald Campbell attempt to break the world water speed record?

38 In which Welsh city is Queen Street Station located?

39 In 1929, which UK south-coast resort added the word 'Regis' to its name after King George V convalesced there?

40 'Per ardua ad astra', or 'through struggle to the stars', is the motto of which of the UK's armed services?

41 Which academic title do Punch and Judy puppeteers give themselves?

42 Laurence Olivier and David Garrick are both buried in which London church?

43 By which alpha-numeric abbreviation is the Secret Intelligence Service, or SIS, better known?

44 Which Scottish city was once famous for its 'Three Js' – Jute, Jam and Journalism?

45 Which city in north-west England has an historic racecourse in the area called the Roodee?

46 In the UK honours system, which title can the wife of a knight adopt?

47 In which century did postage stamps first appear in Britain?

48 The sheltered anchorage called Scapa Flow is in which Scottish island group?

49 Which London district is noted for a park and a famous dogs' home?

50 Housed in St Stephen's Tower at the Palace of Westminster, what is Big Ben?

———————— SET 26 POLITICS ————————

1 In 1978, who said it was 'like being savaged by a dead sheep' when criticized by Geoffrey Howe in the House of Commons?

2 To which political party does US President George W. Bush belong?

3 In 1911, which prime minister was responsible for the Parliament Act, which limited the powers of the House of Lords?

4 In 1927, which Russian revolutionary was expelled from the Communist Party after helping Lenin organize the Red Army?

5 In the 2004 US presidential election, whose campaign did actress Scarlett Johansson support?

6 US President George W. Bush's daughter Jenna has a twin sister with which first name?

7 In 1981, the so-called 'Gang of Four' left which UK political party to form the Social Democratic Party?

8 Who was the founder and first president of the Democratic Republic of Vietnam?

9 What is the typical length of the term of office of the UN's Secretary-General?

10 Between 1949 and 1976, Mao Zedong was the Communist leader of which country?

11 Traditionally, the head of the Secret Intelligence Service, or MI6, is referred to by which single letter?

12 Which first name is shared by UK politicians Prescott, Major and Hutton?

13 The Bolsheviks were a political group in which twentieth-century revolution?

14 In which Latin American country did the Sandinista Revolution take place in 1979?

15 In 1950, which senator famously accused the US government of being infiltrated by Communists?

16 In which decade was Harold Wilson first elected as British Prime Minister?

17 In British politics, which name is usually used to refer to the Secretary of State for the Home Department?

18 Which animal is the established symbol of the Democratic Party in the US?

19 Which twentieth-century politician was known as the Iron Lady?

20 In the 1997 UK general election, which BBC war correspondent was elected as an independent MP?

21 Which song has long been regarded as the traditional anthem of Labour Party conferences?

22 The public gallery in the Houses of Parliament is officially known by which name?

23 The Dáil is the name of one of the chambers of parliament in which country?

24 In 1999, Thabo Mbeki became President of which African country?

25 In 1975, which southern European dictator finally relinquished power after a thirty-six-year reign?

26 In which month of the year are American presidential elections held?

27 Of which political assembly is an MEP a member?

28 Once led by Nelson Mandela, what is the full name of the South African party known as the ANC?

29 Which political party is known by the acronym UKIP?

30 The type of notice requiring MPs to attend a House of Commons vote is called a 'Three-line . . .' what?

31 In 1999, Helen Clark was elected Prime Minister of which country?

32 Which Oscar-winning actress has been MP for the Hampstead and Highgate constituency since 1992?

33 By which other title is the US Commander in Chief of the Armed Forces better known?

34 The holder of which Cabinet position gives the annual Budget speech to the House of Commons?

35 Which twentieth-century US president was nicknamed 'the great communicator'?

36 What colour 'paper' is a UK government report giving information or legislation proposals on a particular issue?

37 Which United Nations agency has the initials FAO?

38 Which Amendment to the US Constitution are criminal suspects said to 'plead' if they remain silent?

39 The town of Rambouillet in northern France is the official summer residence of the holder of which political office?

40 Which politician held the UK 100m record between 1967 and 1974?

41 In the eighteenth century, which political party was in opposition to the Tory party?

42 Which branch of the United States Congress has one hundred members, each of whom sits for six years?

43 The International Court of Justice normally meets in which Dutch city?

44 In September 2006, Fredrik Reinfeldt replaced Göran Persson as the prime minister of which European country?

45 In UK politics, the election of an MP to the Commons at any time other than a general election is known as a . . . what?

46 Vince Cable and Lembit Opik are leading members of which political party?

47 In order to resign, holders of which office first apply for the stewardship of the Chiltern Hundreds?

48 In 1997, Kofi Annan succeeded which Egyptian politician as Secretary-General of the United Nations?

49 In which decade was Sir Anthony Eden Prime Minister of the UK?

50 In US politics, who was Defense Secretary under President Ford in the 1970s and then again under George W. Bush from 2001 to 2006?

───── SET 27 **ROYALTY** ─────

1 Of which English county is Prince Charles the Duke?

2 Which king was the father of the English queen known as Bloody Mary?

3 The British Crown Jewels are housed at which royal fortress?

4 In 1917, the British Royal Family changed its surname from Saxe-Coburg and Gotha to what?

5 Prince Charles and Lady Diana Spencer were married at which cathedral?

6 Who was the first monarch to take up residence at Buckingham Palace?

7 What is the name of the ceremony held at Buckingham Palace in which the New Guard exchanges duty with the Old?

8 What is the title of the British national anthem?

9 Born in 1940, Queen Margrethe II is which European country's reigning monarch?

10 Anne Elizabeth Alice Louise Laurence is better known by what name?

11 In 1974, which of the Queen's children was the subject of an attempted kidnap in Pall Mall?

12 King Albert II and his wife Queen Paola are the sovereigns of which European country?

13 Which 'royal' title did Pocahontas hold within the Algonquian Indian tribe?

14 Who became Queen of Scotland in December 1542 when she was only six days old?

15 Who was the first person pictured on a British postage stamp?

16 What relation was the late Princess Margaret to the Queen?

17 Which British king reigned throughout the Second World War?

18 According to legend, which English king held his court at Camelot?

19 Who was the sixth wife of Henry VIII who outlived him?

20 Which member of the Royal Family is the president of the charity Save the Children?

21 From 1714 to 1837, the British monarch also ruled which state in northern Germany?

22 In 1921, on which Greek island was the Duke of Edinburgh born?

23 Who was the first monarch to be crowned at Westminster Abbey?

24 In the year 2000, which birthday was celebrated by the Queen Mother?

25 How many kings of England have been called Richard?

26 What is the name of the eldest daughter of the Duke of York?

27 Henry VII and Elizabeth I were members of which English royal dynasty?

28 Anna Anderson Manahan famously claimed to be which member of the Russian royal family?

29 Which future king was created the first English Prince of Wales in 1301?

30 Which English monarch was crowned King of France in Paris in 1431?

31 Who is the third child and second son of Queen Elizabeth II and the Duke of Edinburgh?

32 Whom did Lieutenant Philip Mountbatten marry in November 1947?

33 Which medieval king ordered the building of castles at Harlech, Conwy, Caernarfon and Beaumaris?

34 The Babington Plot of 1586 was a plan to assassinate which English monarch?

35 Who was King of England from 1042 to 1066 and later made a saint by the Church in Rome?

36 Which king was the father of Queen Elizabeth II?

37 Beatrice and Eugenie are the daughters of which male member of the Royal Family?

38 Of which Asian country is Akihito the emperor?

39 Which medieval English king had the nicknames 'Longshanks' and 'Hammer of the Scots'?

40 Whom did Captain Mark Phillips marry in 1973?

41 In 1521 the Pope granted which English king the title 'Defender of the Faith'?

42 In 1588, which Spanish monarch was responsible for sending the Spanish Armada to battle against the English navy?

43 Which British monarch was on the throne when the American colonies were lost?

44 Which duke won the Battle of Blenheim in 1704?

45 Which king led the English army to victory at the Battle of Agincourt in 1415?

46 Of which European country is Juan Carlos I king?

47 The Mausoleum in the gardens of Frogmore House contains the remains of which British monarch?

48 Who was the first Tudor monarch of England?

49 Which king of England was forced to limit his royal powers by signing the Magna Carta?

50 What was Diana, Princess of Wales's middle name?

──────────── *SET 28* **CELEBRITY** ────────────

1 Which US rapper was born Marshall Bruce Mathers III?

2 In 2006, which Rolling Stones legendary rock guitarist injured himself by falling out of a palm tree?

3 In which country of the UK did Madonna and Guy Ritchie get married in 2000?

4 Which British-born entertainer, who died in 2003 at the age of 100, was nicknamed 'Old Ski Nose'?

5 Which US actor was originally called Christian Michael Leonard Hawkins?

6 In 2000, which *Carry On* star wrote an autobiography entitled *All of Me: My Extraordinary Life*?

7 Born in 2000, Mia Honey is the daughter of which British actress?

8 In 2006, which US socialite topped the animal rights organization PETA's worst-dressed list for wearing fur?

9 'Not 'arf!' was a catchphrase of which legendary disc jockey?

10 In 2005, which actress separated from fellow Hollywood star Charlie Sheen?

11 What is the surname of Dec in the popular TV presenting duo, Ant and Dec?

12 Which Australian rock star was the father of Paula Yates's fourth child, Heavenly Hiraani Tiger Lily?

13 Which pianist and entertainer, unperturbed by bad reviews, famously said: 'I cried all the way to the bank'?

14 Which British TV comedy actor was born David Williams?

15 In 2005, which actress did Tom Cruise publicly criticize for her 'misguided' use of anti-depressant drugs?

16 In 1988, which US actor set a new benchmark for actors' salaries when he was paid $5 million for the film *Die Hard*?

17 In 2005, which England footballer married his childhood sweetheart, Louise Bonsall?

18 Which US male actor has a daughter named Shiloh Nouvel, born in 2006?

19 In 2006, which singer and reality TV star won the prestigious Rear of the Year award?

20 In March 2005, which cook issued a half-time rallying cry to supporters during a Norwich City football game?

21 In 2003, which US illusionist spent forty-four days suspended in a glass box by the river Thames?

22 In 1990, the film and TV make-up artist Sunetra Sastry married which English comedian and *Blackadder* star?

23 During her time with the Spice Girls, what was Melanie Brown's nickname?

24 In 2006, which Hollywood actor did *People* magazine name Sexiest Man Alive for the second time?

25 Between 1992 and 1996, the Major League baseball player David Justice was married to which *X-Men* actress?

26 In which US state was actress Nicole Kidman born?

27 World Wrestling Entertainment veteran star Terrence Bollea is better known by what name?

28 Which TV presenter won the Sport Relief series *Only Fools on Horses* in 2006?

29 Which Hollywood heartthrob actor did actress Jennifer Garner marry in 2005?

30 Which Swedish actress married English comedian Peter Sellers in 1964?

31 Which American heiress released the single 'Stars Are Blind' in 2006?

32 In 2006, which US rocker spoke about 'the huge hole in the ozone layer' his flamboyant 1980s hairstyles created?

33 In 2006, which blonde US actress was forced to hire more security after appearing in the hit film *Borat*?

34 In 2006, which British actress provoked controversy by claiming pregnant women could drink alcohol?

35 In 2006 the *Forbes* Celebrity 100, showcasing the world's most powerful stars, featured which US socialite at number 56?

36 Which *Star Wars* actress is the daughter of Hollywood stars Debbie Reynolds and Eddie Fisher?

37 Which actor turned politician famously said in a 2004 speech, 'Don't be economic girlie men!'?

38 Which famous US film director is the godfather of actress Gwyneth Paltrow?

39 How is the English singer-songwriter Florian Cloud de Bounevialle Armstrong, born in 1971, better known?

40 The author Santa Montefiore is the older sister of which British It girl?

41 Which TV chef plays drums in the band Scarlet Division?

42 Which US female pop singer was the star of TV's *Newlyweds: Nick and Jessica*?

43 In 2006, which actress famously made remarks which offended the residents of the city of Pittsburgh?

44 Which former 'Playboy Playmate' and actress married the billionaire octogenarian J. Howard Marshall II in 1994?

45 Born in 2004, Apple Blythe Alison Martin is the daughter of which Coldplay singer?

46 In 2006, which *Sex and the City* actress expressed regret at the decision to wear black at her wedding?

47 Which Scottish female vocalist's real name is Marie McDonald McLaughlin Lawrie?

48 In 2006, supermodel Jodie Kidd raced for which motor racing team?

49 Which European monarch has sisters called Caroline and Stephanie?

50 Which Asian country has designated 6 October 2006 as Tom Cruise Day?

──────── *SET 29* **TV SITCOMS AND SOAPS** ────────

1 Which TV soap featured the characters Jack Sugden, Mandy Dingle and Seth Armstrong?

2 Which 1980s and 90s US TV sitcom centred on the Bundy family?

3 Which former *EastEnders* actor went on to play Gabriel Kent in TV's *The Bill*?

4 Which British actor starred as Antony, the put-upon member of *The Royle Family*?

5 Which British actress has appeared in both the TV comedy series *Are You Being Served?* and the soap opera *EastEnders*?

6 Starring Sheila Hancock, what was the name of the British adaptation of the hit US TV show *The Golden Girls*?

7 *LA Confidential* star Guy Pearce first came to fame playing Mike Young in which Australian TV soap?

8 What was Sharon's married name in the TV sitcom *Birds of a Feather*?

9 The theme tune of the TV sitcom *One Foot in the Grave* was written and sung by which of the Monty Python team?

10 Which TV comedy show featured a group of Irish priests and their housekeeper, Mrs Doyle?

11 Which actor starred as time-traveller Gary Sparrow in the TV sitcom *Goodnight Sweetheart*?

12 What is the name of the street in which the Australian TV soap *Neighbours* is set?

13 *Grace and Favour* was the spin off of which TV sitcom of the 1970s and 80s?

14 Actress June Whitfield played June Medford alongside Terry Scott in which TV sitcom?

15 Which slang name for the garment business was also the title of a popular 1960s and 70s TV sitcom?

16 Rimmer, Cat and Lister were the principal characters in which TV sitcom?

17 In which 1990s TV sitcom did Patricia Routledge play a snobbish, social-climbing character?

18 In the TV sitcom *Only Fools and Horses*, what was the name of Del Boy and Rodney's business?

19 What is the name of the paper merchant's that is the setting of the TV sitcom *The Office*?

20 Which actress plays Robert Lindsay's wife in the popular TV sitcom *My Family*?

21 In which 1970s TV sitcom did Ronnie Barker star as London 'lag', Norman Stanley Fletcher?

22 Which British TV sitcom of the 1960s featured a horse called Hercules?

23 In which US TV series did Kelsey Grammer's character Frasier first appear?

24 What is the name of the fictional borough in which the TV soap *EastEnders* is set?

25 In the TV comedy series *Are You Being Served?*, what was the name of the character played by John Inman?

26 The first ever episode of which TV soap series was broadcast on 9 December 1960?

27 In which 1980s US TV soap did Priscilla Presley play the character Jenna Wade?

28 Which long-running TV sitcom starred Bill Owen, Kathy Staff and Thora Hird?

29 In the TV series *The Good Life*, which actor played Tom Good?

30 In which classic TV sitcom could the characters Olive, Stan Butler and Inspector 'Blakey' be found?

31 Which British actress starred opposite Freddie Frinton in the TV sitcom *Meet The Wife*?

32 Which actress played Sharon in the TV sitcom *Birds of a Feather*?

33 In the TV sitcom *Dad's Army*, what was the surname of the platoon's sergeant?

34 In which TV sitcom did Su Pollard play chalet maid Peggy Ollerenshaw?

35 Which TV sitcom, set in a Peckham barber's shop, featured the characters Shirley Ambrose and Porkpie?

36 In the 1980s and 90s US TV sitcom, how were Dorothy, Blanche, Rose and Sofia collectively known?

37 In which TV sitcom did the characters Bombardier 'Gloria' Beaumont and Gunner 'Lofty' Sugden appear?

38 In the TV sitcom *Diff'rent Strokes*, which diminutive actor played Arnold Jackson?

39 Which 1970s TV sitcom featured the characters of CJ, Doc Morrissey and Joan Greengross?

40 How was the character Arthur Fonzarelli more commonly known in the TV sitcom *Happy Days*?

41 In which US city is the TV medical drama *ER* set?

42 What was the name of the character played by Adrian Edmondson in the TV comedy *The Young Ones*?

43 In the classic Australian TV drama, the inmates were held in *Prisoner: Cell Block . . . what*?

44 In which 1970s and 80s US TV sitcom did Danny DeVito star as a cantankerous taxi dispatcher in New York City?

45 In which US TV drama, running between 1981 and 1989, did John Forsythe play the character Blake Carrington?

46 In the US TV sitcom *Frasier*, what was the name of Jane Leeves's character?

47 What is the name of the politician played by Paul Eddington in the sitcoms *Yes, Minister* and *Yes, Prime Minister*?

48 Which TV soap was set in the fictitious village of King's Oak in the West Midlands?

49 Which actor played 'Dirty Den', in the TV soap *EastEnders*?

50 Shane Richie played the role of Alfie Moon in which TV soap?

SET 30 CLASSIC TV

1 Which former James Bond actor played the title role in the 1950s TV series *Ivanhoe*?

2 Which 1980s and 90s late-night music TV show was presented by Pete Waterman and Michaela Strachan?

3 Which actress played the part of Aunt Sally in the 1980s TV series *Worzel Gummidge*?

4 Actress Gina Bellman played the title role in which 1989 Dennis Potter TV drama?

5 Which Warner Brothers cartoon pig had a stutter?

6 In the US TV series *The Dukes of Hazzard* what was the name of the Duke Boys' Dodge Charger?

7 Complete the title of the 1950s and 60s TV sci-fi show, *The Twilight* . . . what?

8 Which TV gameshow featured the catchphrase, 'Stay out of the black and into the red'?

9 Arthur Negus, Hugh Scully and Michael Aspel have all presented which long-running TV series?

10 In 1984, which member of the Royal Family appeared on *Jackanory*?

11 At the end of which long-running TV show were subjects presented with a 'big red book'?

12 Which cartoon bird's catchphrase was 'I tawt I taw a puddy tat'?

13 In which children's TV show does the character Windy Miller feature?

14 Which satirical show of the 1980s and 90s featured puppets lampooning celebrities and politicians?

15 In which 1960s TV series did Robert Vaughn and David McCallum fight the evil forces of THRUSH?

16 In which country of the UK was the TV series *Dr Finlay's Casebook* set?

17 Complete the title of Mike Leigh's famous 1977 TV play, *Abigail's . . .* what?

18 Complete the title of the 1970s and 80s music TV show presented by Bob Harris, the *Old Grey Whistle . . .* what?

19 Which Scottish actor played Fitz in the TV drama *Cracker*?

20 In the children's TV cartoon, what was the name of Dangermouse's hamster sidekick?

21 Who was the original presenter of TV's *Question Time*?

22 In which classic children's TV show did small, pink creatures live underground protected by saucepan lids?

23 'Your starter for ten' is a phrase most closely associated with which TV quiz show?

24 In the 1970s, which newscaster high-kicked her way through a dance routine on TV's *The Morecambe and Wise Show*?

25 TV presenter Stuart Hall is well known for his role on which pan-European TV game show?

26 Who was the original host of TV's *The Generation Game*?

27 In the TV show *The Simpsons*, what relation is Abraham Simpson to Bart?

28 *The Two Ronnies* was a comedy duo featuring the talents of Ronnie Corbett and who else?

29 In the TV cartoon series *Scooby-Doo*, what was the nickname of the van the gang travelled around in?

30 In the TV show *Jim'll Fix It*, who was the 'Jim'?

31 Who was the original host of TV's *Mastermind*?

32 Who played the part of Edmund Blackadder in the TV sitcom *Blackadder*?

33 *Monty Python* star, John Cleese, memorably portrayed a civil servant from the 'Ministry of Silly . . .' what?

34 Starring Jack Warner, which police drama series ran on British TV from 1955 to 1976?

35 'Boom! Boom!' was the catchphrase of which TV puppet fox?

36 Which English astronomer and writer has presented the TV series *The Sky at Night* since 1957?

37 Which 1990s TV sitcom was known colloquially as *Ab Fab*?

38 In which 1982 TV drama series did the unemployed Yosser Hughes say 'Gissa job'?

39 Which TV programme cycle broadcast in the 1950s featured Muffin the Mule and Andy Pandy among others?

40 The 'Cybermen' and 'The Ice Warriors' are enemies in which BBC TV series?

41 Which classic 1960s TV puppet series featured the Tracy family?

42 In the TV series *Star Trek*, which character has the middle name Tiberius?

43 What was the first name of the star of the classic TV series *Hancock's Half Hour*?

44 Which Australian was the main presenter of the TV show *Animal Hospital* for nine years?

45 Herman, Grandpa and Eddie Wolfgang were characters in which 1960s TV comedy series?

46 Who played the title role in the 1960s TV series *Dr Kildare*?

47 Originally played by Jack Webb, Sergeant Joe Friday was the main character in which US TV police series?

48 Featuring nineteenth-century ships, which shipping line was the subject of a popular UK TV drama series of the 1970s?

49 How many contestants are there at the start of an episode of TV's *The Weakest Link*?

50 In the TV comedy *Little Britain*, what is the surname of the teenage delinquent, Vicky?

──────── SET 31 **TV STARS** ────────

1 Barney, Betty, Fred and Wilma are characters in which 1960s US TV cartoon series?

2 As a professional wrestler, which late Yorkshire-born actor went by the name of 'Leon Arras the Man From Paris'?

3 Which TV personality famously went on strike, during 2005's *Celebrity Big Brother*, for not receiving his fizzy drinks?

4 Which comedian is known for his pub landlord character?

5 Exploring the globe for authentic culinary delights, TV chefs Simon King and David Myers are better known as which duo?

6 In her 2006 TV series, Anthea Turner was the *Perfect . . .* what?

7 In the 1970s, which *Royle Family* actor served time in prison as a result of his trade union activities?

8 Who presented the UK version of the car make-over series, *Pimp My Ride*?

9 In October 2006, which TV newsreader provoked a media storm by wearing a crucifix on air?

10 During his act, which kind of hat was worn by English comedy magician, Tommy Cooper?

11 Which of his fellow cast members in the TV drama *New Tricks* did James Bolam marry in real life?

12 In 2006, *Children In Need* was co-presented with Terry Wogan by which female BBC newsreader?

13 In 2006, which actor played the role of Charlie Edwards in the TV drama series *Hotel Babylon*?

14 Which future 'Bond' actor played the role of Geordie in the 1990s TV drama *Our Friends in the North*?

15 In 2006, which actress was chosen to replace Billie Piper as the new assistant in *Doctor Who?*

16 Linda Robson, Jenny Eclair and Janet Street Porter have all appeared in the comic TV series *Grumpy Old . . .* what?

17 To which famous TV magician was the supermodel Claudia Schiffer engaged during the 1990s?

18 The journalist and television presenter Kirsty Wark originates from which country of the UK?

19 Wine expert Jilly Goolden presented which TV programme for nearly two decades?

20 Which TV presenter was nicknamed 'Twice Nightly Whiteley' for appearing on two different shows on the same night?

21 In 1917, which comedian and TV sitcom star was born Francis Alick Howerd in York?

22 In 1990, US comic actor Tom Arnold married which larger-than-life US comedienne?

23 What is the name of the frog presenter of *The Muppet Show?*

24 In the popular TV series *Dynasty,* which British actress played the vindictive Alexis Carrington?

25 English actor Mackenzie Crook starred as Gareth in which TV comedy series featuring Ricky Gervais?

26 'Eric and Ernie' were better known as which iconic comedy duo?

27 Which presenter of TV's *Top Gear* is nicknamed 'Hamster'?

28 Keith Allen played the Sheriff of Nottingham in which 2006 TV drama series?

29 Which BBC6 Radio DJ and comedian was the presenter of *Big Brother's Big Mouth* in 2006?

30 Which female TV presenter became a host of *Stars in Their Eyes Kids* in 2003?

31 With over twenty-five years of unbroken appearances, who became the UK's longest-serving TV weather forecaster?

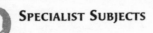

32 Who played the character Oz in the TV series *Auf Wiedersehen, Pet?*

33 In 1999, which ex-footballer took over presenting TV's *Match of the Day?*

34 Who did Angela Lansbury play in the TV series *Murder, She Wrote?*

35 Which stand-up comedian had a TV series entitled *The Man From Auntie?*

36 Which 1970s TV cop was famous for his liking of lollipops?

37 Which comic actor played Brian Potter in the TV comedy *Phoenix Nights?*

38 Which Scottish comedian sang the theme tune to the 1980s TV comedy *Supergran?*

39 In which Stephen King TV horror series did Tim Curry play Pennywise the Clown?

40 Who was the original UK presenter of TV's *Supermarket Sweep?*

41 In 2006, which Welsh female singer hosted her own comedy talk-show?

42 In 2006, who won a reality TV talent show to take the lead role of Maria in Andrew Lloyd-Webber's *The Sound of Music?*

43 In 2003, which illusionist hit the headlines for performing a 'live Russian Roulette' stunt on TV?

44 Bubbly TV personality Jo Frost is commonly known as Super . . . what?

45 Which Liverpudlian drag-queen character was created by comedian, Paul O'Grady?

46 The 2005 series of *Strictly Come Dancing* was won by which former England cricketer?

47 Which TV cookery game show was first presented by Fern Britton?

48 Which English comic actor and musician partnered Peter Cook on TV and on the stage?

49 By what name was the British comedian Alfred Hawthorne Hill better known?

50 Which fellow comedienne partners Dawn French in a TV comedy sketch series?

———————— SET 32 **THE STAGE** ————————

1 Complete the title of the Broadway musical based on Charles Schulz's comic strip, *You're a Good Man . . .* ?

2 Which US comedian and star of vaudeville was born Benjamin Kubelsky in Chicago in 1874?

3 Which Broadway musical features the showgirl Miss Adelaide, the long-suffering girlfriend of Nathan Detroit?

4 In which play by Shakespeare is King Duncan of Scotland murdered?

5 Which UK rock band's history and hits are the basis for the stage show *We Will Rock You*?

6 'Summertime' and 'It Ain't Necessarily So' are songs from which 1935 musical play by George and Ira Gershwin?

7 In which famous Oscar Wilde comedy does the character of 'Lady Bracknell' appear?

8 Kabuki is a traditional type of theatre that originated in which country?

9 Which *Riverdance* star went on to create the stage show *Lord of the Dance*?

10 In the theatre, an apron stage allows audience seating on how many sides?

11 Since 1977, which city has been the base of the Royal Shakespeare Company in the north of England?

12 Eliza Doolittle is the name of the cockney flower-seller in which musical adaptation of a George Bernard Shaw play?

13 In 2006, which US actor made his West End début in Richard Alfieri's *Six Dance Lessons in Six Weeks*?

14 In the musical *Little Shop of Horrors*, the plant from outer space, Audrey II, requires a diet of fresh what?

15 Featuring dancing storm troopers, the infamous song 'Springtime For Hitler' appears in which hit musical?

16 Founded by Louis XIV in 1680, what is the name of the French national theatre?

17 Which playwright made the claim, 'All the world's a stage'?

18 Set during the Vietnam War, which musical features a romance between an American GI and a Vietnamese bar girl?

19 In 2006, which former UK Eurovision Song Contest performer opened in the West End stage musical *Daddy Cool*?

20 In which country is the stage musical *Evita* based?

21 William Shakespeare's play *Romeo and Juliet* is set in which Italian city?

22 The style of drama known as 'Pinteresque' is named after which English playwright?

23 Which member of the band Steps has played Joseph in the musical *Joseph and the Amazing Technicolor Dreamcoat*?

24 Which Russian playwright wrote the plays *The Three Sisters* and *Uncle Vanya*?

25 From which Shakespeare play is the line, 'Cry, God for Harry! England and Saint George!'?

26 What is the name of the hit Monty Python musical that opened at the Palace Theatre London in 2006?

27 First staged in the UK in 2006, which musical tells the untold story of the Witches of Oz?

28 Which London theatre, situated off the Strand, opened in 1881 and is particularly associated with Gilbert and Sullivan?

29 By which stage name was the French actress Henriette-Rosine Bernard better known?

30 Which stage musical featured Michael Crawford and Sarah Brightman in the lead roles when it premiered in 1986?

31 Which US film star has been artistic director of London's Old Vic theatre since 2003?

32 Which song, from the musical *Sweet Charity*, begins with the line, 'The minute you walked in the joint'?

33 *Look Back in Anger* and *The Entertainer* were early successes for which twentieth-century British playwright?

34 The American 1940s Broadway hit play about two murderous old women is entitled *Arsenic and Old . . .* what?

35   Richard O'Brien played the character Riff-Raff in which musical theatre production?

36   Whose stage plays of *Educating Rita* and *Shirley Valentine* were later made into feature films?

37   The Broadway musical *Thoroughly Modern Millie* is set in which decade of the twentieth century?

38   The stage musical *Rent* is based on which Puccini opera?

39   In which stage musical does 'prisoner number 24601' feature?

40   Which play by Agatha Christie has been running in London's West End since 1952?

41   Which street in Manhattan, famous for its theatres, is nicknamed the Great White Way?

42   Which famous London theatre was home to the National Theatre from 1963 to 1976?

43   In 2004, which US actor played Randle P. McMurphy in the West End production of *One Flew Over the Cuckoo's Nest*?

44   What nationality is the popular composer Andrew Lloyd Webber?

45   Which Shakespearean tragic hero is also known as the 'Moor of Venice'?

46   Which pantomime features the characters Buttons, Dandini and two ugly sisters?

47   'Aquarius' is a song that features in which hippy musical theatre production?

48   In the theatre, what name is given to an afternoon performance of a play?

49   In a play by Edmond Rostand, which long-nosed French hero falls in love with Roxanne?

50   Which Lerner and Loewe stage musical concerns a fictional Scottish village that only appears every hundred years?

—————— *SET 33* **ACTORS AND ACTRESSES** ——————

1 Which US actress starred as Mirabelle alongside Steve Martin in his 2005 self-penned film *Shopgirl*?

2 In the 1998 film *Primary Colours*, which Hollywood actor starred as a US governor running for president?

3 Which 2004 film starred Michael Gambon, alongside Daniel Craig, as the gangster Eddie Temple?

4 Which veteran US actor played 'old' Number Two in the *Austin Powers* series of film comedies?

5 Which 1980 film comedy, set on a golf course, starred Bill Murray as a grounds keeper trying to exterminate gophers?

6 Which US actor played lawyer Sam Bowden in the 1962 film thriller *Cape Fear*?

7 Which 1991 film stars Kurt Russell and William Baldwin as firefighting brothers?

8 Which 1987 film starred Richard Dreyfuss and Emilio Estevez as cops staking out the home of a convict's ex-girlfriend?

9 Which Hollywood heart-throb and star of TV's *The West Wing* was born Robert Hepler Lowe in 1964?

10 In which 2002 British film does Jim, played by the actor Cillian Murphy, walk through a completely abandoned London?

11 In which decade of the twentieth century was the English film star Roger Moore born?

12 Glenda Jackson's first Best Actress Oscar was for her performance in which 1969 film?

13 Which British pop icon appeared in the 2006 film *The Prestige*?

14 Which deceased martial arts film star is to have a memorial theme park built in his south-east China ancestral home?

15 Which US actress, born Margarita Carmen Cansino, starred in the films *Gilda* and *The Lady from Shanghai*?

16 For which series of films were the actors Kenneth Williams and Sid James best known?

17 In which 2005 romantic comedy film did actress Diane Keaton star as Sybil Stone?

18 Which Dutch star of the 1982 film *Blade Runner* appeared in a series of TV adverts for Irish stout?

19 Which US actor directed the 2006 film *Rocky Balboa*?

20 Who played Baby Face in the film *Bugsy Malone* at age ten and Tony Casemore in TV's *Hotel Babylon* thirty years later?

21 Which British actor won an Oscar for his portrayal of Christy Brown in the 1989 film *My Left Foot*?

22 Which English character actor won an Oscar for his role as John Bayley in the 2001 film *Iris*?

23 *Goodness Had Nothing to Do with It* was the title of the 1959 autobiography of which notorious actress?

24 In 1996, actress Melanie Griffith married which Spanish actor?

25 'Here's another nice mess you've gotten me into' was the catchphrase of which US comedy film star?

26 Which Oscar-winner is the daughter of actress Phyllida Law?

27 Hollywood actress Kate Beckinsale is the daughter of which star of the TV sitcom *Porridge*?

28 Who was the actor husband of US actress Mary Pickford with whom she built the Hollywood mansion known as 'Pickfair'?

29 In which 1990 film comedy do Eric Idle and Robbie Coltrane play men who dress up as nuns in order to escape gangsters?

30 With which Hollywood actor did Katharine Hepburn have a well-known love affair for twenty-seven years?

31 In which country was movie heart-throb Colin Farrell born?

32 Which British actress played the title role in the 2005 film *Domino*?

33 In the *Harry Potter* series of films, which role has been played by Tom Felton?

34 Which comic actor directed and starred in the 1994 film *Staggered*, about the victim of a stag night prank?

35 Which English actress became engaged to director Tim Burton in 2001?

36 In which 1984 film did Tom Hanks play Walter Fielding, a recently married man struggling to fix his dilapidated house?

37 Who was the child star of the films *The Sixth Sense* and *AI: Artificial Intelligence*?

38 In how many *Superman* films did Christopher Reeve play the lead role?

39 In which Oscar-winning film did Robin Williams say, 'We read and write poetry because we are members of the human race'?

40 Actor Richard Kiel is best known for playing which character in two different Bond films?

41 Who won a Best Supporting Actress Oscar for a performance of less than eight minutes on screen in a 1998 film?

42 Which screen legend was born Marie Magdalene Dietrich in Berlin in 1901?

43 Which Oscar-winning British actress voiced the Queen in the film *Shrek 2*?

44 On New Year's Eve 1997, which British actress married US film director and producer Taylor Hackford?

45 In the 2005 film *Three*, which British actress plays Jennifer, the wife of Billy Zane's character, Jack?

46 In 2005, actress Michelle Williams starred in which Oscar-winning Ang Lee film?

47 Which French actress is famous for her role as Amélie Poulain in a 2001 film?

48 Which hellraising actor played the role of Athos in the 1973 film version of *The Three Musketeers*?

49 By what name is the Scottish actor born Thomas Connery better known?

50 Which Australian film star provided the voice of a penguin called Norma Jean in the 2006 animation *Happy Feet*?

────── SET 34 **BLOCKBUSTERS** ──────

1 In which 1965 film musical did Julie Andrews play the spirited young nun Maria?

2 Who played The Joker in the 1989 film *Batman*?

3 To which US city did the title character travel in the 1998 Hollywood film *Godzilla*?

4 What is the name of the second film in the original *Star Wars* trilogy released in 1980?

5 In two hit films, Cameron Diaz, Drew Barrymore and Lucy Liu are collectively known as what?

6 Which English actress starred in the 1997 film *Titanic*?

7 In the 1939 film *The Wizard of Oz*, what was the first name of the character played by Judy Garland?

8 In the Jim Carrey film *The Mask*, what colour did the lead character's face become when he put on the mask?

9 What type of fish is Nemo in the animated film *Finding Nemo*?

10 Who produced and directed the 1982 Oscar-winning film *Gandhi*?

11 In the 2002 film musical *Chicago*, which Welsh star played the character Velma Kelly?

12 In the 1993 film *The Firm*, what is the profession of Mitch McDeere?

13 Which US comedy actor was the voice of Donkey in the 2001 film animation *Shrek*?

14 Which action film star played Korben Dallas in the 1997 blockbuster *The Fifth Element*?

15 The 1998 film *Deep Impact* centred on which type of celestial body colliding with the Earth?

16 In the Harry Potter films, which actor succeeded the late Richard Harris in the role of Professor Albus Dumbledore?

17 The 2006 animation film *Happy Feet* centres around a community of which flightless birds?

18 Who played the little girl, Gertie, in the film *ET the Extra-Terrestrial*?

19 Which hit 1993 Steven Spielberg film is about scientists cloning dinosaurs to populate a theme park?

20 Which 2004 film animation directed by Brad Bird featured a family of undercover superheroes?

21 In the 2001 film *Ocean's Eleven*, the three targeted casinos were in which US city?

22 Which British actor, who appeared in TV's *The Office*, also featured in the hit film *Pirates of the Caribbean*?

23 Bill Pullman played the American President in which hit 1996 film about aliens invading Earth?

24 The line 'I'm the king of the world!' comes from which 1997 Leonardo DiCaprio film?

25 Which 1994 British film comedy featured the number one hit 'Love Is All Around' from the group Wet Wet Wet?

26 In 2005, actor Tom Cruise starred in which sci-fi film directed by Steven Spielberg?

27 Which British actor played a mutant called Magneto in the *X-Men* series of feature films?

28 Which 1990 US comedy film told the story of Kevin, a young boy left at home by mistake when his family flies to Paris?

29 In the 2006 Bond film *Casino Royale*, which actress played Vesper Lynd, the title character's love interest?

30 Which US comedy actor played film-maker Carl Denham in the 2005 film *King Kong*?

31 Which hit 1997 film drama featured an FBI agent and a criminal who swapped faces?

32 In the 1992 film *The Addams Family*, what colour was Morticia Addams's hair?

33 In which live action and animated 1988 film comedy is an animated rabbit accused of murder?

34 *Forrest Gump* and *Back to the Future* were hit films for which Hollywood director?

35 Which 2003 hit film comedy followed the lives of eight very different couples?

36 In the 2000 film *Gladiator*, which actor starred as Maximus?

37 In the 2006 film comedy *The Devil Wears Prada*, which US actress played the character of Andy Sachs?

38 Tom Hanks and Matt Damon starred as soldiers in which 1998 Oscar-winning Second World War film?

39 In the film *Ghostbusters*, what was the green ghost called?

40 Which 1994 film had the tagline, 'Life's greatest adventure is finding your place in the Circle of Life'?

41 US actress Liv Tyler starred alongside Ben Affleck and Billy Bob Thornton in which 1998 space drama?

42 Which American composer wrote the original scores for the films *Star Wars* and *ET the Extra-Terrestrial*?

43 In the blockbuster film *Notting Hill*, who played the character Anna Scott?

44 Which 2004 hit film featured Dennis Quaid as a climatologist trying to find a way to save the world from global warming?

45 Which actor played the character Morpheus in *The Matrix* trilogy?

46 In the 1995 film epic *Braveheart*, which French actress played the character of Princess Isabelle?

47 Which muscular hero was played by Sylvester Stallone in the 1982 film *First Blood*, and two further sequels?

48 Who played Colin Farrell's mother Olympias in the 2004 film *Alexander*?

49 The line 'I see dead people' comes from which 1999 Bruce Willis film?

50 Which Oscar-winning US actor played Lex Luthor in the 2006 film *Superman Returns*?

—————————— *SET 35* **CLASSIC FILM** ——————————

1 Which classic British car featured as a getaway vehicle in the 1969 crime comedy *The Italian Job*?

2 Which 1953 film, set in Hawaii during the Second World War, starred Burt Lancaster and Montgomery Clift?

3 Which 1941 classic film features a sled called 'Rosebud'?

4 In the 1984 film *Gremlins*, the three rules for the new pet were no food after midnight, no bright light, and no what?

5 The song 'Windmills Of Your Mind' came from which 1960s film?

6 By what name was the film comedian Daniel David Kaminsky better known?

7 In the 1973 film *Papillon*, which actor starred alongside Steve McQueen as fellow convict Louis Dega?

8 In the 1958 film *Frankenstein 1970*, which actor played Baron Victor von Frankenstein?

9 In which 1979 Franc Roddam film does Phil Daniels play a scooter-riding Jimmy Cooper?

10 Which 1994 movie set in a prison contains the line, 'Get busy livin', or get busy dyin''?

11 Which actor played geeky Louis Tully in the 1984 film *Ghostbusters*?

12 In the 1976 spoof gangster film *Bugsy Malone*, what was the name of the nightclub gangster owner?

13 In which 1987 film romance did Baby nervously say to Patrick Swayze's character, Johnny: 'I carried a watermelon'?

14 Which 1992 Sharon Stone film is famous for a controversial leg-crossing scene?

15 In both the stage and the film versions of *Grease*, what was the name of the high school?

16 In which 1988 comedy film set in New York did Tom Hanks play on a giant keyboard?

17 In the 1938 film *Angels with Dirty Faces,* which actor starred alongside James Cagney as the character Jim Frazier?

18 In the 1984 film *Splash,* what type of mythical creature did Daryl Hannah play?

19 In the 1951 film *A Streetcar Named Desire,* which British actress won an Oscar for her role as Blanche DuBois?

20 In the 1963 film musical *Summer Holiday,* which European city is the final destination of Cliff Richard and his friends?

21 Which classic 1973 British horror film was remade in 2006, starring Nicholas Cage?

22 In which 1955 film comedy do a gang of crooks pose as musicians to rent a house from the elderly Mrs Wilberforce?

23 Which British comedian played the toymaker in the 1968 film *Chitty Chitty Bang Bang*?

24 Which 1995 film thriller starred Kevin Spacey as the mysterious 'Verbal' Kint?

25 In which series of films did Carl Weathers play boxer Apollo Creed?

26 In which 1986 historical murder mystery did Sean Connery play a monk turned sleuth?

27 In which 1972 film, starring Burt Reynolds, do four friends go on a dangerous canoe trip through the US back-country?

28 The 1981 film *Das Boot* was set during which war?

29 The 1963 film *The Great Escape* was set during which war?

30 Which child star played the title role in the 1968 film *Oliver!*?

31 For which 1988 film did Dustin Hoffman win a Best Actor Oscar for his portrayal of Raymond Babbitt?

32 In the 1994 action film *Speed,* what speed must the bus not go below?

33 Complete the title of the 1968 horror film directed by Roman Polanski, *Rosemary's . . .* what?

34 In which 1970 disaster movie with an aerial theme did Burt Lancaster star alongside Dean Martin?

35 Which classic 1980s film featured the characters Mikey, Brand, Chunk, Mouth and Data?

36 In the 1977 film blockbuster *Star Wars*, which US actor played the character Han Solo?

37 Which 1964 film, based on a play by George Bernard Shaw, ends with the line, 'Eliza, where the devil are my slippers?'?

38 Jessica Tandy became the oldest Oscar-winning actress for her role in which 1989 film?

39 In a famous scene from the 1960 film *La Dolce Vita*, which Swedish actress bathed in Rome's Trevi Fountain?

40 Which Disney film features a toy maker called Gepetto?

41 Which Russian director made the hugely influential 1925 film *The Battleship Potemkin*?

42 In 2000, the film *Crouching Tiger, Hidden Dragon* was set in which country?

43 In 1927, which US actor and singer spoke and sang on the first sound film, *The Jazz Singer*?

44 Which actor played the role of Britt in the 1960 film *The Magnificent Seven*?

45 Which Bond character in the 1963 film *From Russia with Love* was famous for her poison-tipped shoes?

46 In the 1960 film thriller *Psycho*, what is the name of the motel managed by Norman Bates?

47 In the film *The Wizard of Oz*, in which fictional city does the wizard live?

48 In the 1956 film *The Searchers*, which US actor, famed for his cowboy portrayals, played Ethan Edwards?

49 In the 1950s, who was the director of the films *Sunset Bvd* and *Some Like It Hot*?

50 Which 1976 horror film stars Sissy Spacek as a girl with telekinetic powers?

─── SET 36 **AWARDS** ───

1 Who was nominated for a best director award at the 2006 Oscars for the film *Munich*?

2 Ang Lee won the Best Director award at the 2006 Oscars for which film?

3 Which film won the Best Picture Oscar in 2006?

4 Which actress was nominated for an Oscar for her performance as Ginger McKenna in the 1995 film *Casino*?

5 Make-up artist Rick Baker won his first Oscar for Best Make-Up for his work on which 1981 horror movie?

6 In 1996, which musical won both the Pulitzer Prize for Drama and four Tony awards for tackling the subject of HIV?

7 Given for distinguished achievement in the US theatre, by what name are the Antoinette Perry Awards better known?

8 Which two stars of *Jeeves and Wooster* won the first Perrier Award at the Edinburgh Fringe festival?

9 Which 1954 film won Marlon Brando his first Best Actor Oscar?

10 Which Irish poet won the Nobel Prize for Literature in 1995?

11 Who has won a Best Director Oscar four times, including for the 1940 film *The Grapes of Wrath*?

12 In 1988, who won a Grammy for Best Concept Music Video for 'Fat', a parody on Michael Jackson's 'Bad'?

13 Which US pop star's Grammy award-winning album was entitled *The Emancipation of Mimi*?

14 In 1957, which future US president won the Pulitzer Prize for History for his book *Profiles in Courage*?

15 Which Briton won a 2006 Tony Award for Leading Actor for his Broadway role in *The History Boys*?

16 In October 2006, Indian-born novelist Kiran Desai won which prestigious UK literary award?

17 Which 2000 Oscar-winning film had the tagline, 'What we do in life echoes in eternity'?

18 Whose first novel *Behind the Scenes at the Museum* won the Whitbread Book of the Year award in 1995?

19 Who was the first African-American actress to win the Oscar for Best Actress?

20 Which Hollywood star won a Best Actress Oscar for her role in the 2003 movie *Monster*?

21 Which 1991 Disney classic was the first animated film to be nominated for a Best Picture Oscar?

22 Which 1996 film, staring Kristin Scott Thomas, was adapted from a Michael Ondaajte novel and won nine Oscars?

23 At the 2006 British Independent Film Awards, which Dame was given a special award for film achievement?

24 At the 2004 Press Awards, which former newspaper editor did Jeremy Clarkson famously punch?

25 At the 1992 Oscar ceremony, which elderly actor famously performed one-armed press-ups?

26 In which creative field are the Ivor Novello Awards presented?

27 Which supermodel won the title of Model of the Year at the 2006 British Fashion Awards?

28 Reese Witherspoon won a 2006 Best Actress Oscar for her portrayal of June Carter in which hit movie?

29 At the 2006 World Music Awards in London, which male UK singer-songwriter won the award for Best New Artist?

30 Which 1993 Oscar-winning film has the line said by Itzhak Stern: 'The list is an absolute good. The list is life'?

31 Which author wrote the 1978 Booker Prize-winning novel entitled *The Sea, The Sea*?

32 Which controversial author won the 1995 Whitbread Novel Award with his novel *The Moor's Last Sigh*?

33 At the 2006 World Music Awards, which US pop diva won the award for Best Pop Artist?

34 In 1964, which French philosopher declined the Nobel Prize for Literature?

35 The plot of the 2004 Oscar-winning film *Million Dollar Baby* is based around which sport?

36 In 1990, which pop duo were forced to give up their Grammy award after revelations of lip synching?

37 Which Irish author won the Booker Prize for his 1993 novel *Paddy Clarke Ha Ha Ha*?

38 Which *Harry Potter* book won the 2001 Hugo Award?

39 For which 1981 film did Henry Fonda and Katharine Hepburn win the Best Actor and Actress Oscars?

40 Hollywood movie star Paul Newman won his only Best Actor Oscar for which 1986 film?

41 In October 2006, Turkish writer Orhan Pamuk won which prestigious international literature prize?

42 Which US actor won an Oscar for his role as Rod Tidwell in the 1996 film, *Jerry Maguire*?

43 Which novel, set during the American Civil War, won the 1937 Pulitzer Prize?

44 Which Wallace and Gromit film won the Best Film award at the 2006 Children's BAFTAs?

45 Who won a Golden Globe for his performance of the character Ray Say in the film *Little Voice*?

46 Born Riley King, which blues guitarist won a Grammy Lifetime Achievement Award in 1987?

47 Along with Matt Damon, which actor won a Best Screenplay Oscar for co-writing the film *Good Will Hunting*?

48 In 1998, which film director's Oscar acceptance speech included the line 'I'm king of the world'?

49 Which former South African archbishop was awarded the Nobel Peace Prize in 1984?

50 Which Hollywood star won a Best Actor Oscar for his performance as Melvin Udall in the 1997 movie *As Good as It Gets*?

——————— *SET 37* **FOOD AND DRINK** ———————

1 Which fruit is the main ingredient of Melba sauce?

2 Which US city is nicknamed Beantown for its association with baked beans?

3 Known as the 'herb of the angels', angelica is a member of which herb family?

4 In November 2006, which British celebrity chef opened his first New York restaurant in the London NYC Hotel?

5 Feltham First, Kelvedon Wonder and Sugar Snap are varieties of which vegetable?

6 A nectarine is a smooth-skinned variety of which fruit?

7 In the title of a TV series, how were celebrity cooks Clarissa Dickson-Wright and Jennifer Paterson known?

8 The Chablis district of Burgundy makes high quality white wine from which grape variety?

9 Gaelic coffee is coffee traditionally served with cream and which alcoholic component?

10 A French delicacy, which nut is iced in a *marron glacé*?

11 What name is given to the type of plastic bowls that were introduced by American chemist Earl Tupper in the 1940s?

12 Which light, fluffy confection made from coloured spun sugar is usually held on a stick?

13 Which English county is the home of the lamb and potato dish known as 'hotpot'?

14 In the US, with which confectionery is the name Ghirardelli most closely associated?

15 The white wine retsina comes from which European country?

16 In France, a charcuterie is a shop that traditionally sells meat taken from which animal?

17 In the UK, the sour boiled sweets, popular with children, are known as Acid . . . what?

18 Which city in Israel gives its name to an artichoke that belongs to the sunflower family?

19 Which Welsh 'bread' is made from a type of seaweed, mixed with oatmeal and fried in flat cakes?

20 The Benedictine monk Dom Perignon is believed to be associated with the development of which French sparkling drink?

21 Gubbeen and Cashel Blue are cheeses originating in which country?

22 Of what is Lapsang Souchong a variety?

23 Which English lakeland town is famous for its mint cake?

24 *Fromage* is the French word for which food?

25 The vineyards that make the French wines called Châteauneuf-du-Pape and Hermitage are in the valley of which river?

26 Which fish is traditionally an ingredient of a Caesar salad?

27 What flavour is the liqueur known as Curaçao?

28 Which village, in the Mendip Hills in Somerset, has given its name to a famous cheese?

29 Which fruit has a variety known as Bartlett?

30 The Bellini cocktail was invented in the famous Harry's Bar of which Italian city?

31 Which Portuguese island in the Atlantic gives its name to a type of fortified wine that is made there?

32 What is the name of the sweet bun, decorated with a cross, traditionally eaten at Easter?

33 In Britain, which beef product is preserved in brine, chopped, pressed and sold in tins?

34 Which TV chef owns the Michelin starred 'Fat Duck' restaurant in Bray?

35 The wine 'vinho verde' comes from which European country?

36 In food terms, what name is given to the V-shaped bone between the neck and breast of a cooked bird?

37 Popular in Mediterranean cuisine, what is the English word for *calamari*?

38 In which European country did the dish fondue originate?

39 Which female cookery writer is credited with introducing Mediterranean food to Britain after the Second World War?

40 What is the common name for the green vegetable that is sometimes called 'ladies' fingers', used in Indian cuisine?

41 To which group of animals does whitebait belong?

42 Which herb is a symbol of remembrance?

43 What does the word *dolce* on an Italian bottle of wine mean?

44 The Spanish festival of 'La Tomatina' is a battle involving throwing which fruit?

45 In the UK how are fava beans more commonly known?

46 By what name is the sauce Crème Anglaise more commonly known in Britain?

47 Which vegetable is served with or added to a dish that is described as 'Parmentier'?

48 In the food industry, what do the letters GM stand for?

49 The small portable brazier for heating and cooking food, known as the hibachi, is originally from which Asian country?

50 Which citrus fruit is traditionally added to make a 'vodka gimlet'?

———————————— *SET 38* **FOOTBALL** ————————————

1 Which Premiership soccer club has a station on the Piccadilly line of the London Underground named after it?

2 In October 2006, who was the first forty-year-old to score a goal in the Premiership?

3 At which cricket ground was the first FA Cup final played in 1872?

4 In 2002, whom did Mick McCarthy replace as manager of the Republic of Ireland national football team?

5 In 2006, which former Director General of the BBC became non-executive chairman of Brentford Football Club?

6   What was the iconic architectural feature of the old Wembley Stadium?

7   Which Lancashire town has a football club with the nickname 'Stanley'?

8   In 2002, Victoria Beckham challenged which English football team over the rights to her 'posh' nickname?

9   Former Chelsea and Newcastle United coach Ruud Gullit played international football for which country?

10   By which acronym is the 'Fédération Internationale de Football Association' better known?

11   The name of which spice is used in football as a term for playing the ball between an opponent's legs?

12   Which Premiership football team is nicknamed 'The Hornets'?

13   Upton Park is the home ground of which London football club?

14   For which European country did Peter Schmeichel play international football?

15   How many feet off the ground is the crossbar of the goalposts in senior football?

16   In 1923, the FA Cup final was held in which stadium for the first time?

17   Which English city has football grounds called Hillsborough and Bramall Lane?

18   The Spanish football club Real Madrid traditionally play at home in a kit that is predominantly which colour?

19   Which Scottish football club plays its home matches at Pittodrie?

20   Which Spanish football club won the European Cup final on the first five occasions it was held?

21   Which song, sung by David Baddiel and Frank Skinner, was the anthem for the England football team's Euro '96 campaign?

22   In 2006, Martin O'Neill joined which West Midlands football club as manager?

23   In 2006, Paul Scholes made his 500th appearance for which football club?

24 Which Merseyside Premiership football team's home strip is royal blue shirts?

25 In the 2002 FIFA Football World Cup, which South American nation knocked England out of the tournament?

26 In June 2003, England footballer David Beckham agreed a four-year deal with which Spanish club?

27 Held in France, the 1998 FIFA World Cup was won by which European nation?

28 Which German footballer was the first to win the FIFA World Cup both as a player and as a manager?

29 Bobby Moore played for which London football club throughout the 1960s?

30 Which Premiership football team is nicknamed the 'Villains'?

31 Which ex-footballer was the German team head coach during the 2006 FIFA World Cup?

32 Alex Ferguson won the European Cup Winners' Cup in 1983 as manager of which Scottish football club?

33 Which football team won the Scottish Premier League in April 2006?

34 Which Premiership football club signed Andriy Shevchenko from AC Milan in 2006?

35 Which English city has one football club known as County, and another called Forest?

36 Which London football club won the FA Cup in 1988 with a shock victory over Liverpool in the final?

37 During the 2006 FIFA World Cup, which team did Marcello Lippi coach?

38 Ajax are a leading football club based in which Dutch city?

39 Craven Cottage is the home ground of which London football club?

40 Brian Clough twice managed which football club to victory in the European Cup?

41 In the England football team's 5–1 victory over Germany in 2001, which England player scored a hat-trick?

42 The footballer Cristiano Ronaldo plays for which European country?

43 In the 1986 FIFA Football World Cup, which Argentinian credited 'The Hand of God' for a goal he scored against England?

44 Which London football club moved to the Emirates Stadium in 2006?

45 During the 2006 FIFA Football World Cup, who was England's manager?

46 'Becks' is the nickname of which former England football captain?

47 In which country will the 2010 Football World Cup be held?

48 'Gazza' is the nickname of which former England football player?

49 What nationality is Chelsea Football Club manager José Mourinho?

50 In 2004, England footballer Wayne Rooney left Everton to join which club?

——————— SET 39 THE WORLD OF SPORT ———————

1 In 1966, who was the first player ever to score a hat-trick in a World Cup final?

2 In which city will the 2012 Olympic Games be held?

3 The St Moritz Tobogganing Club races on which famous ice run?

4 In tennis, what term is used to describe a score of forty points each in a game?

5 The England cricketer Andrew Flintoff plays for which county?

6 The 1974 Zaire boxing match between Muhammad Ali and George Foreman was nicknamed 'The Rumble in the . . .' what?

7 Which Olympic sport requires competitors to vault over a horse?

8 Which nation did England beat to win the 2003 Rugby World Cup?

9 With which sport is Lindsay Davenport most closely associated?

10 The sport of sumo wrestling originated in which country?

11 Which Gloucestershire spa town is home to the famous annual Gold Cup horse race?

12 How many players compete in an equestrian polo team?

13 In which European country was the jockey Frankie Dettori born?

14 How many players are there on a women's lacrosse team?

15 The name Prince Naseem is most closely associated with which sport?

16 In 1976, which British figure-skater won the country's first Olympic Gold in that sport?

17 For which country did Imran Khan captain at cricket?

18 Which nation will host the 2007 Rugby World Cup?

19 In 2005, which England cricketer was voted BBC Sports Personality of the Year?

20 In both the 1980 and 1984 Olympics, which British athlete claimed decathlon gold medals?

21 In which sport is the America's Cup contested?

22 New Zealand's national rugby team is better known by what nickname?

23 Sylvester Stallone and which boxing legend present the boxing reality show *The Contender*?

24 The Harlem Globetrotters played their first game in which sport in 1927?

25 Which high-speed vehicles are raced during the Isle of Man TT races?

26 Built in time to hold the 1970 Commonwealth Games, in which Scottish city is the Meadowbank Stadium?

27 At which distance did Sally Gunnell win her hurdling gold medal at the 1992 Olympics?

28 In the UK, the Lonsdale Belt is a prize awarded in which sport?

29 For which Wimbledon tennis title is the champion awarded the Venus Rosewater Dish?

30 In which sport is Spain's Sergio Garcia a leading competitor?

31 With which sport is Ian Botham most closely associated?

32 With which sport is Zinedine Zidane most closely associated?

33 In which sport was American Lance Armstrong a leading competitor?

34 Which Spanish driver won the 2006 Formula 1 World Champion title?

35 How many metres in length is an Olympic-sized swimming pool?

36 In the 1980s, Eddie 'The Eagle' Edwards became a household name in which Olympic winter sport?

37 The US baseball team called the Yankees is based in which city?

38 During the 1990s, Russia's Alexander Popov was a dominating figure in which Olympic sport?

39 In 1997, Mike Tyson infamously bit off part of which boxer's ear during a title fight?

40 As well as showing plays, the Crucible Theatre, Sheffield is famous for competitions of which indoor sport?

41 In which country did the sport of Gaelic football originate?

42 Which 'C' is the name given to the electronic line judge at Wimbledon?

43 In cricket, what do the initials 'MCC' stand for?

44 Ireland's Aiden O'Brien is one of the leading figures in which sport?

45 How many coloured rings are there on the Olympic flag?

46 In 1975, who was the first African-American man to win the Wimbledon singles championship?

47 Which oath is taken by one athlete from the host country on behalf of all athletes at the start of the Olympic Games?

48 The cricketer Shane Warne plays for which country?

49 In the 2004 Olympic Games, which British athlete won double track gold in the women's 800m and 1500m?

50 With which football club did George Best win the 1968 European Cup?

———————— SET 40 **SPORTING HEROES** ————————

1 In World Wrestling, who is known as 'Stone Cold'?

2 Which American won the women's singles title at Wimbledon eight times between 1927 and 1938?

3 Which Scottish golfer has won seven successive European Order of Merits?

4 During the 1970s, Annemarie Moser-Pröll of Austria dominated which sport?

5 Which Panamanian world champion boxer had the nickname 'Hands of Stone'?

6 Which US cyclist won the Tour de France in 1986, 1989 and 1990?

7 Which British driver never won the Formula 1 World Championship but was runner-up four years in a row in the 1950s?

8 Which rider has the record for being the National Hunt Champion Jockey on the most occasions?

9 At the 1980 Olympic Games, which British athlete won the gold medal in the 100m?

10 In 1974, which runner broke the 3,000m world record and won the BBC Sports Personality of the Year award?

11 Victorian sporting hero Fred Archer dominated which sport with thirteen years of consecutive titles?

12 In 1985, which Irish boxer defeated Eusebio Pedroza to win the world featherweight title?

13 Which former World Darts champion is nicknamed the 'Viking'?

14 Famous for his exploits in the 1920s and 1930s, what breed of dog was Mick the Miller?

15 What type of sports ball did Nolan Ryan once throw at a record speed of over 100 miles per hour?

16 In 1984, which duo won BBC Sports Personality of the Year award, the first time it had been won jointly by two people?

17 Which world heavyweight boxing champion of the 1970s was nicknamed 'Smokin' Joe'?

18 Which left-handed American golfer won the 2006 US Masters?

19 For which country has swimmer Ian Thorpe won several Olympic titles?

20 In which sport has Peter Nicol been ranked number one in the world, and played for both England and Scotland?

21 Which British showjumping family has international riders called John, Michael, Robert, William and Ellen?

22 What is the nationality of cross-country skier Bjorn Daehlie, who won eight gold medals at the Winter Olympics in the 1990s?

23 Which famous jockey's only win in the Epsom Derby came in 1953 on Pinza?

24 Which Austrian skiing star was nicknamed the 'Herminator'?

25 In 1977, who did Virginia Wade defeat in the Ladies' Singles final at Wimbledon?

26 In the 2004 Paralympics, which British athlete won two gold medals in wheelchair events?

27 After recovering from cancer, jockey Bob Champion rode which horse to win the 1981 Grand National?

28 Which boxer became the youngest Heavyweight World Champion when he won the title in 1986?

29 Which legendary manager of Manchester United retired in 1969?

30 Which British driver won the 1992 Formula 1 World Championship?

31 During nineteen days in 1985, which British athlete broke world records in the 1500m, 2000m and Mile?

32 In which sport was Canadian Wayne Gretzky known simply as 'The Great One'?

33 In October 2006, Liverpudlian Beth Tweddle won Britain's first ever World Championship gold medal in which sport?

34 Which Olympic rower famously said, 'If anyone sees me near a boat again they have my permission to shoot me'?

35 In 2005, which British woman became the fastest person to sail solo non-stop round the world?

36 The football World Cup has been won a record five times by which nation?

37 In 1929, three-times Wimbledon champion Fred Perry won the world title in which other sport?

38 What was the nationality of track athlete Paavo Nurmi who won nine gold medals in three Olympic Games in the 1920s?

39 In 1996, which British golfer came from six shots behind Greg Norman to win the US Masters?

40 In the 1960 Olympic Games, Anita Lonsborough won a gold medal for Britain in which sport?

41 Which jockey won the Epsom Derby on the horses Grundy, Golden Fleece and Quest for Fame?

42 Which heavyweight boxing champion earned the nickname 'The Louisville Lip' for his outspoken personality?

43 In 1995, Scotsman Colin McRae was world champion in which form of motorsport?

44 With which US sport are the names David Wright and Willie Randolph most associated?

45 What nationality is the tennis player, winner of the 2001 Wimbledon singles title, Goran Ivanisevic?

46 In 1980, which country did Bill Beaumont captain to win the Grand Slam in Rugby Union?

47 In the Victorian era, the Renshaw twins dominated which sport?

48 Which Irish cyclist won the Tour de France in 1987?

49 In which sport did US player Ben Hogan win nine major championships?

50 At the 1976 Winter Olympics, which Austrian skier won the men's downhill title?

Part 4
In the Spotlight

SOMETIMES PEOPLE give the silliest answers when they're on the spot. Faced with a full studio and our panel of celebrity quiz whizzes, are you sure you wouldn't do the same?

Q: According to the nursery rhyme, little girls are made of sugar and spice and what?
A: *Jelly Delights*

Q: The Essex coast lies on which sea?
A: *Southend-on-Sea*

Q: The four Gospels of the New Testament are Matthew, Mark, Luke and what?
A: *Harry*

Q: How many letters in the word five?
A: *Five*

Q: Pug, Pointer and Pekinese are all breeds of which animal?
A: *Penguins? Birds? Fishes? I really don't know.*

Q: Who composed Handel's *Water Music*?
A: *Beethoven*

Q: What is the penultimate letter of the alphabet?
A: *A*

Q: What does the 'G' stand for in 'G & T'?
A: *Guinness*

Q: Which animal is often described as 'the ship of the desert'?
A: *Rat*

Q: In which city is *Casablanca* set?
A: *Tangiers*

Q: Finish the title of the 1980s song 'Last Night A DJ . . .' what?
A: *Swam*

Q: In the tale 'The Princess and the Pea' what did the queen put under the mattress?
A: *A ring*

Q: Who is the mother of model and actress Elizabeth Jagger?
A: *Elizabeth Taylor*

Q: Complete the saying – 'One man's meat is another man's . . .' what?
A: *Vegetable*

Q: Which member of the bear family is white but has black eye patches, ears, legs, feet, chest and shoulders?
A: *Polar bear*

Q: How many stars are there on the Union Jack?
A: *Six*

Q: What type of food is a macadamia?
A: *A sausage*

Q: A 'stinking bishop' is a type of what?
A: *Cocktail . . . no idea . . . an insect . . . I've seriously got no idea . . . skunk?*

Q: Who is Elizabeth Windsor?
A: *Is she an actress?*

Q: Who is Elizabeth Windsor?
A: *A dinner lady*

Q: Maris Piper is a type of what?
A: *Cleaning equipment*

Q: Who wrote Handel's *Messiah*?
A: *Jane Austen*

Q: How many legs does a spider have?
A: *One . . . nine . . . never really counted how many legs a spider has.*

Q: In the children's nursery rhyme, which small carnivorous mammal is said to 'pop'?
A: *Tiger*

Q: In the *Mrs Merton Show* who was asked, 'What first attracted you to the millionaire Paul Daniels'?
A: *Anne Robinson*

Q: What type of boot is named after the victorious general at the Battle of Waterloo?
A: *Ugg Boot*

Q: 'A, p, e' is an anagram of which tiny vegetable?
A: *Pie*

Q: How long did the Six Day War between Egypt and Israel last?
A: *Four (days)*

Q: In which US city is *LA Law* set?
A: *San Francisco*

Q: Complete the phrase, 'Never look a gift horse in the . . .' what?
A: *Eye*

Q: What type of animal is Dogmatix?
A: *A sheep*

Q: What is a Maris Piper?
A: *Yer one from Doctor Who*

Q: Who wrote Shakespeare's 'Macbeth'?
A: *Hamlet*

Q: Which invaders of Gaul are the enemies of the cartoon character Asterix?
A: *The Klingons*

Q: In Greek mythology, the Gorgon Medusa's hair was made up of which creatures?
A: *Cows*

Q: Which word connects a salad ingredient and the name of a steam locomotive built by George Stephenson?
A: *Tomato*

Q: In dating, what does the abbreviation GSOH stand for?
A: *Get Some Over Here*

Part 5
Answers

PART 1 The Auditions Answers

Under 25s SET 1

1 Majorca
2 J. K. Rowling
3 Twelve
4 Robot Wars
5 Robert Burns
6 Giant Panda
7 Blue
8 Tea
9 Michael Owen
10 Notting Hill

Under 25s 2

1 Reese Witherspoon
2 Plumbing
3 Vincent van Gogh
4 Prince Harry
5 Rugby Union
6 Warren
7 Zebra
8 George Michael
9 Conservative
10 Cat Deeley

Under 25s SET 3

1 Eight
2 Jim Carrey
3 Italy
4 William I
5 Moses
6 Scotland
7 Vodka
8 Blur
9 Garage
10 Mr T

Under 25s SET 4

1 Moon
2 Weasel
3 Blue Peter
4 English
5 United States of America
6 Jackie Chan
7 Dishwasher
8 Gorillaz
9 The Alamo
10 Belfast

Under 25s SET 5

1 Jamaica
2 Live and Kicking
3 George Frideric Handel
4 Poseidon
5 White
6 Scratchings
7 Outkast
8 Pi
9 Flies
10 Jamie Foxx

Under 25s SET 6

1 Pink
2 Roses
3 Snooker
4 The Little Mermaid
5 Harp
6 Wales
7 Abraham Lincoln
8 The Royle Family
9 Alkaline
10 Poison

Under 25s SET 7

1 Daleks
2 Snicket
3 Equilateral
4 Julie Andrews
5 White
6 Flour
7 British
8 Art nouveau
9 Cairo
10 Dog

Under 25s SET 8

1 Antarctica
2 Euro
3 Real Madrid
4 Sixteenth
5 Youth Hostel Association
6 Five
7 New York
8 Gary Rhodes
9 Pinocchio
10 Alan Davies

Under 25s SET 9

1 Pablo Picasso
2 Anfield
3 Boomerang
4 Cleopatra
5 David Blaine
6 Gin
7 British prime minister
8 Robbie Coltrane
9 Ronan Keating
10 The Lost Boys

Under 25s Set 10
1 France
2 Four
3 Italy
4 EastEnders
5 All Saints
6 Carbon monoxide
7 Gary Kemp
8 Rachel Weisz
9 Peter Stringfellow
10 Superman

Under 25s Set 11
1 Take That
2 Birmingham
3 Tree
4 Halle Berry
5 Barcelona
6 Gladiators
7 Pocahontas
8 Buff
9 The Pope
10 Pub

Under 25s Set 12
1 Kelly
2 Steven Gerrard
3 Latitude
4 The Colosseum
5 Two
6 Rum
7 Rafael Nadal
8 Cardiff
9 Love Actually
10 Monday

Under 25s Set 13
1 Love You
2 Strawberry
3 Sherwood Forest
4 Margaret Thatcher
5 Rio de Janeiro
6 Red
7 UEFA
8 John Cleese
9 Peaches Geldof
10 Spooks

Under 25s Set 14
1 Kylie Minogue
2 Back to the Future
3 Balmoral
4 Motorcycling
5 Knock
6 William Shakespeare
7 Hypothermia
8 Rosé
9 Dame Helen Mirren
10 Ruby Allen

Under 25s Set 15
1 Sugababes
2 Shoulder blade
3 Saddle
4 Rugrats
5 Bill Gates
6 Ligament
7 France
8 Jennifer Lopez
9 Punnet
10 Potato

Under 25s Set 16
1 Braille
2 George W. Bush
3 Atomic Kitten
4 Feet
5 Inflation
6 Stalactite
7 Chicken
8 Ireland
9 Gwyneth Paltrow
10 Neighbours

Under 25s Set 17
1 Leo
2 Steps
3 The Truman Show
4 A pea
5 Toilet
6 Victoria Cross
7 Wayne Rooney
8 Roadrunner
9 Steven
10 Tangerine

Under 25s Set 18
1 Bob the Builder
2 Red
3 Massachusetts
4 Four
5 Charles Darwin
6 Alsatian
7 Malaria
8 Kate Moss
9 Walk the Line
10 Oprah Winfrey

Under 25s SET 19

1 Prague
2 Caterpillar
3 Aristocats
4 Ant and Dec
5 Joey Tribbiani
6 Karl
7 Florence Nightingale
8 Heart
9 Moguls
10 Nicole Kidman

Under 25s SET 20

1 'N SYNC
2 Matthew Pinsent
3 Victoria and Albert Museum
4 Loch Ness
5 Che Guevara
6 Spanish
7 Water
8 Chugger
9 Elle Macpherson
10 Peter Kay

Under 25s SET 21

1 Trent
2 Greece
3 Thirty-one
4 Barking
5 Charles Darwin
6 Edinburgh
7 Jennifer Lopez
8 Dido
9 Barbara Windsor
10 Christopher Eccleston

Under 25s SET 22

1 Destiny's Child
2 Bamboo
3 Aberdeen
4 Floor
5 Sex and the City
6 New York
7 Flute
8 Nelson Mandela
9 Squeak
10 Nicole Kidman

Under 25s SET 23

1 Achilles
2 Tennis
3 George Michael
4 Johnny Depp
5 New Zealand
6 Whale
7 Two
8 Eiffel Tower
9 Big Brother
10 Philip

Under 25s SET 24

1 Indiana Jones
2 Green
3 JFK
4 Steps
5 Isambard Kingdom Brunel
6 Switzerland
7 The Simpsons
8 'The Hokey Cokey'
9 Michael Jordan
10 Penélope Cruz

Under 25s SET 25

1 Samson
2 Wales
3 Rudolph
4 Acute
5 All Saints
6 Vegan
7 Own goal
8 Paris Hilton
9 Potato
10 Arachnophobia

Under 25s SET 26

1 Nicole Kidman
2 Robert the Bruce
3 Ring a Ring o'Roses
4 Feet
5 Republic of Ireland
6 Yorkshire
7 Teri Hatcher
8 American
9 Matthew Perry
10 Theo Walcott

Under 25s SET 27

1 Julia Roberts
2 Ronald Reagan
3 Goldilocks
4 Royal Mint
5 ER
6 Take That
7 Football
8 California
9 Teri Hatcher
10 Toast

Under 25s SET 28

1 CND
2 Queen Elizabeth the Queen Mother
3 Shakespeare
4 China
5 Green
6 Chicken
7 Futurama
8 Bail
9 Gareth Gates
10 The Rock

Under 25s 29

1 Spice Girls
2 Elizabeth I
3 Badger
4 Martina Navratilova
5 Tarot
6 United Nations
7 TARDIS
8 Egypt
9 Pamela Anderson
10 Johnny

Under 25s SET 30

1 Six
2 Bermuda Triangle
3 Prime number
4 Animal Farm
5 Madonna
6 Sleep
7 Semi-final
8 Star Trek
9 Poaching
10 The Vicar of Dibley

Under 25s SET 31

1 Two
2 Radiohead
3 Tweedledee
4 Beijing
5 Patsy Palmer
6 USA
7 Ocean's Twelve
8 Pea
9 Chris Martin
10 Thursday

Under 25s 32

1 Penny Black
2 Charlotte's Web
3 Neon
4 S Club 7
5 Rome
6 Dog
7 April
8 Ear lobe
9 Matthew
10 £5

Under 25s SET 33

1 Scotland
2 Alfred the Great
3 Saudi Arabia
4 Bicycle
5 Four
6 Lucy Liu
7 Hairdressing
8 Ten
9 Red
10 Dead Poets Society

Under 25s SET 1

1 Wales
2 South America
3 'Dancing Queen'
4 Dijon
5 Stephen Hendry
6 Vertebrate
7 Renaissance
8 Two
9 Claudia Winkleman
10 Lock, Stock and Two Smoking Barrels

Under 25s SET 2

1 Michael Douglas
2 One
3 Pocahontas
4 Italy
5 Peter Kay
6 Earl Grey
7 Amsterdam
8 Horse
9 Sigmund Freud
10 Bullseye

Under 25s SET 3

1 Miss Marple
2 Snakes
3 S
4 Football
5 Tea
6 Aberdeen
7 Coco Chanel
8 Typhoon
9 Will Young
10 Japan

25–40 SET 4

1 Wardrobe
2 Mullet
3 Johnny Depp
4 Harvard
5 London
6 Omega-3
7 Fifteen
8 Take That
9 Wales
10 Sue Johnston

25–40 SET 5

1 Edwina Currie
2 Melon
3 Canary Islands
4 Manchester United
5 Four
6 Roseanne
7 Christina Aguilera
8 The Magnificent Seven
9 American
10 Draco Malfoy

25–40 SET 6

1 London Bridge
2 Nell Gwyn
3 Prince Charles
4 Manchester United
5 Susan Sarandon
6 Sunday
7 Cologne
8 Adelaide
9 Endeavour
10 Justin Timberlake

25–40 SET 7

1 The Office
2 Al fresco
3 World Cup
4 Pole vault
5 M
6 Leeds
7 Automobile Association
8 Simply Red
9 Coventry
10 German

25–40 SET 8

1 Alicia Keys
2 Holby City
3 Thistle
4 2008
5 Gloucester
6 Science fiction
7 Milan
8 Ballet
9 Citric
10 Hugh Jackman

25–40 SET 9

1 Rodney
2 EastEnders
3 Radio 3
4 Brighton and Hove Albion
5 Snow White and the Seven Dwarfs
6 Great Bear
7 Charles I
8 Damon Albarn
9 Grapefruit
10 German

25–40 SET 10

1 Cliff Richard
2 Dublin
3 Wonder Woman
4 Scotland
5 Dame Vera Lynn
6 Hansard
7 Randy Crawford
8 Don Quixote
9 Spain
10 Bonnie and Clyde

25–40 SET 11

1 Jonathan Ross
2 Peter Sellers
3 Olympic Games
4 Bakewell
5 Michael Jackson
6 Head
7 King Arthur
8 David Lloyd George
9 Red
10 Gesundheit

25–40 SET 12

1 Gloria Estefan
2 Dumbo
3 Kenya
4 Demi Moore
5 Canute
6 Ice hockey
7 Architecture
8 Romans
9 Phil Mitchell
10 Front

25–40 Set 13

1 Dame Edna Everage
2 Dad's Army
3 Elizabeth I
4 Lance Armstrong
5 Repetitive Strain Injury
6 London
7 Bern
8 Daniel Bedingfield
9 Viz
10 St Elmo's Fire

25–40 Set 14

1 Dr John H. Watson
2 Tyra Banks
3 Islas Malvinas
4 Aqua
5 Damon Hill
6 Alf Garnett
7 Neil Armstrong
8 Home
9 Beyoncé Knowles
10 EasyJet

25–40 Set 15

1 Sylvester Stallone
2 Mozart
3 Torquay
4 New York
5 Mary
6 Henry VIII
7 Manchester
8 Great Barrier Reef
9 Minnie Driver
10 Gordon Brown

25–40 Set 16

1 Jessica Simpson
2 Doncaster
3 Cats
4 Monday
5 Ludwig van Beethoven
6 USA
7 Sir Thomas More
8 Rice
9 Tokyo
10 Abba

25–40 Set 17

1 Woody Allen
2 Romeo and Juliet
3 China
4 The Netherlands
5 Persona non grata
6 Blue
7 Sodium
8 Kate Bush
9 Robert
10 Curling

25–40 Set 18

1 Madonna
2 Bewitched!
3 Tequila
4 Japan
5 Channel Tunnel
6 Scorpio
7 Pacific Ocean
8 Robbie Coltrane
9 Texas
10 John Le Carré

25–40 Set 19

1 Stiletto
2 George Michael
3 Beavis
4 Tina Turner
5 Horse riding
6 The Beatles
7 Switzerland
8 Massachusetts
9 Niagara Falls
10 John Major

25–40 Set 20

1 Nelly Furtado
2 Les Dawson
3 Out of Africa
4 Galaxy
5 White
6 Sundial
7 Apple
8 Black Sea
9 ASBO
10 Tennis

25–40 Set 21

1 Eye
2 Crèche
3 Sven-Göran Eriksson
4 Kirsten Dunst
5 Edinburgh
6 Madonna
7 George Orwell
8 Sydney
9 Physical Education
10 Bruce Forsyth

25–40 SET 22

1 Rudyard Kipling
2 MI5
3 Clyde
4 Sandra Bullock
5 10 Downing Street
6 Dolly Parton
7 Pasta
8 Golf
9 Quarantine
10 Catwalk

25–40 SET 23

1 Avocado
2 Cliff Richard
3 Chitty Chitty Bang Bang
4 The Vicar of Dibley
5 Tiger Woods
6 Prince Harry
7 Venice
8 Jackie
9 Fish
10 Japan

25–40 SET 24

1 USA
2 Romeo and Juliet
3 Spain
4 Liverpool
5 William I
6 Judaism
7 German
8 Edinburgh Castle
9 Omnivore
10 The Beatles

25–40 SET 25

1 Friday
2 Pavement
3 Travis
4 Golf
5 Heart
6 Scotland
7 June
8 Dame
9 Bob Holness
10 Brad Pitt

25–40 SET 26

1 Deborah Harry
2 Sharon
3 Oakley
4 Moby Dick
5 Houses of Parliament
6 Bob Monkhouse
7 Demi Moore
8 Straw
9 Ninety minutes
10 Mediterranean Sea

25–40 SET 27

1 Corgi
2 Mark Thatcher
3 Bee
4 Changing Rooms
5 Leo Tolstoy
6 Swedish
7 Mike Myers
8 Argentina
9 Dire Straits
10 Spain

25–40 SET 28

1 The Three Musketeers
2 Pet Shop Boys
3 Fourteen
4 Red
5 Robin Williams
6 Elizabeth I
7 1980s
8 François Mitterrand
9 George W. Bush
10 Hallowe'en

25–40 SET 29

1 Queen Victoria
2 Morocco
3 1,000
4 Apple
5 Dog
6 Ostrich
7 Still
8 Plot
9 My Fair Lady
10 Queen

25–40 SET 30

1 Whale
2 Eleven
3 French Franc
4 Italy
5 Morgan Freeman
6 The First World War
7 Song
8 Dog
9 Dandelion
10 EastEnders

25–40 SET 31

1 R Kelly
2 Antarctica
3 Theatre
4 Red
5 Lawrence Of Arabia
6 Sixteen
7 Mark Twain
8 Horse
9 Diana Ross
10 Wombles

25–40 SET 32

1 Air Force One
2 Japan
3 Aintree
4 David Hasselhoff
5 Greenwich Mean Time
6 King Lear
7 Mariah Carey
8 Compact Disc
9 Five o'clock
10 Minnie Driver

25–40 SET 33

1 Choux pastry
2 John F. Kennedy
3 King Kong
4 August
5 Louisiana
6 Cheshire
7 Haka
8 Antlers
9 Minder
10 Flute

25–40 SET 34

1 The Shining
2 Chickpea
3 Leeds
4 Bullfighting
5 Phil Collins
6 Famous Five
7 Harrods
8 Intelligence Quotient
9 Bon voyage
10 Leonardo da Vinci

40+ SET 1

1 Seven
2 Franklin D. Roosevelt
3 Pakistan
4 Darlington
5 Bayeux Tapestry
6 J. R. R. Tolkien
7 George Gershwin
8 Scotland
9 David Bowie
10 Giant

40+ SET 2

1 Shergar
2 Bishop
3 Istanbul
4 The Second World War
5 Dolly Parton
6 Pacific Ocean
7 Soldiers
8 Patrick
9 Kidney
10 Andy Warhol

40+ SET 3

1 Uranus
2 Mrs Slocombe
3 Home
4 John Cleese
5 New Zealand
6 Italy
7 Anna Pavlova
8 Michael Crichton
9 Duchess
10 'Candle In The Wind'

40+ SET 4

1 Anna Ford
2 Carrot
3 Unicorn
4 Rugby Union
5 Giuseppe Verdi
6 China
7 North Atlantic Treaty Organization
8 Galway
9 Executor
10 Charles I

40+ SET 5

1 American
2 The A-Team
3 Egypt
4 Peter Piper
5 Francis Chichester
6 Lawrence of Arabia
7 Rum
8 Oedipus
9 Anthony Hopkins
10 Show Boat

40+ SET 6

1 Boston
2 Margaret Thatcher
3 Sherlock Holmes
4 Detective
5 Mary Rose
6 Meat Loaf
7 Michael Moore
8 Mickey
9 Italian
10 Death of a Salesman

40+ SET 7

1 Gordon Ramsay
2 Harold Wilson
3 Harpo
4 Skegness
5 Iron
6 British Museum
7 Eggs
8 CCTV
9 Hot Chocolate
10 Dallas

40+ SET 8

1 David Niven
2 Romania
3 Billy Bunter
4 Scotland
5 Boris Becker
6 Potato
7 Forty
8 Wet Wet Wet
9 Thomas Alva Edison
10 This Is Spinal Tap

40+ SET 9

1 Spandau Ballet
2 Florence Nightingale
3 Mary Celeste
4 Apple
5 Deerstalker
6 France
7 South Park
8 Barbados
9 Halloween
10 Courage

40+ SET 10

1 Sheena Easton
2 Toad
3 Curling
4 Poldark
5 Cider
6 Italy
7 Elba
8 Silver
9 Chest
10 Rouge

40+ SET 11

1 Rasputin
2 Charles de Gaulle
3 Tarzan
4 Spoon
5 Marlene
6 Oxford
7 Papaya
8 Los Angeles
9 Indian Ocean
10 Robin Williams

40+ SET 12

1 Buffy the Vampire Slayer
2 London
3 Gymnastics
4 Henry Ford
5 John Grisham
6 Teddy boys
7 BLT
8 Africa
9 Sweden
10 Jilly Goolden

40+ SET 13

1 Benjamin Disraeli
2 Boeing
3 Barbra Streisand
4 Beijing
5 Lion
6 Pied-à-terre
7 Chess
8 Six inches
9 Raymond Burr
10 May

40+ SET 14

1 Princess Anne
2 Bristol
3 Thelma and Louise
4 Italy
5 Errors
6 Gordon Kaye
7 Egg
8 Gooseberry
9 Austrian
10 Scorpio

40+ SET 15

1 Teletubbies
2 Geese
3 Poland
4 Calum
5 Brazil
6 By the way
7 Rod Stewart
8 Baltic Sea
9 Bill Bryson
10 Spartacus

40+ SET 16

1 Boy
2 Steve McClaren
3 Steven Spielberg
4 Genie
5 Dukes of Norfolk
6 Westie
7 Ballykissangel
8 Sight
9 John F. Kennedy
10 Trousers

40+ SET 17

1 Maggie Smith
2 Indianapolis
3 Good sense of humour
4 Yellow Pages
5 Shakin' Stevens
6 Delight
7 Forest of Dean
8 1980s
9 Bat
10 Aled Jones

40+ SET 18

1 Supremes
2 Harare
3 The Italian Job
4 Peter Carl Fabergé
5 White
6 USA
7 Elephant
8 David
9 Snow
10 Kenneth Grahame

40+ SET 19

1 Ingrid Bergman
2 Fifty metres
3 Puppet
4 American
5 University of St Andrews
6 Fish
7 Labour
8 Dawn French
9 Lesley Garrett
10 Canary Islands

40+ SET 20

1 Horse
2 Grease
3 Golf
4 Mel Gibson
5 Six
6 Men Behaving Badly
7 Herman Melville
8 William Shakespeare
9 Jacket
10 Balsamic vinegar

40+ SET 21

1 Lamb
2 Germany
3 Katrina
4 French
5 Penzance
6 India
7 Frank Whittle
8 Versace
9 Charlie Chan
10 Tog

40+ SET 22

1 China
2 Lionheart
3 Belfast
4 New Zealand
5 Joanna Lumley
6 Rudyard Kipling
7 Circus
8 George Formby
9 Tea
10 Frankie Dettori

40+ SET 23

1 Ireland
2 Liverpool
3 Chess
4 Halle Berry
5 Have I Got News For You
6 Germany
7 Cassius Clay
8 Franciscan Order
9 The waterspout
10 Thirty

40+ SET 24

1 Apple
2 Philadelphia
3 Sahara
4 Fingers
5 Horse
6 Pacific
7 Harry Potter
8 Adieu
9 Libra
10 Lovejoy

40+ SET 25

1 Boils
2 Australia
3 Jane Fonda
4 Leonardo DiCaprio
5 Ten
6 France
7 Ordnance Survey
8 Bram Stoker
9 The Jam
10 Almond

40+ SET 26

1 Horseradish
2 Sisters
3 100m
4 Owl
5 Lizard
6 Magpie
7 Germany
8 Mediterranean Sea
9 A, E, I, O and U
10 George Bernard Shaw

40+ SET 27

1 Richard Wagner
2 Cars
3 Marlon Brando
4 Sebastian Coe
5 Bernadette
6 Ultravox
7 Eddie Munster
8 Germany
9 MI5
10 Rome

40+ SET 28

1 Cloud
2 Marilyn Monroe
3 Banbury Cross
4 Arkansas
5 Alexander
6 Calista Flockhart
7 1980s
8 Greg Norman
9 New Zealand
10 Hands

40+ SET 29

1 Mel Brooks
2 Horatio Hornblower
3 Lake District
4 Bilbao
5 Phil Spector
6 Fish
7 Sevens
8 Rob Roy
9 German
10 Dixon of Dock Green

40+ SET 30

1 Mini skirt
2 Sean Connery
3 Ballet
4 Oscar Wilde
5 Jordan
6 Jellystone Park
7 Journalism
8 Elvis Presley
9 Butterfly
10 Richard Gere

40+ SET 31

1 British
2 China
3 Ad infinitum
4 Choosers
5 Plonk
6 Scissor Sisters
7 Diamond
8 Idi Amin
9 Asia
10 Emilia Fox

40+ SET 32

1 Newcastle United
2 Scotland
3 Jesus Christ Superstar
4 Boney M
5 USA
6 Lesotho
7 Cheese
8 Edward
9 Ricky Gervais
10 Fox

40+ **SET 33**

1 Brazil
2 Court
3 Walt Disney
4 Indian
5 Jane Eyre
6 Air conditioning
7 Bette Davis
8 1950s
9 One Man and His Dog
10 U2

PART 2 General Knowledge Answers

SET 1

1 Greyhound racing
2 Julian Fellowes
3 B*witched
4 Velvet Revolution
5 Dove
6 Spooks
7 Rod Stewart
8 Earthquake
9 Dan Quayle
10 Digital Audio Broadcasting
11 Violin
12 Princess Anne
13 Republic of Ireland
14 Christopher Marlowe
15 Mussels
16 Rhea
17 Pentagon
18 Australia
19 Ludwig van Beethoven
20 River Thames
21 Cigar
22 Edith Piaf
23 Jeremy Thorpe
24 Three
25 Sean Connery
26 Lions
27 Andy Robinson
28 1918
29 Saint Peter
30 Yorkshire pudding
31 Dormouse
32 Pyrotechnics
33 Dallas
34 Eardrum
35 Hackney
36 Australia
37 USA
38 Cow
39 Coffee
40 Scotland
41 Harold Macmillan
42 New Zealand
43 Polaris
44 Thesaurus
45 Stansted
46 Supermarket Sweep
47 Marilyn Manson
48 India
49 Margo Leadbetter
50 Siblings

SET 2

1 Caterpillar
2 British
3 Mauritius
4 Chrissie Hynde
5 Japan
6 Naomi Campbell
7 Putter
8 Lancaster
9 BB King
10 Aberdeenshire
11 The Jungle Book
12 Mike Leigh
13 Greenwich
14 Boris Karloff
15 Franklin D. Roosevelt
16 Horse
17 Extras
18 Pamela Anderson
19 France
20 Ludo
21 Mae West
22 Catcher in the Rye
23 Seafood
24 Stevie Wonder
25 Golf
26 Warsaw
27 United Nations
28 Arthur Sullivan
29 Saltaire
30 Horatio Kitchener
31 J. R. R. Tolkien
32 Frankie Goes To Hollywood
33 Brian O'Driscoll
34 Ronaldo
35 Boxing

36 Fondue

37 Aerobics

38 Oxford

39 Charles II

40 Cockles and mussels

41 Swan

42 Aesop

43 Nineteenth

44 Esther Rantzen

45 Balearics

46 Rats

47 SuperTed

48 'The Power Of Love'

49 Pig

50 Six

SET 3

1 RADA

2 Shoes

3 Pac-Man

4 Rouge

5 Dangermouse

6 World

7 Inca

8 Monosodium glutamate

9 Nobel Prize

10 Helium

11 'Clint Eastwood'

12 Republic of Ireland

13 Baguette

14 Chesney Hawkes

15 Amnesty International

16 Nicholas Breakspear

17 France

18 Colditz

19 Leonard Rossiter

20 Birds' eggs

21 Elmer Fudd

22 USA

23 Timmy

24 Cheese plant

25 Steve Coogan

26 New York City

27 Stamps

28 The Invisible Man

29 Australia

30 Harry S. Truman

31 Andrew Neil

32 Allsorts

33 Scotland

34 Austria

35 Kent

36 1960s

37 Cheese

38 Brazil

39 Elton John

40 Ciccone

41 Van Morrison

42 Blue

43 Baton Rouge

44 Gerry and the Pacemakers

45 Theodore Roosevelt

46 Division

47 Jeffrey Archer

48 Charlie Dimmock

49 Bolshoi

50 Massachusetts

SET 4

1 Gin

2 Frank Sinatra

3 Bird

4 Glasgow

5 Gardeners' Question Time

6 Red and white

7 Don Bradman

8 Leap year

9 Aristotle

10 Route 66

11 Indianapolis

12 Sussex

13 John Simpson

14 Nero

15 Greece

16 In vitro

17 Germany

18 Mexico

19 Jerry Hall

20 Brussels sprout

21 Pumice

22 Water

23 France

24 Cribbage

25 Giacomo Puccini

26 Horse

27 Macaulay Culkin

28 Baltic States

29 Germany

30 Oliver Twist

31 Piranha

32 Italy

33 Scotland

34 Henry James

35 China

36 U2

37 Tower of London

38 Indonesia

39 Painting

40 Funny Face
41 Vesta
42 Henry Ford
43 French
44 Ducklings
45 Middlesex
46 Britney Spears
47 Robert Walpole
48 Asia
49 Graeme Dott
50 Eight

SET 5

1 Trains
2 Crow
3 Winston Churchill
4 Snoopy
5 Ottoman
6 Bordeaux
7 Wuthering Heights
8 Spanish
9 Japan
10 Sir Winston Churchill
11 Gospel of St Matthew
12 Ear
13 France
14 Pantheon
15 1980s
16 Belgium
17 Echo
18 Sanhedrin
19 French
20 The League of
    Gentlemen
21 Sir Richard Branson
22 Postage stamp
23 Bruce Forsyth

24 Jackson
25 David Tennant
26 The Taming of the
    Shrew
27 Smokey Robinson and
    the Miracles
28 The Hood
29 Fox
30 New York
31 Archaeologist
32 Connecticut
33 Canaletto
34 Rick
35 Xylophone
36 Walker Brothers
37 Italian Grand Prix
38 Italia Conti
39 Kendo
40 Crash
41 Green
42 1970s
43 Umpire
44 Manchester United
45 Magnesium
46 Mikhail Gorbachev
47 Antony Worrall
    Thompson
48 Ang Lee
49 Wrestling
50 'Can't Get You Out Of
    My Head'

SET 6

1 October
2 Iron Maiden
3 Sun protection factor
4 Appleby
5 Tennis

6 William Shakespeare
7 Bob Hope
8 The Oaks
9 Pawnbroker's
10 Royal Shakespeare
    Company
11 Margaret Thatcher
12 FBI
13 Island
14 Rugby League
15 Rolling Stones
16 Liechtenstein
17 Lilli Marlene
18 John Gordon Sinclair
19 Honor Blackman
20 Roger Moore
21 Chippendale
22 Be prepared
23 Barbican
24 November
25 Dutch
26 Cate Blanchett
27 Clarence
28 Shooting stars
29 Lancashire
30 Anne Boleyn
31 Territorial Army
32 Heath Ledger
33 Horse racing
34 Lamb
35 Sidney Poitier
36 Australian
37 South Georgia
38 Robinson Crusoe
39 Twenty-eight
40 Billy Idol
41 'Er indoors

42 *Linda Eastman*

43 *70 mph*

44 *Princess Anne*

45 *German*

46 *Fosse Way*

47 Cheers

48 *El Greco*

49 *Shakespear's Sister*

50 *Coldplay*

SET 7

1 *Barbie*

2 *Orchid*

3 *Sheep*

4 *The Bangles*

5 *Tara*

6 *Comic Relief*

7 Red Dwarf

8 *Imran Khan*

9 *South Africa*

10 Get Carter

11 *Jujitsu*

12 *'Summer of '69'*

13 La Traviata

14 *Sixty*

15 *Horse*

16 *Flowers*

17 *Katharine Hepburn*

18 *Japan*

19 *Greece*

20 *Lambeth Walk*

21 *Canada*

22 *Kenya*

23 *Reptiles*

24 *July*

25 *Mark Ramprakash*

26 *Temperature*

27 *Japan*

28 *Ellis Island*

29 *Republic of Ireland*

30 *The Queen*

31 *Danny Wallace*

32 *Williams*

33 *Germany*

34 *Whisky*

35 *Kelly Holmes*

36 *Wimbledon*

37 *Left-hand*

38 *John Hancock*

39 *Common Agricultural Policy*

40 *Rubber plant*

41 *Jewish*

42 *Bolivia*

43 *Mahjong*

44 *New York*

45 *South Africa*

46 *Cashew*

47 *Aladdin*

48 *Table tennis*

49 *Edinburgh*

50 *Jeff Goldblum*

SET 8

1 *Michael Bolton*

2 *Wales*

3 *Mosaic*

4 *Spain*

5 *Canute*

6 *Land's End*

7 *Richard Whiteley*

8 *Rumpole of the Bailey*

9 Hustle

10 *Mel Gibson*

11 *Cricket*

12 *Noel's House Party*

13 *Gareth Gates*

14 *T.S. Eliot*

15 *Cancer*

16 *Grouse*

17 *Bullfighting*

18 *Cooking*

19 *Butler*

20 *Carrie Fisher*

21 *Sunflower*

22 *Ingmar Bergman*

23 *USA*

24 *Butterfly*

25 *Balloon*

26 *Aswad*

27 *Germany*

28 *Germany*

29 *Jackson*

30 *Japan*

31 It's a Wonderful Life

32 *Dry*

33 *Hamlet*

34 *Turkey*

35 *Water*

36 *Two*

37 Twelve Angry Men

38 *Caroline Aherne*

39 *Charles I*

40 *Ray Alan*

41 *Japan*

42 *Aqua*

43 *Anne Robinson*

44 *Coffee-table*

45 *Rugby Union*

46 JK and Joel
47 Donald Duck
48 King Arthur
49 United Kingdom
50 Sirius

SET 9

1 South America
2 Newcastle-upon-Tyne
3 Tolpuddle
4 Guys and Dolls
5 Knitting
6 Tank
7 Cilla Black
8 Sir Anthony Eden
9 Willy Brandt
10 Fleetwood Mac
11 Jayne Torvill and
    Christopher Dean
12 Roy Orbison
13 Graceland
14 South Africa
15 Otto von Bismarck
16 Baseball
17 Blue
18 Rudyard Kipling
19 Giovanni Giacomo
    Casanova de Seingalt
20 Sally Field
21 Steve Martin
22 Left
23 The Archers
24 Duke of Wellington
25 Triple jump
26 Queen Victoria
27 Rat Pack
28 Steps

29 The Wombles
30 Princess Anne
31 Billy Wright
32 Also Known As
33 Bob the Builder
34 Colchester
35 Garp
36 Teri Hatcher
37 Seal
38 Thirty-one
39 Bobby Brown
40 Romeo and Juliet
41 The Wall
42 Paul Young
43 'Waterloo Sunset'
44 France
45 Angelina Jolie
46 Sherlock Holmes
47 Cardinal Richelieu
48 Ray Charles
49 New Zealand
50 1950s

SET 10

1 Mascarpone
2 Josip Tito
3 Garibaldi
4 Hypotenuse
5 Soprano
6 Sooty
7 Mensa
8 Twenty-two
9 Dances with Wolves
10 Dundee
11 Football
12 Ludwig van Beethoven
13 Mormon

14 Aubergine
15 Bart's
16 Fearne Cotton
17 Jamaica
18 Horse
19 Theodore Roosevelt
20 Stalagmite
21 Rajiv Gandhi
22 Twist
23 Thirty-nine
24 George Orwell
25 Princess Eugenie of York
26 Peacock
27 Shirley Bassey
28 National Health Service
29 Pasta
30 Tsunami
31 Tyburn
32 King
33 Gold
34 Mint sauce
35 Lifeboat
36 Canada
37 Goat
38 Felix
39 Oscar Wilde
40 What Not To Wear
41 Brasilia
42 Imelda Marcos
43 Heracles
44 Republic of Ireland
45 Fourth
46 Grateful Dead
47 Sandringham
48 Shirley Conran
49 Benjamin Disraeli
50 Paul Keating

SET 11

1 Isadora Duncan
2 Nick Robinson
3 The Lion King
4 Infernal
5 Jack Rosenthal
6 Opera glasses
7 Zorro
8 Phil Collins
9 The periodic table
10 September
11 Charles I
12 Edward Heath
13 Pocahontas
14 Mary, Queen of Scots
15 Fiddler on the Roof
16 Crescendo
17 John McEnroe
18 Preston
19 Heston Blumenthal
20 Jeremy Paxman
21 Oasis
22 William Hague
23 Plum
24 Fish
25 Edinburgh
26 Kentucky
27 Dusty Springfield
28 St Hilda's
29 Tom Petty
30 Spider
31 Dan Brown
32 John Le Carré
33 Seal
34 Naples
35 Twentieth

36 Harrison Ford
37 Toledo
38 Ronald Reagan
39 Egypt
40 Italy
41 Flytrap
42 Horatio
43 Poland
44 New Zealand
45 Tina Turner
46 Typhoon
47 Pinocchio
48 Setter
49 The Godfather: Part II
50 George Harrison

SET 12

1 Austria
2 Intensive care unit
3 George
4 Sir Walter Scott
5 China
6 Adrian Mole
7 Scarborough
8 Israel
9 Kindness
10 Australia
11 December
12 The Omen
13 Canada
14 Zoolander
15 Sausages
16 24 Hour Party People
17 Bat
18 Charles Dickens
19 World Rally
   Championship

20 Trumpton
21 Lizard
22 Crimean War
23 Clangers
24 Austria
25 Paul Gauguin
26 December
27 Bark
28 100 to 30
29 Single white female
30 India
31 Daniel Craig
32 Earl of Warwick
33 Boxing
34 Pointe shoes
35 Spandau Ballet
36 Anna Ford
37 Carol Smillie
38 Poland
39 Egypt
40 The Police
41 Searchers
42 Talking Heads
43 Gardening
44 Kate Moss
45 Motorcade
46 Mary Rand
47 Staffordshire Bull
   Terrier
48 Ian Botham
49 Juliette Lewis
50 Caryn Franklin

SET 13

1 Arm
2 Joey
3 Berlin

4 Showjumping

5 Kate Humble

6 Football

7 Heart

8 Benjamin Britten

9 Bergamot

10 The Second World War

11 Brian Connolly

12 Tom Conti

13 Chequers

14 Christopher Wren

15 Gwyneth Paltrow

16 Coriander

17 Sheep

18 India

19 Seoul

20 Black Lace

21 Wigan

22 Africa

23 Australia

24 Reg Presley

25 Gordon Ramsay

26 One

27 Stratford-upon-Avon

28 Noughts and Crosses

29 Kate Moss

30 European Free Trade Association

31 Michael Johnson

32 Artichoke

33 Calendar

34 Chalet

35 Poteen

36 Robert Bunsen

37 Puffin

38 French

39 Groundhog Day

40 Young Women's Christian Association

41 Il Divo

42 Talking Heads

43 Walker

44 Richard I

45 Fawns

46 Mr Chips

47 Othello

48 The Killers

49 Remus

50 Santa Claus

SET 14

1 Sunderland

2 Aardvark

3 Michael Parkinson

4 Wolf

5 Hungary

6 Barcelona

7 1950s

8 Spaghetti bolognese

9 China

10 Croesus

11 William Wallace

12 Agatha Christie

13 Butcher

14 John Major

15 Trinidad

16 Jack Lemmon

17 Spider

18 Electrical current

19 Jamaica

20 Black

21 Paulo Coelho

22 India

23 Fish

24 Canary

25 Hands

26 Cheese

27 Aled Jones

28 Public limited company

29 'Auld Lang Syne'

30 Johnny Vegas

31 Neptune

32 John Terry

33 1960s

34 Spain

35 Madame de Pompadour

36 Edward VII

37 Crystal Palace

38 Judi Dench

39 Edward Woodward

40 Tiger

41 Frankie Valli

42 Dwight D. Eisenhower

43 Woody Harrelson

44 10pm

45 'Show Me Heaven'

46 European Economic Community

47 George I

48 Hanover

49 Edward Heath

50 James Ramsay MacDonald

SET 15

1 David Copperfield

2 Sarah Michelle Gellar

3 Boy George

4 John Webster

5 Andrew Lloyd Webber

6   Human League
7   The Netherlands
8   Omar Sharif
9   Nose
10 Jelly Baby
11 Switzerland
12 Pope
13 Newcastle Falcons
14 Charlotte Church
15 Ricky Tomlinson
16 M60
17 Dean Martin
18 Draughts
19 Dog
20 Edvard Grieg
21 Surrey
22 Liberty
23 Johnny Rotten
24 Fourteenth century
25 William the Conqueror
26 Savage Garden
27 Specials
28 Lois
29 Poland
30 Copenhagen
31 Jetsam
32 Haile Selassie
33 Jonathan Dimbleby
34 Jessica Simpson
35 Ballet
36 Anthony Minghella
37 Tony Bennett
38 Orang-utan
39 Limey
40 Basketball
41 French Revolution

42 Daniel Radcliffe
43 Ear, nose and throat
44 East Germany
45 John Major
46 Winston Churchill
47 Portugal
48 London
49 Nobel Prize
50 West Point Academy

SET 16

1   Acorn
2   Gremlins
3   The Who
4   Stephen Sondheim
5   The Magic Roundabout
6   British Broadcasting Corporation
7   Beef
8   Edward V
9   Hebrew
10 Marie Curie
11 Steamboat Willie
12 Unicorn
13 Prince Charles
14 Neil Diamond
15 John Forsythe
16 The Taming of the Shrew
17 Kiss
18 Magnum opus
19 Diana Ross
20 Pink Floyd
21 Skiing
22 Cellophane
23 ZZ Top

24 Sheffield
25 Javelin
26 The US President
27 Jane Horrocks
28 George Burns
29 Baccara
30 Cecil Day Lewis
31 Kenya
32 Homer
33 Bananarama
34 Charlize Theron
35 Operation Overlord
36 Edward VI
37 Anne Robinson
38 Tennis
39 Pro rata
40 Mr Bumble
41 Rugby Union
42 Germany
43 Marianne
44 Dry
45 Cat
46 Joan of Arc
47 Golf
48 English Civil War
49 Germany
50 Richard Briers

SET 17

1   Utopia
2   Liverpool
3   Henry VII
4   State Registered Nurse
5   Andy Warhol
6   Balsa
7   Flying Squad

8   Big Breakfast

9   Frankie Howerd

10 Elm

11 'The Star-Spangled Banner'

12 Paris Hilton

13 Spanish

14 Violin

15 1980s

16 Isle of Man

17 2 Unlimited

18 Anthea Turner

19 Golf

20 Holmfirth

21 James II

22 Blue and red

23 Neve Campbell

24 White Star Shipping Company

25 Anything Goes

26 Harold Pinter

27 Bluebird K7

28 Name

29 Louis Pasteur

30 Warsaw Pact

31 1950s

32 Odyssey

33 Air battles

34 Lead

35 Little Shop of Horrors

36 Johannesburg

37 Five

38 France

39 Panna cotta

40 John Humphrys

41 Dick Turpin

42 Wimbledon

43 Duke

44 Twentieth century

45 Argentina

46 Eggheads

47 Happy Families

48 Waldorf

49 Gymnastics

50 X

SET 18

1   Italy

2   Pork

3   Blondie

4   China

5   Bus

6   Belgium

7   Bismarck

8   Vancouver

9   Twelve

10 Eight

11 William Hartnell

12 Tim Westwood

13 Golf

14 Karaoke

15 Paris

16 360°

17 Tony Hart

18 Wine

19 Bob Marley

20 Plutonium

21 Ireland

22 Cyrano de Bergerac

23 London Palladium

24 Commedia dell'Arte

25 Wales

26 Boxing

27 Estimated time of arrival

28 Broomsticks

29 Pamela Anderson

30 China

31 Mont-Saint-Michel

32 Garry Kasparov

33 America

34 Shameless

35 Extraordinary General Meeting

36 Steve McQueen

37 Gilbert O'Sullivan

38 Hot Chocolate

39 Mahatma Gandhi

40 Clint Eastwood

41 Bus

42 Yellow

43 Lord Haw Haw

44 David Moyes

45 Jane Fonda

46 John Profumo

47 Red

48 Barnes Wallis

49 Bill Oddie

50 River Avon

SET 19

1   Harold Pinter

2   Jacques Villeneuve

3   Wood

4   Beverley Knight

5   Inigo Jones

6   Amanda Burton

7   Fruit

8   1940s

9   Busy Lizzie

10 Absinthe

11 Wine

12 Mortarboard

13 David Copperfield

14 1980s

15 Hawaii

16 Stephen Hawking

17 Smurfette

18 China

19 Michael Hutchence

20 Underground Railroad

21 Napoleon Bonaparte

22 Glasnost

23 Jack O' Lantern

24 Australia

25 Super Girl

26 Badminton

27 March

28 France

29 Two

30 Japan

31 Paris

32 Robert De Niro

33 Clive Woodward

34 Edward

35 Cher

36 Bath

37 Vinyl

38 The Full Monty

39 Cat Deeley

40 Blood

41 Middlesbrough

42 British

43 Margaret Thatcher

44 July

45 Peter Pan

46 Richard E. Grant

47 Boyzone

48 June Whitfield

49 Bird-watching

50 Snow

SET 20

1 Alan Bleasdale

2 Scotland

3 Kate Winslet

4 Alaska

5 Hop

6 Bonsai

7 Cambridge

8 Drew Barrymore

9 Photography

10 Rugby Union

11 Rowan Atkinson

12 No-man's-land

13 Sugar

14 Philadelphia

15 To Kill a Mockingbird

16 QED

17 £50 note

18 Republic of Ireland

19 1994

20 Blue

21 Republic of Ireland

22 Bertie Wooster

23 Pet Shop Boys

24 Palm Sunday

25 Ten

26 Milk

27 Saturday

28 Dead or Alive

29 Sir Thomas More

30 Sir Elton John

31 Otto von Bismarck

32 Hong Kong

33 Sangria

34 Dick Dastardly

35 Lion

36 The Borrowers

37 Two

38 Football

39 'Jingle Bells'

40 Jersey

41 Ploughman's lunch

42 Italy

43 Speakeasy

44 Ricky Tomlinson

45 Casino Royale

46 Eamonn Andrews

47 Yellow

48 Hand

49 Beluga

50 Paula Yates

SET 21

1 Harrison Ford

2 Glühwein

3 Argentina

4 White

5 Charles Dickens

6 Mickey Blue Eyes

7 Crème de cassis

8 Mali

9 Ginger Baker

10 Our Friends in the North

11 Mangetout

12 Exodus

13 Nanny

14 Cork

15 *Tour de France*

16 *Three*

17 *Frank Spencer*

18 *Albert Einstein*

19 *Fanny Cradock*

20 *John Rennie*

21 *Detroit*

22 *Leg*

23 *Steve Wright*

24 *Birds*

25 *Golf*

26 *House of Stuart*

27 *Helium*

28 *Claudia Winkleman*

29 *Sugababes*

30 *Bruce Willis*

31 Daddy Cool

32 *Helen Hunt*

33 *Murder*

34 *Motor racing*

35 The Riddle of the
Sands: A Record of
Secret Service Recently
Achieved

36 *Golf*

37 *Ice hockey*

38 *Italy*

39 *Abraham Lincoln*

40 *Donald Rumsfeld*

41 *Daffodil*

42 Bottom

43 *George Dawes*

44 *0°C*

45 *Dennis Potter*

46 Kramer vs Kramer

47 *Gilbert and George*

48 *Russian*

49 *Showaddywaddy*

50 *River Café*

SET 22

1 *Thailand*

2 *Absinthe*

3 *Paper*

4 *Eiffel 65*

5 *Pinewood*

6 *Jimmy Nail*

7 *Sweden*

8 *Barbara Windsor*

9 *Vegetarian*

10 *Antilock Braking
System*

11 *BOGOF*

12 *Art*

13 A Fish Called Wanda

14 *Cheetah*

15 *Rose*

16 *Baritone*

17 Days of Thunder

18 *Carpet*

19 *Padraig Harrington*

20 *Alec Guinness*

21 Me

22 *Quasimodo*

23 *Elle Macpherson*

24 Fish

25 *Arc de Triomphe*

26 *Mushroom*

27 *James I*

28 *Bicycles*

29 *Peanut*

30 *Mr Burns*

31 *Hungary*

32 *Italy*

33 *William Shatner*

34 *Tennis*

35 *Horseracing*

36 *Boy George*

37 *Germany*

38 *Tessa Jowell*

39 *Jordan*

40 *Bray*

41 *Mediterranean*

42 *Bruce Willis*

43 *Mouse*

44 *Iceni*

45 *Father*

46 *France*

47 *John Hurt*

48 *Green*

49 *Thomas Gainsborough*

50 *Girls Aloud*

SET 23

1 *Port Sunlight*

2 *Germany*

3 *Arabic*

4 Bleak House

5 *Black*

6 *Methane*

7 *Nick Faldo*

8 *Japanese*

9 *Pygmalion*

10 *Tomato*

11 *Radio 4*

12 *Words Per Minute*

13 *Fred Astaire*

14 *Morrissey*

15 *Tin*

16 *Lithium*

17 *Malaria*

18 *Brazil*

19 Pink

20 Newmarket

21 Haricot

22 Indian

23 Newmarket

24 Sid Waddell

25 Yellow

26 Princess Anne

27 1950s

28 Italy

29 Damien Hirst

30 Calypso

31 Prince Charles

32 Star fruit

33 Biró

34 Italian

35 Angelis

36 Debbie McGee

37 Pontefract

38 Gin

39 Red

40 Makarios III

41 Jimmy Carr

42 Mowgli

43 Gordon Ramsay

44 Angel

45 Berlin

46 Germany

47 Grace

48 The Raccoons

49 Scalene

50 Russian

SET 24

1 Ford Motor Company

2 George Bernard Shaw

3 Grange Hill

4 Boxing

5 Monkey puzzle

6 White

7 Eric Sykes

8 Geriatrics

9 Cheese

10 Liverpool

11 Terry Jones

12 Caddie

13 Teenage Mutant Ninja Turtles

14 Red

15 China

16 Greece

17 Bradford

18 Bruce Forsyth

19 Calcium

20 Republic of Ireland

21 Dr Tanya Byron

22 Republic of Ireland

23 White

24 Captain Pugwash

25 North

26 Beer

27 Wayne Rooney

28 Harry Belafonte

29 'Rule, Britannia!'

30 The Good Old Days

31 Genoa

32 Chardonnay

33 Ronald Reagan

34 Greece

35 Lance Armstrong

36 Kylie Minogue

37 India Pale Ale

38 Jilly Goolden

39 Nookie

40 Des O'Connor

41 John McEnroe

42 Handbag

43 David and Victoria Beckham

44 Little Jack Horner

45 Dinosaur

46 Martin Clunes

47 Latin

48 Marcel Marceau

49 Cheshire

50 Anita Ward

SET 25

1 Venus

2 James Callaghan

3 Great Britain

4 Catherine Deneuve

5 Anne Brontë

6 Weft

7 Popemobile

8 Glen Campbell

9 Zara Phillips

10 Buzz Aldrin

11 Simon Schama

12 Football

13 Tarantula

14 Turkey

15 The Rocky Horror Show

16 Italy

17 France

18 Teri Hatcher

19 Clement Attlee

20 Fairies

21 Golf

22 Mao Zedong

23 Sunset Boulevard

24 Swimming

25 Anthony Quinn

26 BBC

27 Teeth

28 Action on Smoking and Health

29 Thailand

30 Nine

31 Reese Witherspoon

32 Charles II

33 Niña

34 Titanic

35 Jimmy Young

36 London Eye

37 Sylvester

38 Jackanory

39 Golf

40 Robert Burns

41 Ex libris

42 Cream

43 Duck

44 Beijing

45 Sarah Michelle Gellar

46 Salt

47 Dutch

48 Cat Stevens

49 Nigella Lawson

50 Jonathan

SET 26

1 Millennium Bridge

2 Visa

3 Celine Dion

4 Kirsty Young

5 Smack the Pony

6 The Power

7 Lebanon

8 How to Eat

9 New York

10 Madonna

11 Texas

12 Britannia

13 Nero

14 Piano

15 Brideshead Revisited

16 Portugal

17 Henrik Ibsen

18 Claudia Roden

19 Penicillin

20 Zoe Ball

21 Albert Einstein

22 Barber shop

23 Peter Ilyich Tchaikovsky

24 Bob Hoskins

25 Lacrosse

26 Russia

27 Italy

28 Eric Sykes

29 Richard Brinsley Sheridan

30 Canterbury Cathedral

31 Africa

32 Japan

33 Sherry

34 Literature

35 Iceland

36 Germany

37 Vote

38 Gunpowder Plot

39 'Wonderwall'

40 Small cup

41 China

42 Britney Spears

43 LA

44 Costa Rica

45 British

46 Houston

47 Jack Klugman

48 Madonna

49 Melvyn Bragg

50 Perry

SET 27

1 Desert Storm

2 The Queen

3 Portugal

4 Kevin Federline

5 Crackerjack

6 Tartan

7 February

8 Cole Porter

9 Danish

10 Cerberus

11 Family Guy

12 Glasgow

13 April

14 Bruce Springsteen

15 Edwin Starr

16 Tennis

17 Feta

18 Boxing

19 France

20 China

21 Monaco

22 Mona Lisa Smile

23 Theodore Roosevelt

24 Francis Drake

25 Los Angeles

26 'The Winner Takes It All'
27 Toad
28 Jack-in-the-box
29 Great Britain
30 Wendy
31 Watch
32 Gideon Bible
33 René Descartes
34 Manchester
35 Burgundy
36 Motor racing
37 Middlesbrough
38 Razorlight
39 Manchester
40 Flute
41 Four
42 Poppy
43 Apples
44 Ned
45 Mayflower
46 Lyndon Baines Johnson
47 Shanghai
48 Tony Blair
49 Snow White and the Seven Dwarfs
50 Jason

SET 28

1 Mississippi River
2 Helmut Kohl
3 Laura Ingalls Wilder
4 'Jealous Guy'
5 1967
6 Cuneiform
7 China
8 Bletchley Park

9 Eight
10 Black
11 Stanley Kubrick
12 Mumps
13 Steve Ovett
14 Greece
15 Shamrock
16 Prince Edward
17 Normandy
18 Christmas
19 Wolfgang Amadeus Mozart
20 Italy
21 Midnight Caller
22 Larry David
23 Uma Thurman
24 Croquet
25 Slade
26 Spain
27 Two
28 Depeche Mode
29 The Bronx
30 Comets
31 Frank Lampard
32 Guide Dogs for The Blind
33 New Orleans
34 France
35 House of Representatives
36 Thomas Newcomen
37 Country
38 The Queen
39 James Brown
40 Nazi Germany
41 Liverpool
42 Arabic

43 Parker
44 Curling
45 Wales
46 Gangs of New York
47 October
48 Old Bailey
49 Montenegro
50 Martin Scorsese

SET 29

1 Japan
2 Italy
3 1952
4 Jacques Delors
5 Les Misérables
6 Malta
7 Roger Moore
8 Fred Durst
9 The Three Degrees
10 Bali
11 Goat
12 Vic Reeves
13 Jon Bon Jovi
14 Sweden
15 Anne
16 Birmingham
17 The Second World War
18 Octet
19 Thirty
20 Antarctica
21 Willow
22 Yosemite
23 Chickpea
24 Alexandria
25 Venice
26 Miroslav Klose

27 Six
28 Pennsylvania
29 Look Back in Anger
30 The Phantom of the Opera
31 Brazil
32 Gordon Brown
33 Fahrenheit
34 Greenpeace
35 Max Beesley
36 Pasta
37 Bluegrass
38 J. B. Priestley
39 Gary Rhodes
40 Athletics
41 Orange
42 Legally Blonde
43 Idi Amin
44 January
45 Four
46 The Elephant Man
47 Annual
48 Atlantic
49 France
50 Honey, I Shrunk the Kids

SET 30

1 Patton
2 Muhammad Ali
3 Republic of Ireland
4 Renée Zellweger
5 Alfred Hitchcock
6 Unfinished (Symphony)
7 Munro
8 Jordan
9 Iona

10 English Channel
11 Jasper Carrott
12 Little Women
13 Hallowe'en
14 Emma Bunton
15 Ronald Reagan
16 Chlorine
17 James Callaghan
18 Antarctica
19 Manfred Mann
20 Swiss
21 Sir Robert Peel
22 Piano
23 Kuwait
24 Copper
25 Hilary
26 Ava Gardner
27 Nice
28 Steel
29 Alan Ayckbourn
30 Foot and mouth
31 Eyes
32 Oxygen
33 'Band of Gold'
34 Paul Newman
35 Rainbow
36 Norway
37 Peterborough United
38 Waking the Dead
39 France
40 Elvis Costello
41 Tiger
42 Nickel
43 HMS Victory
44 Dame Nellie Melba
45 Gary Lineker

46 Nose
47 Chickpea
48 Phil Taylor
49 Cutty Sark
50 Coconut

SET 31

1 Male
2 White
3 Six
4 France
5 Racehorse
6 Rainbow
7 Carmen
8 1980s
9 Fox
10 Henry VI
11 Richard Gere
12 Lasagne
13 Tuesday
14 Ten
15 Oxford
16 Pollux
17 University Challenge
18 Oberon
19 Rice
20 Denzel Washington
21 RoboCop
22 Perspiration
23 Atlantic
24 Cubs
25 Sausage
26 Italy
27 Alvin Stardust
28 Locomotives
29 Clannad

30 Richard Nixon

31 Rickshaw

32 English Civil War

33 Ken Dodd

34 Japan

35 Doldrums

36 Louisiana

37 Ben Jonson

38 David Lloyd George

39 Penélope Cruz

40 Connie Booth

41 Katie Price

42 Ray Parker Jr

43 'Mack the Knife'

44 French

45 Scotland

46 Robert De Niro

47 Love Story

48 Liverpool

49 The Shadows

50 Immanuel Kant

SET 32

1 Sophia Loren

2 Australia

3 French

4 Zeppelin

5 Winona Ryder

6 Jools

7 Wright

8 Channel Islands

9 Are You Being Served?

10 Glasgow

11 LL Cool J

12 Robert Lindsay

13 Australia

14 USA

15 Margaret Beckett

16 Baseball

17 Kenya

18 Italy

19 Caernarvon

20 Paradise Lost

21 British

22 Sound

23 Grandmother

24 Florence

25 Futurama

26 Melbourne

27 French

28 Michael Howard

29 Blackpool

30 Finland

31 Derren Brown

32 Henry Kissinger

33 Equity

34 Anastasia

35 Eighteen

36 Hovercraft

37 Björk

38 Australia

39 The Ordinary Boys

40 Space

41 Jane Seymour

42 Dennis Waterman

43 Balaclava

44 Wine

45 Sweeney Todd

46 Italy

47 Henry

48 Toque

49 Vasco da Gama

50 Carbon dioxide

SET 33

1 Football

2 Saint Luke

3 Riverdance

4 David Dimbleby

5 Bridget Jones's Diary

6 Sebastian

7 Liam Gallagher

8 UB40

9 Women's Auxiliary Army Corps

10 William IV

11 Yellow

12 Olympia

13 Chipmunks

14 Long John Silver

15 Harvey Nichols

16 World Trade Organization

17 Cactus

18 Shells

19 James Stewart

20 Pebbles

21 Tarte tatin

22 Eskimos

23 Miss Moneypenny

24 Poland

25 London

26 Golf

27 Lee Harvey Oswald

28 Giant

29 British Air Line Pilots Association

30 'Love Me Do'

31 Blue

32 Apple

33 Lard

34 *Edward III*
35 *Runner bean*
36 *Neurology*
37 *Dressing*
38 *Sickle*
39 *Earthquake*
40 *Poinsettia*
41 The Kid
42 On The Town
43 *Italy*
44 Elizabeth I
45 Edward Albee
46 Tennis
47 Remains of the Day
48 Chelsea
49 Honduras
50 Watling Street

SET 34

1 *Madonna*
2 *Red Devils*
3 *Face*
4 *Ophelia*
5 *Malawi*
6 *Charles Rennie Mackintosh*
7 *Horse racing*
8 *Fish roe*
9 *Scotland*
10 The Ivy League
11 Quentin Tarantino
12 Jimmy Carter
13 'O Come, All Ye Faithful'
14 Judaism
15 Royal Albert Hall
16 Pamela Anderson

17 *Prodigy*
18 *Gregorian calendar*
19 *Johann Sebastian Bach*
20 *Bobby Moore*
21 *India*
22 *Bargain Hunt*
23 *Trinny Woodall*
24 *Miss World*
25 *Aluminium*
26 *Borzoi*
27 *Three*
28 *Britney Spears*
29 *Margaret Thatcher*
30 *Howard Keel*
31 *Dean Martin*
32 *Jackie Chan*
33 *Chickpea*
34 Stoppit and Tidyup
35 *Hedgehog*
36 *Italy*
37 *Israel*
38 *Rings*
39 *India*
40 *Dover*
41 *Asia*
42 Sleeping Beauty
43 Sir Jimmy Savile
44 Christina Aguilera
45 Henry Winkler
46 Bluetooth
47 Chess
48 Toad Hall
49 Korea
50 London

SET 35

1 *Chris Evans*
2 *Limbo*
3 *Pig*
4 *Silk*
5 *Chameleon*
6 *Australia*
7 *Kenneth Branagh*
8 *Poland*
9 Seven Brides for Seven Brothers
10 Keith Richards
11 Arnold Wesker
12 *Staccato*
13 *Italy*
14 Terence Rattigan
15 Miss Hoolie
16 Peeping Tom
17 Eddie Merckx
18 Auf Wiedersehen, Pet
19 Austria
20 Vampire
21 1980s
22 George Burns
23 Condensation
24 Gypsy Rose Lee
25 Ben Affleck
26 Bee Gees
27 Venezuela
28 ERNIE
29 Orkney Islands
30 Victoria Cross
31 Philip II
32 Robert the Bruce
33 Jacques-Yves Cousteau
34 Juan Carlos I
35 Canada

36 Barry Humphries

37 Leonard Bernstein

38 Curling

39 Liam Gallagher

40 Department for Constitutional Affairs

41 Tuxedo

42 Lizard

43 What Not To Wear

44 Belgrade

45 1066

46 Lucy Ewing

47 Eleanor Roosevelt

48 Laos

49 Richard Burton and Elizabeth Taylor

50 Haiti

SET 36

1 Israel

2 Isaac Newton

3 Gilbert and Sullivan

4 'The Stonk'

5 Eton

6 Rocky Marciano

7 Bill Clinton

8 Peter Andre

9 Goose

10 Boston

11 Merlin

12 Long Wave

13 Farfalle

14 Oklahoma!

15 Sir Alec Douglas-Home

16 Terry Scott

17 Queen Mother

18 Pole position

19 Mercia

20 Queen Mary

21 Osprey

22 Peter Andre

23 Gorgonzola

24 Rob Brydon

25 Ottawan

26 Guns n' Roses

27 Ian Carmichael

28 Nobel Prize

29 'Spirit In The Sky'

30 Chilli pepper

31 Czech Republic

32 Uncle Albert

33 Gerald Ford

34 Tudor

35 Malawi

36 Rasher

37 Colonel

38 Half A Sixpence

39 Drawing

40 Lisa Marie Presley

41 The Lark

42 Liverpool

43 Richard

44 Germany

45 Mile

46 Love

47 Simply Red

48 Choreography

49 Pacific

50 Sherry

SET 37

1 Sophie Ellis-Bextor

2 Annie

3 Sinbad

4 Helmut Kohl

5 Tennis

6 Russell Watson

7 Seven

8 Football Association

9 Cacao

10 Epsom

11 Fleur-de-lis

12 Pasta

13 Canada

14 Foreign and Commonwealth Office

15 Peru

16 Jean-Paul Sartre

17 Cardinal Wolsey

18 Gondola

19 Toothache

20 International Olympic Committee

21 St Helens

22 White

23 Snooker

24 Day of the Triffids

25 Carp

26 Greece

27 Ascot

28 Pink

29 Perth

30 Edinburgh

31 Edgar Allan Poe

32 Cast Away

33 Kangaroo

34 Ricky Gervais

35 Joseph Mallord William Turner

36 Snooker

37 Cayenne

38 Aardvark

39 Scotland

40 Neighbours

41 Alexander Dubček

42 Sir Alec Douglas-Home

43 Robert Redford

44 Australian

45 Denis

46 Prince Adam

47 Guernsey

48 Red

49 Oranges and lemons

50 Samuel L. Jackson

SET 38

1 Pressure

2 Captain Jack Harkness

3 Jealous

4 Photography

5 'Home Sweet Home'

6 Ethiopia

7 Basketball

8 Ukraine

9 French

10 Rugby

11 Camelot

12 First Amendment

13 Sporty Spice

14 Ants

15 White

16 La Dolce Vita

17 Paul McCartney

18 Andy Roddick

19 Denis

20 The Tempest

21 Ten

22 Cornwall

23 Hair

24 Arlene Phillips

25 Pony

26 Aborigine

27 US Masters

28 Rupert Everett

29 Italy

30 Patricia Cornwell

31 A Streetcar Named Desire

32 Watch

33 Christopher Cazenove

34 Ballet

35 Charles I

36 Roy Lichtenstein

37 Oxford University

38 Telly Savalas

39 River Phoenix

40 Michael Grade

41 Henry VIII

42 Ofcom

43 Skateboarding

44 Herbivore

45 Casualty

46 Wine

47 Skin

48 Gorilla

49 The Second World War

50 Woodwind

SET 39

1 Formula 1

2 Charlie Chaplin

3 Ivor the Engine

4 Italy

5 Glastonbury Music Festival

6 Noble gases

7 Virgo

8 Phillip Glass

9 Lake

10 Shaggy

11 Porridge

12 Eight

13 Chicken

14 Heavy goods vehicle

15 Erwin Rommel

16 Destiny's Child

17 Pogo

18 Ghee

19 Woodpecker

20 'You're fired!'

21 Simon Cowell

22 Lou Reed

23 Beer

24 Mia Farrow

25 Lester Piggott

26 Harry

27 Kirsch

28 Shoulder

29 Spamalot

30 Oxford University

31 TLC

32 US Open

33 Whiskey

34 Ice cream

35 Indianapolis

36 Bull

37 Italy

38 Little Miss Sunshine

39 Superman

40 'Colonel Bogey'

41 The Beautiful Game

42 *Baize*

43 Star Trek

44 *France*

45 *Squeeze*

46 *100*

47 *Stanley Laurel*

48 *Canada*

49 *Marseille*

50 *Nashville*

SET 40

1 *Christie Brinkley*

2 *Model*

3 *Cabbage*

4 *Leeds*

5 *Kiwi*

6 *Japan*

7 *Triple jump*

8 *Hurling*

9 *Just Fontaine*

10 *Teaching English as a Foreign Language*

11 *Sue Barker*

12 *Doop*

13 *1918*

14 *Forty*

15 *Wrestling*

16 *Country*

17 *Supertramp*

18 *Macbeth*

19 *Spanish*

20 *Lethe*

21 *Englishmen*

22 *Ship*

23 *Penguin*

24 *Hellespont*

25 *Colin Powell*

26 *Cod*

27 *Peloponnese*

28 *Frank Skinner*

29 *Cat*

30 *George V*

31 *Alexandra Palace*

32 *Luciano Pavarotti*

33 *Guy*

34 *Policeman*

35 *Buddy Holly*

36 *August*

37 *Hopscotch*

38 *Celsius*

39 *Sir Tom Stoppard*

40 *Danger*

41 *Ruth Madoc*

42 *Mollusc*

43 *Wings*

44 *Salvation Army*

45 *Netherlands*

46 *Dog*

47 *Palm*

48 *Andy Warhol*

49 *David Cameron*

50 *Last*

PART 3 Specialist Subject Answers

SET 1 WORDS AND LANGUAGES

1 *Simile*

2 *Work*

3 *Queen*

4 *Flags*

5 *Smirting*

6 *People*

7 *Skirt*

8 *Colour blindness*

9 *Née*

10 *Krump*

11 *French*

12 *Pangram*

13 *Italian*

14 *Hospital*

15 *Boardwalk*

16 *Phil Hill*

17 *Who*

18 *German*

19 *En suite*

20 *Acronym*

21 *Alma mater*

22 *Mothballs*

23 *Japanese*

24 *Window*

25 *Spanish*

26 *German*

27 *Witches*

28 *Dyslexia*

29 *Guerrilla*

30 *Bear*

31 *Zenith*

32 *Vodka*

33 *Smog*

34 *Brunch*

35 *For your information*

36 *Bonanza*

37 *Othello*

38 *Vandal*

39 *Bunker*

40 *Alcohol*

41 Talk

42 Cineplex

43 Pie

44 1984

45 E

46 Red

47 Cosmonaut

48 Kindergarten

49 Palindrome

50 Royal Horticultural Society

SET 2 WELL-KNOWN PHRASES

1 Imitation

2 Moss

3 Needle

4 Iron

5 In memoriam

6 Down

7 Fatal Attraction

8 Marriage

9 Busman's

10 Pony

11 Manger

12 Short Wave

13 Boats

14 Goodnight

15 Grind

16 Fat cat

17 Ivory

18 Spade

19 Bona fide

20 Oyster

21 Fingers

22 Caveat emptor

23 Tear

24 Coup d'état

25 Beaver

26 Glass

27 Master of none

28 Head

29 Sailor

30 Olive branch

31 Water

32 Race

33 Tape

34 Chaise longue

35 Egg

36 Riley

37 Swallow

38 Worms

39 Spoon

40 Caesar's

41 Haute cuisine

42 Elephant

43 Bread

44 Je ne sais quoi

45 Cat

46 Running

47 Deep blue sea

48 Phone

49 Absolutely

50 Conquered

SET 3 LITERATURE

1 Adam Smith

2 Michael Palin

3 The Crucible

4 Alfred Lord Tennyson

5 Japan

6 Sherlock Holmes

7 Niccolò Machiavelli

8 USA

9 Katherine

10 Homer

11 Alexander Pope

12 Maya Angelou

13 The Time Machine

14 Virgil

15 Mr Jones

16 Peter Kay

17 Charles Dickens

18 The Canterbury Tales

19 The Artful Dodger

20 1984

21 The Shire

22 Windmills

23 Marcel Proust

24 Ernest Hemingway

25 Salem

26 Hiawatha

27 David Livingstone

28 Tennessee Williams

29 Phileas Fogg

30 Robert Burns

31 Venice

32 Book of Common Prayer

33 Bill Clinton

34 Sex and the City

35 Ann Widdecombe

36 Hogwarts School of Witchcraft and Wizardry

37 Dan Brown

38 Erich Maria Remarque

39 Victor Frankenstein

40 Heaven

41 Tarzan

42 Poetry

43 William Shakespeare
44 Salman Rushdie
45 Aslan
46 Limerick
47 London
48 Whisky Galore
49 Forty-two
50 London

SET 4 CHILDREN'S LITERATURE

1 Peter Pan in Scarlet
2 The Little Prince
3 White
4 Bucket
5 Sleep
6 The Water-Babies
7 Garden
8 In the meadow
9 5 November
10 Elephant
11 The Wind in the Willows
12 Grimm
13 Thomas
14 Drury Lane
15 Raymond Briggs
16 Grandmother
17 Mr Men
18 Julia Donaldson
19 Wolf
20 Mould
21 Feather
22 His smile
23 Carlo Collodi
24 Canada
25 Plum

26 Violet Beauregarde
27 Four
28 Nightgown
29 Flour Babies
30 Rudyard Kipling
31 Doctor Dolittle
32 Owl
33 Tarts
34 Wales
35 Dr Seuss
36 Marmalade
37 Quentin Blake
38 Mr McGregor
39 Candlestick maker
40 Prince Charles
41 Edith Nesbit
42 Shoe
43 Roald Dahl
44 Spider
45 Shoe
46 Mr Nosey
47 The giant
48 Grace
49 Hans Christian Andersen
50 Red

SET 5 PRESS AND PUBLISHING

1 Dilbert
2 Daily Telegraph
3 Constantine
4 Stan Lee
5 Kingpin
6 Michael Winner
7 Jim Davis
8 Morning Star
9 Dennis the Menace

10 Arlene
11 Spider-Man
12 Great Dane
13 Wonder Woman
14 Radio Times
15 The Independent
16 Metropolis
17 Rupert Murdoch
18 Beano
19 The Guardian
20 Yellow
21 Financial Times
22 Italy
23 Smallville
24 Oxford
25 Piers Morgan
26 Obituary
27 France
28 The Sun
29 The Sun
30 The Mirror
31 Daily Express
32 Garry Trudeau
33 Film
34 Bridget Jones's Diary
35 New Yorker
36 Hamster
37 Fantastic Four
38 Crossword
39 The Guardian
40 The Observer
41 Viz
42 Medical profession
43 Pravda
44 Tom Ford
45 Juliette Binoche

46 *Fleet Street*

47 *Leader*

48 *Robert Crumb*

49 *The Sun*

50 *Orson's Farm*

SET 6 ART AND ARTISTS

1 *Titian*

2 *Andy Warhol*

3 *Glasgow*

4 *Easel*

5 *Slade*

6 *Peter Blake*

7 *Turner Prize*

8 *Michelangelo*

9 *Antony Gormley*

10 *Column*

11 *Amsterdam*

12 *St Ives*

13 *Red*

14 *British Museum*

15 *Paper*

16 *Thomas Gainsborough*

17 *Claude Monet*

18 *Michelangelo*

19 *Henry VIII*

20 *Cubism*

21 *Austrian*

22 *National Portrait Gallery*

23 *Photography*

24 *China*

25 *Edvard Munch*

26 *Chippendale*

27 *Frank Lloyd Wright*

28 *Milton Keynes*

29 *Deer*

30 *Sculpture*

31 *Spanish*

32 *Ronnie Wood*

33 *English*

34 *Dutch*

35 *Orange*

36 *David Hockney*

37 *Sister Wendy*

38 *Museum of Modern Art*

39 *Photography*

40 *Tate Modern*

41 *Lord Snowdon*

42 *Tate Modern*

43 *Blue*

44 *Mona Lisa*

45 *Damien Hirst*

46 *Fresco*

47 *Babies*

48 *Gustav Klimt*

49 *Beryl Cook*

50 *Paul Gauguin*

SET 7 RELIGION

1 *Lourdes*

2 *Pope Benedict XVI*

3 *Judaism*

4 *Diwali*

5 *Thirteen*

6 *China*

7 *Catholic Church*

8 *Sistine*

9 *Juggernaut*

10 *Sikhism*

11 *Hair shirt*

12 *Advent calendar*

13 *Rastafarians*

14 *Lent*

15 *Sikhism*

16 *Franciscans*

17 *Five*

18 *Sikhism*

19 *Jesuits*

20 *Judaism*

21 *Sikhism*

22 *Ten Commandments*

23 *Mecca*

24 *Habit*

25 *Four*

26 *Judaism*

27 *Joan of Arc*

28 *Monkey*

29 *Jesus Christ*

30 *Twelve*

31 *Nine*

32 *Three Wise Men*

33 *Genesis*

34 *India*

35 *Church of Jesus Christ of Latter-day Saints*

36 *Peter*

37 *Mormons*

38 *Pope*

39 *Lambeth Palace*

40 *Abraham*

41 *France*

42 *Tibetan Buddhism*

43 *Archbishop of Canterbury*

44 *Saul*

45 *James I*

46 *Exodus*

47 *Assisi*

48 *Aaron*

49 Amish

50 Saint Nicholas

SET 8
MYTHOLOGY AND ASTROLOGY

1 Cupid

2 Arthur

3 Walpurgis Night

4 Aries

5 Forty

6 Odysseus

7 Libra

8 Friday

9 Vesta

10 Valhalla

11 Orpheus

12 Minotaur

13 Northern Ireland

14 Thursday

15 Heracles

16 Leo

17 Odysseus

18 Egyptian

19 Victory

20 Ladder

21 Dragon

22 Dog

23 September

24 Amazons

25 Trident

26 Mermaid

27 Oedipus

28 Ambrosia

29 Nemesis

30 Cyclops

31 Stone

32 February

33 Valkyries

34 A hair

35 Agamemnon

36 Sagittarius

37 Zeus

38 Prometheus

39 Pan

40 Excalibur

41 Abominable Snowman

42 Eagle

43 Ceres

44 Pan

45 Nine

46 Capricorn

47 Theseus

48 Love

49 Argo

50 Aborigine

SET 9
TECHNOLOGY

1 Weblog

2 Central

3 Valentina Tereshkova

4 U

5 Podcast

6 In case of emergency

7 ABC

8 1,024

9 RADAR

10 Megabytes

11 Hacker

12 Australia

13 Guglielmo Marconi

14 Blind carbon copy

15 Bluetooth

16 Gold

17 International Space Station

18 Photograph

19 Selfridges

20 Gnomon

21 Belgium

22 Lawn mower

23 Beginner's All-purpose Symbolic Instruction Code

24 Computer-aided design

25 SLR

26 Satellite navigation

27 Facsimile machine

28 World wide web

29 Apollo 11

30 Walkman

31 Harvard

32 Beagle 2

33 Sally Ride

34 Definition

35 Hubble space telescope

36 American

37 Microsoft

38 Bill Gates

39 Hong Kong

40 Alexander Fleming

41 Random Access Memory

42 Steel

43 IBM

44 Rupert Murdoch

45 Sir James Dewar

46 Gross Domestic Product

47 Charles Darwin

48 Guillotine

49 Wall Street

50 Mars

SET 10 SCIENCE

1 Googol
2 Triangle
3 C
4 Tenth
5 Silver
6 Ivan Petrovich Pavlov
7 DNA
8 Isobar
9 Infinity
10 Two
11 Cirrus
12 Ursa Major
13 Radius
14 June
15 Oxygen
16 Twelve
17 Alloy
18 Ninety
19 One hundred
20 Potassium
21 Celsius
22 Michael Collins
23 Laughing gas
24 Archimedes
25 Dmitri Mendeleev
26 Ultraviolet
27 Light-emitting diode
28 Mercury
29 Salt
30 Fahrenheit
31 Krypton
32 Four
33 Wind
34 Quinine
35 NASA
36 Marie Curie
37 Two
38 Hydrogen
39 Diamond
40 Bicarbonate
41 Celsius
42 c
43 March
44 Zinc
45 Arsenic
46 Dolly
47 Earthquakes
48 Six
49 Equinox
50 Ribonucleic acid

SET 11 HUMAN SCIENCE

1 Sneezing
2 Long-sightedness
3 Lockjaw
4 Female
5 Leg
6 O
7 Sigmund Freud
8 Adam's apple
9 Insulin
10 Four
11 Sleepwalking
12 Brain
13 Liver
14 Hypothalamus
15 Spinal cord
16 Arms
17 Skin
18 Brain
19 Bones
20 Larynx
21 Vitamin D
22 Foot
23 Polio
24 Liver
25 Twenty-four
26 Skull
27 Tooth
28 Nose
29 Sight
30 Breastbone
31 Ear
32 General Practitioner
33 Mosquito
34 Iris
35 Arm
36 Heart
37 Ear
38 DNA
39 Eye
40 Kneecap
41 Rapid Eye Movement
42 Blood
43 Measles
44 Smallpox
45 Sunlight
46 Femur
47 Twenty-twenty
48 Colour blindness
49 Handwriting
50 Red

SET 12 ANIMALS

1 None
2 Collie
3 Terrier

4 Horse	40 Cat	24 Piano
5 Tail	41 Fish	25 Strings
6 Russia	42 Hummingbird	26 Zither
7 Fox	43 Kids	27 Piccolo
8 Chameleon	44 Tail	28 Miles Davis
9 Kestrel	45 Peahen	29 Black
10 Ballyregan Bob	46 Herbivores	30 Brass
11 Cat	47 St Bernard	31 Billie Holiday
12 Brown	48 Frasier	32 Saxophone
13 Arthropods	49 Camel	33 India
14 Swan	50 Butterfly	34 Horse
15 Australia		35 Leeds
16 Spotted hyena	**SET 13 THE WORLD**	36 Kurt Weill
17 Springbok	**OF MUSIC**	37 Clarinet
18 Komodo	1 Saxophone	38 Louis Armstrong
19 Deer	2 Glenn Miller	39 Piano
20 Bit	3 Drum	40 Glenn Miller
21 Lamb	4 Four	41 Violin
22 Dog	5 Piano	42 Peggy Lee
23 Squirrel	6 Cymbals	43 Pianissimo
24 Four	7 Dizzy	44 Metronome
25 Goliath	8 Duke Ellington	45 Bing Crosby
26 Deer	9 Glockenspiel	46 Jazz
27 Avocet	10 Double bass	47 Cab Calloway
28 Pig	11 Xylophone	48 Percussion
29 Sow	12 Count Basie	49 Eighty-eight
30 Gibraltar	13 Ragtime	50 Trumpet
31 Otter	14 Billie Holiday	
32 South America	15 Triangle	**SET 14 CLASSICAL**
33 Standard	16 Adolphe Sax	**AND OPERA**
34 Gosling	17 Russia	1 'Cinderella'
35 Adder	18 Saxophone	2 Franz Schubert
36 Croatia	19 Harp	3 Rigoletto
37 Tyrannosaurus	20 Violin	4 HMS Pinafore
38 Buck	21 Charlie Parker	5 Madam Butterfly
39 Heifer	22 Woodwind	6 Robert Schumann
	23 George Gershwin	7 Henry Wood

8 *Jenny Lind*

9 *English*

10 *Edward Elgar*

11 *Two*

12 *Westminster Abbey*

13 *Giacomo Puccini*

14 Messiah

15 Il Trovatore

16 *Seventeenth*

17 Carmen

18 *Libretto*

19 *Prima donna*

20 1812

21 *Contralto*

22 *Tchaikovsky*

23 *Australian*

24 Die Fledermaus

25 Boléro

26 *Richard Wagner*

27 *Italian*

28 The Three Tenors

29 *Irving Berlin*

30 Elizabeth I

31 *Felix Mendelssohn*

32 *Gioacchino Rossini*

33 *Antonio Vivaldi*

34 *Egypt*

35 *Ludwig van Beethoven*

36 *Pyotr Ilyich Tchaikovsky*

37 *G*

38 *French*

39 The Pirates of Penzance

40 *Pyotr Ilyich Tchaikovsky*

41 *George Frideric Handel*

42 *Antonín Dvořák*

43 *Piano*

44 *Spanish*

45 *Great Britain*

46 *Vienna*

47 *Frédéric Chopin*

48 *Richard Wagner*

49 *Gustav Holst*

50 *Giacomo Puccini*

SET 15 TOP OF THE POPS

1 *Acapulco*

2 *Green Day*

3 *Otis Redding*

4 The Zutons

5 *Westlife*

6 'Ticket To Ride'

7 'Mamma Mia'

8 Dave Clark Five

9 *Duran Duran*

10 *Eddy Grant*

11 *Boomtown Rats*

12 *Gabrielle*

13 *Backstreet Boys*

14 *Dancer*

15 *Bucks Fizz*

16 *Fugees*

17 *Blur*

18 *Michael Jackson*

19 'With A Little Help From My Friends'

20 *Iron Maiden*

21 An Atomic Bomb

22 UB40

23 *Madonna*

24 Barry White

25 *Small Faces*

26 Star Trek

27 *Sting*

28 *Stevie Wonder*

29 *Undertones*

30 *Molly*

31 *Travis*

32 'I Still Haven't Found What I'm Looking For'

33 *Nirvana*

34 *Village People*

35 *George Harrison*

36 *Pogues*

37 *Buttercup*

38 *Tina Turner*

39 *Dire Straits*

40 *Beach Boys*

41 'It Must Have Been Love'

42 *Frank Sinatra*

43 'My Heart Will Go On'

44 *Jason Donovan*

45 Grease

46 'Walk On By'

47 TLC

48 Chas and Dave

49 2Pac

50 *Take That*

SET 16 POP STARS

1 *Geri Halliwell*

2 *Justin Timberlake*

3 *Shakira*

4 *Little Richard*

5 *Tori Amos*

6 *Tina Turner*

7 *Buddy Holly*

8 Canadian

9 John Lennon

10 Michael Jackson
11 Cliff Richard
12 Jennifer Lopez
13 Shakin' Stevens
14 Julio Iglesias
15 Michael Jackson
16 Frank Ifield
17 Ricky Valance
18 Lenny Kravitz
19 'Fame'
20 Britney Spears
21 Brenda Lee
22 Rod Stewart
23 Phil Collins
24 Donny Osmond
25 Kylie Minogue
26 Sheryl Crow
27 Natalie Imbruglia
28 KT Tunstall
29 Moby
30 Sonia
31 Billy Joel
32 Madonna
33 Adam Faith
34 Joni Mitchell
35 Olivia Newton-John
36 'Beat It'
37 Billy Ocean
38 The King
39 Lisa Stansfield
40 Cilla Black
41 Robert Palmer
42 MC Hammer
43 Cher
44 Alison Moyet
45 Chris De Burgh

46 Rick Astley
47 Shirley Manson
48 Charlotte Church
49 Steve Brookstein
50 Whitney Houston

SET 17 CLASSIC ROCK

1 Guns n' Roses
2 Metallica
3 Aerosmith
4 Ringo Starr
5 U2
6 Slade
7 Rolling Stones
8 Europe
9 Queen
10 David Bowie
11 Oasis
12 Kinks
13 American
14 Status Quo
15 Whitesnake
16 The Who
17 Wizzard
18 Troggs
19 Toto
20 Wild
21 Jethro Tull
22 Fleetwood Mac
23 'Unchained Melody'
24 Simple Minds
25 'Eye Of The Tiger'
26 Jim Morrison
27 Eric Clapton
28 Phil Lynott
29 Alice Cooper

30 Guitar
31 Ozzy Osbourne
32 Foreigner
33 Aerosmith
34 Cream
35 Bon Jovi
36 Van Halen
37 Bruce Springsteen
38 The Police
39 Counting Crows
40 'Total Eclipse Of The Heart'
41 AC/DC
42 Pete Townshend
43 Coldplay
44 Jimi Hendrix
45 White Stripes
46 Mud
47 Foreigner
48 T Rex
49 Pink Floyd
50 The Darkness

SET 18 FASHION AND DESIGN

1 Tyra Banks
2 French
3 The Emmanuels
4 Horse riding
5 French
6 Raglan
7 Hairdressing
8 Madonna
9 Mohican
10 Double-breasted
11 Wrap
12 Cardigan

13 *Heidi Klum*

14 *Anna Wintour*

15 *Dinner jacket*

16 *Italy*

17 *Head*

18 *Cotton*

19 *Vivienne Westwood*

20 *Clog*

21 *Comme Des Garçons*

22 *Feet*

23 The Fifth Element

24 *Imelda Marcos*

25 *Head*

26 *Wayne Hemingway*

27 *Yves Saint Laurent*

28 *Biba*

29 *Coco Chanel*

30 *Linen*

31 *Poncho*

32 *Twiggy*

33 *Christian Dior*

34 *Victoria Beckham*

35 *New York*

36 *Norway*

37 *Trousers*

38 *Bra*

39 *Canada*

40 *Boot*

41 *American*

42 *Elizabeth Hurley*

43 *Italian*

44 *Elle Macpherson*

45 *Haute couture*

46 *Bikini*

47 *Korea*

48 *Paris Hilton*

49 *Gabbana*

50 *Terence Conran*

SET 19 WORLD GEOGRAPHY

1 *Suez Canal*

2 *Rocky Mountains*

3 *Zero*

4 *Connemara*

5 *Africa*

6 *Guernsey*

7 *China*

8 *Pennsylvania*

9 *San Andreas fault*

10 *Italy*

11 *Atlas Mountains*

12 *Greece*

13 *Great Britain*

14 *Montreal*

15 *Dublin*

16 *Public House*

17 *The equator*

18 *Olive*

19 *Luxembourg*

20 *Mississippi*

21 *France*

22 *Salt marsh*

23 *Soweto*

24 *Sahara Desert*

25 *Caves*

26 *Florida*

27 *Flanders*

28 *Spain*

29 *New Zealand*

30 *Estonia*

31 *Japan*

32 *Biscay*

33 *The Falkland Islands*

34 *California*

35 *Hawaii*

36 *India*

37 *Gibraltar*

38 *Pitcairn*

39 *South Africa*

40 *Marco Polo*

41 *Patras*

42 *Italy*

43 *Red*

44 *Spanish*

45 *North Korea*

46 *Egyptian Pound*

47 *White*

48 *Jersey*

49 *Japan*

50 *Red*

SET 20 WATERS OF THE WORLD

1 *Zambia*

2 *Baltic*

3 *Thames*

4 *Atlantic*

5 *Scotland*

6 *Shannon*

7 *Traitor's Gate*

8 *Caribbean Sea*

9 *Pacific*

10 *River Arno*

11 *Sicily*

12 *New Zealand*

13 *Arctic Ocean*

14 *Jordan*

15 *Atlantic Ocean*

16 *Adriatic Sea*

17 France
18 Lough Neagh
19 Caribbean Sea
20 Victoria
21 Germany
22 Indian Ocean
23 Niagara Falls
24 Tigris
25 Loch Lomond
26 Nile
27 Mexico
28 France
29 Wales
30 North Sea
31 River Rhône
32 Thames
33 South Africa
34 Caspian Sea
35 Switzerland
36 The Great Lakes
37 China
38 Atlantic Ocean
39 Niagara Falls
40 Mediterranean
41 Hungary
42 Windermere
43 South America
44 Strait of Magellan
45 Atlantic
46 Sydney
47 Black Sea
48 Kerry
49 Uzbekistan
50 Lake Geneva

SET 21 TOWNS AND CITIES

1 London
2 Germany
3 Moscow
4 Alice Springs
5 The Netherlands
6 Florence
7 Warsaw
8 Detroit
9 Kyoto
10 James Monroe
11 Uruguay
12 Reykjavik
13 New York
14 Istanbul
15 Jerusalem
16 Ho Chi Minh City
17 Oslo
18 Volgograd
19 Morocco
20 Adelaide
21 Mediterranean
22 Prague
23 Denmark
24 New Zealand
25 Belgium
26 Athens
27 Republic of Ireland
28 Paris
29 Bombay
30 New York
31 Calcutta
32 Amsterdam
33 Bull
34 Gdansk
35 Germany

36 Venice
37 Berlin
38 Lake Michigan
39 France
40 Vienna
41 Afghanistan
42 Peru
43 Australia
44 La Paz
45 Hong Kong
46 Singapore
47 London Bridge
48 Madras
49 Vatican City
50 Malaysia

SET 22 TRAVEL AND TOURISM

1 August
2 Croatia
3 Cuba
4 Greece
5 Atlantic Ocean
6 Central Park
7 Jordan
8 Brazil
9 New York
10 London
11 Windsor Castle
12 France
13 Euro
14 Israel
15 Gran Canaria
16 Boat
17 Canterbury
18 Rio de Janeiro
19 Jamaica

20 *Cambridge*

21 *Leicester*

22 *Spain*

23 *Golden Gate*

24 *Algarve*

25 *Costa Brava*

26 *Singapore*

27 *Stonehenge*

28 *John Lennon*

29 *Egypt*

30 *Three*

31 *Corfu*

32 *London*

33 *Mexico*

34 *Bullfighting*

35 *France*

36 *Turkey*

37 *Las Vegas*

38 *Sydney*

39 *Queens*

40 *Athens*

41 *California*

42 *Left-hand side*

43 *EPCOT*

44 *Bangkok*

45 *Egypt*

46 *The Gambia*

47 *Riviera*

48 *Loire Valley*

49 *Italy*

50 *Spain*

SET 23 WORLD HISTORY

1 *Moon*

2 *European Community*

3 *Russian Revolution*

4 *Troy*

5 *Ireland*

6 *Japan*

7 *Costa Rica*

8 *Mexico*

9 *Crimean War*

10 *Babylon*

11 *Claudius*

12 *Kenya*

13 *Pantheon*

14 *Alexandria*

15 *Colonel Thomas Blood*

16 *Kow-tow*

17 *France*

18 *Samantha*

19 *Jim Bowie*

20 *Herculaneum*

21 *Marie Antoinette*

22 *Rosa Parks*

23 *French*

24 *Nikita Khrushchev*

25 *Concorde*

26 *Julius Caesar*

27 *The Beatles*

28 *Rouge*

29 *Conservative Party*

30 *Chile*

31 *Condoleezza Rice*

32 *1989*

33 *Vietnam*

34 *China*

35 *Versailles*

36 *Sri Lanka*

37 *D*

38 *Washington DC*

39 *Albania*

40 *Czechoslovakia*

41 *Salvation Army*

42 *Flora Macdonald*

43 *Crimean War*

44 *Alcohol*

45 *Abraham Lincoln*

46 *Venice*

47 *Papyrus*

48 *Portugal*

49 *Constantinople*

50 *John D. Rockefeller*

SET 24 HISTORICAL FIGURES

1 *Theodore Roosevelt*

2 *Greece*

3 *Al Gore*

4 *Cambridge*

5 *Eva Braun*

6 *Fidel Castro*

7 *Neville Chamberlain*

8 *Willy Brandt*

9 *Malcolm X*

10 *Egypt*

11 *King Edward VII*

12 *Winston Churchill*

13 *Indira Gandhi*

14 *Austrian*

15 *Nero*

16 *Lord Lucan*

17 *Scottish*

18 *Sir Edmund Hillary*

19 *Romans*

20 *King James I*

21 *Plato*

22 *Dallas*

23 *France*
24 *Uganda*
25 *Tokyo Rose*
26 *Willy Messerschmitt*
27 *Cuba*
28 *Italy*
29 *Richard Nixon*
30 *Sir Francis Drake*
31 *Greek*
32 *George V*
33 *Great Fire of London*
34 *Sweeney Todd*
35 *Edith Cavell*
36 *South Africa*
37 *Oliver Cromwell*
38 *Highwayman*
39 *Billy the Kid*
40 *Albert Einstein*
41 *Henry VIII*
42 *Rubicon*
43 *Paul Revere*
44 *Gerhardt Schröder*
45 *Mikhail Gorbachev*
46 *Milton Friedman*
47 *Ghanaian*
48 *Pakistan*
49 *Kim Philby*
50 *Harold Macmillan*

SET 25 BRITAIN

1 *John Major*
2 *Open University*
3 *Three*
4 *Children In Need*
5 *Arthur Scargill*
6 *Poll Tax*
7 *d*
8 *1950s*
9 *Nobel Prize*
10 *Ministry of Defence*
11 *Glasgow*
12 *Geography*
13 *Green*
14 *York*
15 *Royal Society for the Prevention of Cruelty to Animals*
16 *Wales*
17 *Isle of Man*
18 *Bank of England*
19 *Westminster Abbey*
20 *Liver bird*
21 *Lundy*
22 *Victoria Cross*
23 *Lindisfarne*
24 *National Eisteddfod*
25 *Edinburgh*
26 *John Prescott*
27 *Tyne*
28 *Pennines*
29 *Caledonian Canal*
30 *Windsor Castle*
31 *Scotland*
32 *Twenty-pence piece*
33 *Samuel Johnson*
34 *Edinburgh*
35 *Saint Margaret's Church*
36 *Major*
37 *Coniston Water*
38 *Cardiff*
39 *Bognor*
40 *RAF*
41 *Professor*
42 *Westminster Abbey*
43 *MI6*
44 *Dundee*
45 *Chester*
46 *Lady*
47 *Nineteenth*
48 *Orkney Islands*
49 *Battersea*
50 *A bell*

SET 26 POLITICS

1 *Denis Healey*
2 *Republican Party*
3 *Herbert Asquith*
4 *Leon Trotsky*
5 *John Kerry*
6 *Barbara*
7 *Labour Party*
8 *Ho Chi Minh*
9 *Five years*
10 *China*
11 *C*
12 *John*
13 *Russian Revolution*
14 *Nicaragua*
15 *Joseph Raymond McCarthy*
16 *1960s*
17 *Home Secretary*
18 *Donkey*
19 *Margaret Thatcher*
20 *Martin Bell*
21 *'The Red Flag'*
22 *Strangers' Gallery*
23 *Republic of Ireland*
24 *South Africa*

25 General Francisco Franco

26 November

27 European Parliament

28 African National Congress

29 United Kingdom Independence Party

30 Whip

31 New Zealand

32 Glenda Jackson

33 President

34 Chancellor of the Exchequer

35 Ronald Reagan

36 White

37 The Food and Agricultural Organization

38 Fifth

39 President

40 Sir Menzies Campbell

41 Whig

42 Senate

43 The Hague

44 Sweden

45 By-election

46 Liberal Democrat

47 Member of Parliament

48 Boutros Boutros-Ghali

49 1950s

50 Donald Rumsfeld

SET 27 ROYALTY

1 Cornwall

2 Henry VIII

3 The Tower of London

4 Windsor

5 St Paul's Cathedral

6 Queen Victoria

7 Changing of the Guard

8 'God Save The Queen'

9 Denmark

10 Princess Anne

11 Princess Anne

12 Belgium

13 Princess

14 Mary, Queen of Scots

15 Queen Victoria

16 Sister

17 George VI

18 King Arthur

19 Catherine Parr

20 Princess Anne

21 Hanover

22 Corfu

23 William I

24 One hundredth

25 Three

26 Princess Beatrice

27 Tudor

28 Anastasia

29 Edward II

30 Henry VI

31 Prince Andrew

32 Queen Elizabeth II

33 Edward I

34 Elizabeth I

35 Edward the Confessor

36 George VI

37 Prince Andrew

38 Japan

39 Edward I

40 Princess Anne

41 Henry VIII

42 King Philip II

43 George III

44 Duke of Marlborough

45 Henry V

46 Spain

47 Queen Victoria

48 Henry VII

49 King John

50 Frances

SET 28 CELEBRITY

1 Eminem

2 Keith Richards

3 Scotland

4 Bob Hope

5 Christian Slater

6 Barbara Windsor

7 Kate Winslet

8 Nicole Richie

9 Alan Freeman

10 Denise Richards

11 Donnelly

12 Michael Hutchence

13 Liberace

14 David Walliams

15 Brooke Shields

16 Bruce Willis

17 Michael Owen

18 Brad Pitt

19 Javine Hylton

20 Delia Smith

21 David Blaine

22 Rowan Atkinson

23 Scary Spice

24 George Clooney

25 *Halle Berry*

26 *Hawaii*

27 *Hulk Hogan*

28 *Jenni Falconer*

29 *Ben Affleck*

30 *Britt Ekland*

31 *Paris Hilton*

32 *Jon Bon Jovi*

33 *Pamela Anderson*

34 *Rachel Weisz*

35 *Paris Hilton*

36 *Carrie Fisher*

37 *Arnold Schwarzenegger*

38 *Steven Spielberg*

39 *Dido*

40 *Tara Palmer-Tomkinson*

41 *Jamie Oliver*

42 *Jessica Simpson*

43 *Sienna Miller*

44 *Anna Nicole Smith*

45 *Chris Martin*

46 *Sarah Jessica Parker*

47 *Lulu*

48 *Maserati*

49 *Prince Albert of Monaco*

50 *Japan*

SET 29 TV SITCOMS AND SOAPS

1 Emmerdale

2 Married With Children

3 *Todd Carty*

4 *Ralf Little*

5 *Wendy Richard*

6 Brighton Belles

7 Neighbours

8 *Theodopolopoudos*

9 *Eric Idle*

10 Father Ted

11 *Nicholas Lyndhurst*

12 *Ramsay Street*

13 Are You Being Served?

14 Terry and June

15 *Rag Trade*

16 Red Dwarf

17 Keeping Up Appearances

18 *Trotters Independent Traders Co.*

19 *Wernham Hogg*

20 *Zoë Wanamaker*

21 Porridge

22 Steptoe and Son

23 Cheers

24 *Walford*

25 *Mr Humphries*

26 Coronation Street

27 Dallas

28 Last of the Summer Wine

29 *Richard Briers*

30 On the Buses

31 *Thora Hird*

32 *Pauline Quirke*

33 *Wilson*

34 Hi-De-Hi!

35 Desmond's

36 *Golden Girls*

37 It Ain't Half Hot Mum

38 *Gary Coleman*

39 The Fall and Rise of Reginald Perrin

40 *Fonzie*

41 *Chicago*

42 *Vyvyan*

43 H

44 Taxi

45 Dynasty

46 *Daphne Moon*

47 *James Hacker*

48 Crossroads

49 Leslie Grantham

50 EastEnders

SET 30 CLASSIC TV

1 *Roger Moore*

2 Hitman and Her

3 *Una Stubbs*

4 Blackeyes

5 *Porky the Pig*

6 *The General Lee*

7 Zone

8 Bullseye

9 Antiques Roadshow

10 *Prince Charles*

11 This Is Your Life

12 *Tweety Pie*

13 Camberwick Green

14 Spitting Image

15 The Man from U.N.C.L.E.

16 *Scotland*

17 Party

18 Test

19 *Robbie Coltrane*

20 *Penfold*

21 *Sir Robin Day*

22 The Clangers

23 University Challenge

24 *Angela Rippon*

25 It's a Knockout/Jeux Sans Frontières
26 Bruce Forsyth
27 Grandfather
28 Ronnie Barker
29 Mystery Machine
30 Jimmy Savile
31 Magnus Magnusson
32 Rowan Atkinson
33 Walks
34 Dixon of Dock Green
35 Basil Brush
36 Patrick Moore
37 Absolutely Fabulous
38 Boys from the Blackstuff
39 Watch with Mother
40 Doctor Who
41 Thunderbirds
42 Captain Kirk
43 Tony
44 Rolf Harris
45 The Munsters
46 Richard Chamberlain
47 Dragnet
48 The Onedin Line
49 Nine
50 Pollard

SET 31 TV STARS
1 The Flintstones
2 Brian Glover
3 John McCririck
4 Al Murray
5 Hairy Bikers
6 Housewife
7 Ricky Tomlinson

8 Tim Westwood
9 Fiona Bruce
10 Fez
11 Susan Jameson
12 Natasha Kaplinsky
13 Max Beesley
14 Daniel Craig
15 Freema Agyeman
16 Women
17 David Copperfield
18 Scotland
19 Food and Drink
20 Richard Whiteley
21 Frankie Howerd
22 Roseanne Barr
23 Kermit
24 Joan Collins
25 The Office
26 Morecambe and Wise
27 Richard Hammond
28 Robin Hood
29 Russell Brand
30 Cat Deeley
31 Michael Fish
32 Jimmy Nail
33 Gary Lineker
34 Jessica Fletcher
35 Ben Elton
36 Kojak
37 Peter Kay
38 Billy Connolly
39 It
40 Dale Winton
41 Charlotte Church
42 Connie Fisher
43 Derren Brown

44 Nanny
45 Lily Savage
46 Darren Gough
47 Ready Steady Cook
48 Dudley Moore
49 Benny Hill
50 Jennifer Saunders

SET 32 THE STAGE
1 Charlie Brown
2 Jack Benny
3 Guys and Dolls
4 Macbeth
5 Queen
6 Porgy and Bess
7 The Importance of Being Earnest
8 Japan
9 Michael Flatley
10 Three
11 Newcastle
12 My Fair Lady
13 Billy Zane
14 Blood
15 The Producers
16 Comédie Française
17 William Shakespeare
18 Miss Saigon
19 Javine
20 Argentina
21 Verona
22 Harold Pinter
23 H
24 Anton Chekhov
25 Henry V
26 Spamalot
27 Wicked

28 *Savoy Theatre*

29 *Sarah Bernhardt*

30 The Phantom of the Opera

31 *Kevin Spacey*

32 *'Big Spender'*

33 *John Osborne*

34 Lace

35 The Rocky Horror Show

36 *Willy Russell*

37 *1920s*

38 La Bohème

39 Les Misérables

40 The Mousetrap

41 *Broadway*

42 *Old Vic*

43 *Christian Slater*

44 *British*

45 Othello

46 Cinderella

47 Hair

48 *Matinée*

49 *Cyrano de Bergerac*

50 Brigadoon

SET 33 ACTORS AND ACTRESSES

1 *Claire Danes*

2 *John Travolta*

3 Layer Cake

4 *Robert Wagner*

5 Caddyshack

6 *Gregory Peck*

7 Backdraft

8 Stakeout

9 *Rob Lowe*

10 28 Days Later

11 *1920s*

12 Women in Love

13 *David Bowie*

14 *Bruce Lee*

15 *Rita Hayworth*

16 Carry On

17 The Family Stone

18 *Rutger Hauer*

19 *Sylvester Stallone*

20 *Dexter Fletcher*

21 *Daniel Day Lewis*

22 *Jim Broadbent*

23 *Mae West*

24 *Antonio Banderas*

25 *Oliver Hardy*

26 *Emma Thompson*

27 *Richard Beckinsale*

28 *Douglas Fairbanks*

29 Nuns on the Run

30 *Spencer Tracy*

31 *Republic of Ireland*

32 *Keira Knightley*

33 *Draco Malfoy*

34 *Martin Clunes*

35 *Helena Bonham Carter*

36 The Money Pit

37 *Haley Joel Osment*

38 *Four*

39 Dead Poets Society

40 *Jaws*

41 *Judi Dench*

42 *Marlene Dietrich*

43 *Julie Andrews*

44 *Helen Mirren*

45 *Kelly Brook*

46 Brokeback Mountain

47 *Audrey Tautou*

48 *Oliver Reed*

49 *Sean Connery*

50 *Nicole Kidman*

SET 34 BLOCKBUSTERS

1 The Sound of Music

2 *Jack Nicholson*

3 *New York*

4 The Empire Strikes Back

5 *Charlie's Angels*

6 *Kate Winslet*

7 *Dorothy*

8 *Green*

9 *Clown fish*

10 *Richard Attenborough*

11 *Catherine Zeta-Jones*

12 *Lawyer*

13 *Eddie Murphy*

14 *Bruce Willis*

15 *Comet*

16 *Michael Gambon*

17 *Penguins*

18 *Drew Barrymore*

19 *Jurassic Park*

20 The Incredibles

21 *Las Vegas*

22 *Mackenzie Crook*

23 Independence Day

24 Titanic

25 Four Weddings and a Funeral

26 War of the Worlds

27 *Sir Ian McKellen*

28 Home Alone

29 Eva Green

30 Jack Black

31 Face/Off

32 Black

33 Who Framed Roger Rabbit?

34 Robert Zemeckis

35 Love Actually

36 Russell Crowe

37 Anne Hathaway

38 Saving Private Ryan

39 Slimer

40 The Lion King

41 Armageddon

42 John Williams

43 Julia Roberts

44 The Day After Tomorrow

45 Laurence Fishburne

46 Sophie Marceau

47 John Rambo

48 Angelina Jolie

49 The Sixth Sense

50 Kevin Spacey

Set 35 CLASSIC FILM

1 Mini Cooper

2 From Here To Eternity

3 Citizen Kane

4 Water

5 The Thomas Crown Affair

6 Danny Kaye

7 Dustin Hoffman

8 Boris Karloff

9 Quadrophenia

10 The Shawshank Redemption

11 Rick Moranis

12 Fat Sam

13 Dirty Dancing

14 Basic Instinct

15 Rydell High School

16 Big

17 Humphrey Bogart

18 Mermaid

19 Vivien Leigh

20 Athens

21 The Wicker Man

22 The Ladykillers

23 Benny Hill

24 The Usual Suspects

25 Rocky

26 The Name of the Rose

27 Deliverance

28 The Second World War

29 The Second World War

30 Mark Lester

31 Rain Man

32 50 mph

33 Baby

34 Airport

35 The Goonies

36 Harrison Ford

37 My Fair Lady

38 Driving Miss Daisy

39 Anita Ekberg

40 Pinocchio

41 Sergei Eisenstein

42 China

43 Al Jolson

44 James Coburn

45 Rosa Klebb

46 The Bates Motel

47 Emerald City

48 John Wayne

49 Billy Wilder

50 Carrie

Set 36 AWARDS

1 Steven Spielberg

2 Brokeback Mountain

3 Crash

4 Sharon Stone

5 An American Werewolf in London

6 Rent

7 Tony Awards

8 Stephen Fry and Hugh Laurie

9 On the Waterfront

10 Seamus Heaney

11 John Ford

12 Weird Al Yankovic

13 Mariah Carey

14 John F. Kennedy

15 Richard Griffiths

16 Man Booker Prize

17 Gladiator

18 Kate Atkinson

19 Halle Berry

20 Charlize Theron

21 Beauty and the Beast

22 The English Patient

23 Helen Mirren

24 Piers Morgan

25 Jack Palance

26 Music

27 Kate Moss

28 Walk the Line

29 James Blunt

30 Schindler's List

31 Iris Murdoch

32 Salman Rushdie

33 Madonna

34 Jean-Paul Sartre

35 Boxing

36 Milli Vanilli

37 Roddy Doyle

38 Harry Potter and the Goblet of Fire

39 On Golden Pond

40 The Color of Money

41 Nobel Prize

42 Cuba Gooding Jr

43 Gone with the Wind

44 Curse of the Were-Rabbit

45 Michael Caine

46 BB King

47 Ben Affleck

48 James Cameron

49 Desmond Tutu

50 Jack Nicholson

SET 37 FOOD AND DRINK

1 Raspberries

2 Boston

3 Parsley

4 Gordon Ramsay

5 Peas

6 Peach

7 Two Fat Ladies

8 Chardonnay

9 Whisky

10 Chestnut

11 Tupperware

12 Candyfloss

13 Lancashire

14 Chocolate

15 Greece

16 Pig

17 Drops

18 Jerusalem

19 Laver bread

20 Champagne

21 Republic of Ireland

22 Tea

23 Kendal

24 Cheese

25 Rhône

26 Anchovy

27 Orange

28 Cheddar

29 Pear

30 Venice

31 Madeira

32 Hot cross buns

33 Corned beef

34 Heston Blumenthal

35 Portugal

36 Wishbone

37 Squid

38 Switzerland

39 Elizabeth David

40 Okra

41 Fish

42 Rosemary

43 Sweet

44 Tomato

45 Broad beans

46 Custard

47 Potato

48 Genetically modified

49 Japan

50 Lime

SET 38 FOOTBALL

1 Arsenal

2 Teddy Sheringham

3 The Oval

4 Jack Charlton

5 Greg Dyke

6 Twin Towers

7 Accrington

8 Peterborough United

9 The Netherlands

10 FIFA

11 Nutmeg

12 Watford

13 West Ham United

14 Denmark

15 Eight feet

16 Wembley

17 Sheffield

18 White

19 Aberdeen

20 Real Madrid

21 'Three Lions'

22 Aston Villa

23 Manchester United

24 Everton

25 Brazil

26 Real Madrid

27 France

28 Franz Beckenbauer

29 West Ham United

30 Aston Villa

31 Jürgen Klinsmann
32 Aberdeen
33 Celtic FC
34 Chelsea
35 Nottingham
36 Wimbledon
37 Italy
38 Amsterdam
39 Fulham
40 Nottingham Forest
41 Michael Owen
42 Portugal
43 Diego Maradona
44 Arsenal
45 Sven-Göran Eriksson
46 David Beckham
47 South Africa
48 Paul Gascoigne
49 Portuguese
50 Manchester United

SET 39 THE WORLD OF SPORT

1 Geoff Hurst
2 London
3 Cresta Run
4 Deuce
5 Lancashire
6 Jungle
7 Gymnastics
8 Australia
9 Tennis
10 Japan
11 Cheltenham
12 Four
13 Italy

14 Twelve
15 Boxing
16 John Curry
17 Pakistan
18 France
19 Andrew Flintoff
20 Daley Thompson
21 Yachting
22 All Blacks
23 Sugar Ray Leonard
24 Basketball
25 Motorcycles
26 Edinburgh
27 400m
28 Boxing
29 Ladies' Singles
30 Golf
31 Cricket
32 Football
33 Cycling
34 Fernando Alonso
35 Fifty
36 Ski jumping
37 New York
38 Swimming
39 Evander Holyfield
40 Snooker
41 Ireland
42 Cyclops
43 Marylebone Cricket Club
44 Horse racing
45 Five
46 Arthur Ashe
47 The Olympic Oath
48 Australia
49 Kelly Holmes

50 Manchester United

SET 40 SPORTING HEROES

1 Steve Austin
2 Helen Wills-Moody
3 Colin Montgomerie
4 Skiing
5 Roberto Duran
6 Greg LeMond
7 Stirling Moss
8 Tony McCoy
9 Allan Wells
10 Brendan Foster
11 Horse racing
12 Barry McGuigan
13 Andy Fordham
14 Greyhound
15 Baseball
16 Torvill and Dean
17 Joe Frazier
18 Phil Mickelson
19 Australia
20 Squash
21 Whitaker
22 Norwegian
23 Sir Gordon Richards
24 Hermann Maier
25 Betty Stove
26 Tanni Grey Thompson
27 Aldaniti
28 Mike Tyson
29 Sir Matt Busby
30 Nigel Mansell
31 Steve Cram
32 Ice hockey

33 *Gymnastics*

34 *Sir Steven Redgrave*

35 *Ellen MacArthur*

36 *Brazil*

37 *Table tennis*

38 *Finnish*

39 *Nick Faldo*

40 *Swimming*

41 *Pat Eddery*

42 *Muhammad Ali*

43 *World Rally Championship*

44 *Baseball*

45 *Croatian*

46 *England*

47 *Lawn tennis*

48 *Stephen Roche*

49 *Golf*

50 *Franz Klammer*